a Smile in One Eye

Ayliffe Macphail

Smiles and tears...
Seems that life is all
in the balance. Scotland
changed my father's life
and he was always grateful.
Scotland was where he
learned about generosity.

Ralph

November 30, 2016

a Smile in One Eye

a Tear in the Other

Ralph Webster

ISBN-13: 9781533656926
ISBN-10: 1533656924
Library of Congress Control Number: 2016909395
CreateSpace Independent Publishing Platform
North Charleston, South Carolina

Dedication

To those who must flee their homelands for reasons that make no sense. Let you journey to a kinder place to live in freedom and find a better life.

Ralph Webster June, 2016

Would you tell me, please, which way I ought to go from here?
That depends a good deal on where you want to get to, said the Cat.
I don't much care where, said Alice.
Then it doesn't matter which way you go, said the Cat.
So long as I get somewhere, Alice added as an explanation.
Oh, you're sure to do that, said the Cat, if you only
walk long enough.

Lewis Carroll, Alice in Wonderland

Preface

$\mathcal{D}$uring the fall of 2015, my wife Ginger and I took an extended trip across mainland Europe. Ours was a pleasure trip. We were hiking. As we went from place to place, there was something significant happening around us that we couldn't help but notice. The refugee crisis was escalating. Thousands of refugees from Syria and Afghanistan were streaming across Europe in search of safety and security. We watched the international news broadcasts each evening as they displayed image after image and discussed the many sides of the burgeoning, and often complicated, controversial refugee situation. Throughout our trip, we met people from all over the world, and the conversation would frequently continue. There were many varied opinions, sometimes finger pointing, and even a few heated exchanges. It was and is a complicated issue.

On a few occasions, at train stations and on trains, we encountered groups of refugees trying to make their way north. Most were headed to Germany. And, in various countries, there were times we watched the police board our train and remove refugees from our midst. We never felt danger. We saw no disturbance. What we watched were people striving to communicate through the medium of different languages. We saw the stress, the toll that leaving one's homeland takes. Every interaction we watched between police and refugees was civil and polite; we never viewed anything less, only a silent procession of people in search of a new life. We saw mothers, fathers, children, and groups of young men. There was no avoiding this. It was in our face, in front of our eyes.

I am the son of a refugee family, and as Ginger and I watched this crisis unfold, it gave me reason to consider my family's journey to the United States and to telling this story. In doing so, I have learned much that I did not know about this issue and my family. I sympathize with the simple truth that today's refugees become tomorrow's aliens and recognize that can be a complicated topic too. Of late, there has been much political discourse about refugees: where they should go, who should take them, the danger they could bring to our way of life. There are those who believe that refugees and aliens may be wolves hidden in sheep's clothing. As with anything, I suppose there is truth in everything.

The plight and pilgrimage of refugees is not a new story. It is centuries old. And the distrust of aliens within is a much repeated scenario. It happened in America with the Japanese at the beginning of World War II. It happened in Great Britain when German refugees were sent to internment camps. And when Italy and Britain went to war, it happened again when nineteen thousand Italians living in Great Britain were ordered to be rounded up. There are not enough pages here to list all the examples.

Common sense dictates that nations must concern themselves with their own internal security. Who would argue against that? But it also is not unreasonable to suppose that some might overreact in their response. And, like most complex issues, usually the best answer is not as simple as it may first appear.

This book makes no claim as to who is right and who is wrong. That's not the point of this story. As some would say, I have no dog in that hunt. I would only offer that most refugees, if not all, are people like you and me, except for that one single difference. They were forced to leave the land of their fathers and mothers, and for most, this was through no fault of their own. Many had created successful lives and have raised incredible families. Now they hope to live with freedom, dignity, security, and opportunity. They have made sacrifices. They have travelled far. Most ask only for a hand up and not for a handout. Most, given the chance, offer more than they would ever take. I have compassion for these people. My family has lived that life, and that's the story I would like to share. If I can illuminate this journey, then I have accomplished what I set out to do.

Ralph Webster, June, 2016
www.smileinoneeye.com

Part One
Germany

Chapter 1

The Sled

By my fifth winter, I had mastered the skill of riding a sled on my own. With luck and good fortune, December of 1927 in Preussisch Holland was filled with snow beyond the imagination. The hill beyond the old Jewish cemetery, with its craggy imperfections, created the perfect downhill adventure. For the first time, I discovered the competing wonders of independence and daring, a reminder of my first steps, but grander, and so much better. Now my world was expanded. I could roam further than my eyes would take me.

Riding a sled, hurtling downhill, replaced that sense of fear, the safety of being held, with my stubborn desire to be free from protective arms. Here was something I could do alone, a risk I understood and was eager to undertake.

When Father first introduced me to sledding, I was too young to tackle the hill without help. As I climbed aboard the sled and wiggled my small body against his, I felt those uneasy moments of anticipation. I remember shutting my eyes and holding on with all my strength, my hands tightly clenched, as we headed downward. I recall that thrill of riding the sled wrapped in Father's strong arms, so gentle, yet so secure.

We would sit upright atop the sled. Father would be in back. I would ride in front, my small back to his large chest. As we raced down the hill, my eyes would narrow, all else would blur. Flakes of loose snow would cling to my face, frozen with little needles of ice. My nose would drip. Small icicles would form. Steaming hot chocolate, too hot to hold in my cold, gloveless hands, would be the reward that waited to end the day.

Those winter days, even my decade-older sisters would join the fun. Lotte, the middle sister, was fearless, her excitement hard to contain and contagious. She and I would fly down the hill, tumbling over and over each other when we reached bottom. And she would laugh. No matter what, Lotte would laugh. That was the way Lotte was about everything. Lotte always knew how to laugh. Trude, the oldest, would shout the instructions. She was the one who told us what to do. She expected us to listen. Ilse, the youngest, would ride the hill cautiously, taking care with each turn. She was prone to mishaps. With Ilse, anything could happen. Even then, when I was five, I could see how each differed from the other.

That winter, I raced against the older and bigger kids. Everyone would jostle for position at the top. Someone would yell, "Go!" and like a wave, we would all start together and dive down the hill, each fighting against the other. It was a continuing competition to see who could reach bottom first. We would forget the windy cold air and listen only to the sound of the snow as it brushed along the blades. This was my discovery that winter of 1927.

Age provided many privileges. As long as I stayed in the company of others, I was allowed to navigate the three blocks to the hill without a parent or sister holding my hand. My wool mittens were replaced with leather gloves: not that soft leather, but the thick leather with wool linings that kept hands and fingers warm. Mother knitted the perfect cap, one that covered my entire head except for the slits that opened for my eyes, ears, nose, and mouth. We all wore the same. Then, we were all exactly alike, and there was nothing to keep us apart.

It was a different time, and in East Prussia, children, from a young age, were safe to explore on their own. We would run through neighbors' yards, build snowmen and snow forts, and wage war with snowball fights. I felt special but was one of many. My friends and I stayed under the protective guidance and watchful eyes of the older kids. All had younger brothers and sisters they tended. All parents were our parents. I was just one more in the pack of kids racing down that hill. And, in that pack, there was always room for one more.

Snow, deep and dusty white, arrived early that year. On Christmas Eve, I was thrilled when Father and Mother presented me with a new sled replacing the worn and cumbersome hand-me-down my older sisters had used before me. My new sled instantly became my best friend. We shared that sleepless night huddled in deep conversation. Now, nearly eighty years later, I still feel the excitement, anticipation, and pure joy that I felt that Christmas. Whatever my life has encountered, that night and that feeling will always remain. It can never be taken. The heights of happiness deserve to be savored, embraced, and only reluctantly forgotten.

My sled was new, not repaired and worn like the old one. It was sleek, sure to be fast, and handmade just for me. Much different from the sleds I was to give my children years later, this sled had no handles to push to turn left or right. Turning required leaning all your weight in this direction or that, a maneuver those younger could not perform. There was no hand brake to stop. Stopping required a sudden, abrupt lean, almost to the point of turning the sled over, making the sled spin and reverse direction. I still feel my smile, stretched across my face, the first time that remarkable feat was accomplished. And I remember my hands-on-hips, no-big-deal nonchalance when I stood up, hoping, but not wanting, to draw the attention of others.

The sled's runners were wooden and the width of snow skis. The tips were turned like ram's horns, curved to a point that no matter how deep the snow, the sled would glide endlessly. Each ride promised to be the ride of a lifetime. Best of all, the sled belonged to me.

That winter, I waxed the runners and cared for that sled just like Father taught me. We all knew that waxing the runners was the secret to speed. It was a secret only known and carefully shared among our fraternity of downhill racers, passed from older to younger in hushed tones.

Each year through my childhood, that sled and I shared our winters together. As I grew older, skis would compete, both cross country and downhill, but the sled remained my favorite. Each winter, it was my trusted companion.

Even after our world had changed and so many doors were closed, that craggy hill beyond the old Jewish cemetery remained open. Wearing our ski masks and riding our sleds on a cold, wintry, snow-filled day, nothing separated us. For these moments, we were all the same.

⤙

When I was ten, the sled sat on the school stage for the Christmas pageant. I narrated the story of Joseph and Mary, a ritual repeated annually by each class in front of proud parents. That year, my parents sat in the very front row.

Without warning, only months following that Christmas of 1932, I was no longer welcome. I was no longer part of the pack. That pageant would be the last time I ever set foot on any school stage. New rules would be established. I would find myself on the other side of a line that had been drawn, one that I could not cross. It was a matter of race. I no longer belonged.

―⤸

A few years later, when my sister Trude's daughter Ruth was old enough, I shared the magical secrets of my sled with her. My young niece and her parents drove the eighteen kilometers from Elbing to visit us at the farm in Crossen nearly every Sunday afternoon. Oh, how Ruth loved to be pulled on the sled through the snow across the meadow and fields. She would sit so straight and upright, one moment serious, and grinning the next. That winter, when we glided down the hill behind the old cemetery, she would throw her head back and laugh with pure joy just like my sister Lotte would do. I still remember that day Ruth pushed my arms aside and told me that she could do this on her own. I was so proud, and she smiled in the same way I had smiled only a few years before.

With my own sisters older and fully grown, Ruth became my little sister, and I became her older brother. It has always been that way. I have always believed this was good for her. I know it was good for me.

Winter in 1938 was cut short when we quickly left for Berlin, leaving most of our broken possessions and our East Prussia lives behind, never to be retrieved. That day we left, before leaving for the train station, my last gift to Ruth was my prized sled. She was five now and skilled in its use. I hugged her and told her she was old enough to have a sled of her own. I made her whisper and promise to wax the runners just like I had done. Ruth and her parents would not leave Elbing. They stayed through the war. They felt safe and unaffected.

―⤸

By 1941, war had turned our worlds upside down. Their lives in danger, Ruth, her infant brother, and my sister Trude still remained in Elbing. Great Britain had declared war on Germany to stop the horror. Ruth's father, Walter, was serving as a German soldier. I had fled to Scotland and joined the British Army. Now we were enemies. My sister Ilse was in Shanghai with Mother, Father, Arthur, and Frank. As for my sister Lotte, the one who loved to laugh? By then, we had little idea where Lotte was. By then, we had lost touch with one another. We had lost the way to communicate.

And the sled? It was called to serve the war as well. The children of Elbing were instructed to bring their snow sleds to the army supply depot. It was their duty. Sleds were needed to help transport supplies to the German front lines.

Ruth added a tag with her name and reluctantly handed the sled over to the German soldiers. Her wintry days with Uncle Gerhard would have to remain warm memories. To her amazement, the sled was returned within days. The army had more sleds than were needed. The sled was put into the cellar for safekeeping. It would have a life when the war was over.

⟶

It was bitterly cold in January of 1945 when the Russian invasion of Elbing began. That night, as the fires burned and the sky was lit bright orange, Ruth and her mother Trude retrieved the sled. They loaded young Manfred and pulled him down the street. They checked on neighbors to see who remained and who had left, and searched for any food that may have been left behind. They scavenged for kerosene, firewood, and water. My old sled still had a use.

When they returned to their apartment, Ruth, Manfred, and Trude joined others moving into the cellar, the bomb shelter for the ten families who remained nearby. They hoped to survive the overhead battle between their German protectors and the invading Red Army.

Three weeks later, after the Germans had been defeated, the victorious Russians went block to block, searching and freeing civilians who had survived the intense bombing. The cellar doors were thrown open. Ruth, her mother, and her brother emerged into the daylight to learn their fate. They had no knowledge of the destruction that had taken place above their heads. They only knew that they had heard the thundering sounds of bombs and felt the ground shudder. No one could imagine the horrors that would await them.

The sled? The sled would never be seen again.

A generation later...

I, too, learned to ride a sled in my father's arms. This was in the early 1950s, on the hill behind the cemetery at Sinnissippi Park in Rockford. My red Flexible Flyer was much different from the sled Dad had used in East Prussia in 1927. I'm sure the hill was different too. But I bet the feeling was the same, the way the snow felt against my face, the comfort of his big arms wrapped around me, even the drips from my nose forming icicles. I, too, remember the thrill, the pure joy, the pure elation, and the anticipation the first time we set off from the top of the hill.

I learned the story of Dad's sled shortly after I became a grandparent and Dad a great-grandparent. I guess he was feeling sentimental, sharing the story as we walked together along the beach that day. Before, I never thought to ask where or when he learned to sled. Like so many other questions, it never was that important, just another I never thought to ask. I suppose that is true about many things parents teach their children. We take for granted most things taught. We seldom ask questions before the answers are known.

There was much about Dad that I knew little about. Not bad stuff, not great stuff, nothing astonishing, nothing to be hidden. No, the fabric that makes stories, the little details of his life, his history, the family facts, and mostly, his emotions. Dad tended to keep his emotions private. I suppose most parents try to shield their emotions from their children. I know we did and still do. Now I find it hard to remember. Did I ever see him cry? Did I ever know his anguish?

Dad was a quiet, respectful, and unpretentious man. Only when he was older did he speak much. By then, I was away raising my own family. And, as Ginger will attest, I am seldom a very good listener.

I remember, too, the first time: he gave a push, let go, and watched nervously as I traversed the hill on my own. I remember when I did the same for my son, as I am certain he did for his children. Dad always encouraged me to go forward with my life, to stand on my own feet, to be comfortable in my own skin, to take measure of my own risks. He never held me back. He wanted me to be confident that I could care for myself. I always knew that he believed that I would succeed. This was the way he was raised. It was the way I was raised. I hope we raised Zak that way too.

My dad, or Jerry, as his friends and coworkers would call him, was, more than anything else, a good guy. I never met anyone who thought otherwise. He was curious, resourceful, sometimes strangely opinionated, wicked smart in a non-book kind of way, a devoted parent, a loving husband, never a pain in the ass. I can't say he was humble, but he certainly was modest. I never thought of him as stingy, but he was careful and frugal. He had his own sense of humor. Unlike Mom, he could never remember a joke, particularly the punchline. He loved to flirt. He mixed strange drinks. Steady would be a way to describe him. I don't think of him as moody, perhaps Mom did at times. Sometimes he loved to disagree, to pretend to know better. I never disliked him, can't remember ever having an argument with him. He never struck me or any family member, and I never struck him. I cannot say a bad word about him. He was a good provider. He was honest. He was polite. He listened more than he spoke. He had a sense of adventure but was cautious with risk.

With Dad, it was never his way or the highway. He had his opinions and never relinquished his right to be right, but I seldom remember a time when he imposed. He might state his case, but mostly deferred when I stated mine. That was true whether the discussion was bedtime, report cards, or using his car. Topics like religion or politics were generally left for Mom. Dad was never one to debate these unsolvable matters. Even as a child, I was always afforded his respect. The only absolute I can ever remember was this one simple rule: Whatever it was, if it was German made or German sold, he would not buy it.

I always loved my dad. And I knew him better as I grew older. With time, he became my very best friend. Now, perfect cannot be described and is impossible to claim. But close to perfect is the mental picture I ask you to have, not only of Dad, but the rest of my family: my wife, my mother, my sister, my son, his wife, my grandchildren. I would never suggest that we are the best or better than most, nor do I wish to compare to anyone else. I am just offering that, as far as families go, we are pretty typical, pretty happy, and generally satisfied with life. Normal would be the best description. At least, that's my view most of the time.

I know you will ask. No, I am not trying to set you up in the first act for a nasty surprise in the second. I am just trying to describe who we are. No parent is perfect, nor are their children. That pretty much sums it up. That's all I need to say.

Chapter 2

My First Memory

ela and the kids often encourage me to tell my stories, to open up, to share my life. Honestly, that has never interested me too much. Some people wear their heart on their sleeve. That's not me. I am comfortable with letting others do the talking. They can state their opinions. Since I am quiet, others assume I am listening. That's not always true. Usually I choose whether to listen. Some may find my approach annoying or even arrogant, but it is not meant to be. My attitude rarely shows. It is just that sometimes I like to live within my own head. I collect and keep my own thoughts. I suppose we all do, each in our own way, maybe me a bit more than others. I don't know.

There really is not anything in the past that I don't want to share. Other than respect, I'm not particularly concerned about my own privacy. I do think there is little of my past life that is as interesting as the current. Why should I recite my ancient stories? That's what old people do. I was raised to put the past in the past. You can't change what's past. The past is over and done. Don't dwell. I think I enjoy the present more than most. I am content with the here and now. For me, today and tomorrow are more compelling than yesterday. Even today's news has already happened. So, when I do reminisce, I try to keep it in my head, to contain it in my dreams. These are conversations meant to have with myself. Mostly, I believe there is little I can say that would be genuinely interesting to others.

The kids sometimes asked what my first memories were. That's something I enjoy sharing. I remember them clearly. We were at our farm in Crossen. Mother handed me a small bucket filled with grains and seeds, and pointed to the chickens. I knew exactly what to do. My first memories were feeding the chickens. Hardly taller than the tallest chicken, I took handfuls of feed and tossed their food everywhere. I was in charge of the chickens.

How I loved the chickens. They loved me too and followed me everywhere. As they ran all about, my hands could not catch them. It didn't matter how hard I tried or how fast I chased. They laughed at me as I laughed at them. Their language sounded nothing like that of my sisters or Mother or Father. It was a language that only I and the chickens could understand. They were noisy, excited, and constantly chattering. I thought we were giggling together. So happy to see me, they were my first friends. That day, I must have felt I was a chicken too.

Our farm in Crossen was a wondrous place for a small child, full of sounds and smells, not dull and drafty. The farm was so unlike the big house in Preussisch Holland, where we lived through the week. My first words were spoken at the farm. I knew all the animals, and they all knew me. I learned all their languages. I learned all their sounds.

All I remember of my childhood was good and sweet. I was loved. I was protected. I was made to feel special. I was never uncertain. I was always held. My family kept their arms around me, Mother, Father, my three sisters. Those were my first memories.

Of course, all that changed, and then, it changed again. Always is never the same. Mela tells me that life has a smile in one eye and a tear in the other. Although my nature, at times, is to disagree for no reason other than to be disagreeable, on that, I know she was right. Life does find a way to create a balance somewhere between smiles and tears. And, like a pendulum's swing, life seldom stays in one place. Life keeps on moving until, one day, it stops.

Last summer...

One day, Dad told me that he was thinking about having heart bypass surgery again. At the time, I thought it a strange thing to say. But it was the kind of statement he was apt to make. Dad had successfully undergone quadruple bypass surgery seventeen years earlier. Now, as I write, I am wondering if there is any necessity to describe the earlier surgery as successful. I would not be writing now if he had not survived the surgery seventeen years before. In any case, that surgery went very well. He fully recovered and resumed an active life.

When he made the comment, I found myself puzzled. Dad and I had just finished a five mile walk, barefoot on the beach, in 95-degree temperatures. This was a daily ritual when Mom and he visited our home on the Outer Banks of North Carolina. He had not complained. I was the one drenched in sweat, breathing hard, and whose heart was racing. I had kept up with him, not the other way around. Usually, people who can do this are not in need of heart bypass surgery. Dad was eighty-two years old at the time.

Our walk must have been similar to a stress test but in much hotter surroundings. Our pace may have been steady and the speed unvaried, but it was five miles and completed in less than 1 ½ hours. Most would admit that is a reasonably good time when walking the beach. Why did Dad think he should have bypass surgery again? Did I even know anyone who had repeated the procedure? And, anyway, who is able to self prescribe bypass surgery?

In general, Dad didn't talk that much. He was one who typically answered more than he asked. The exception was his health, which he discussed at great length. His comment was not entirely uncharacteristic. Ginger and I often laughed about Dad's preoccupation with his health.

I cannot really say he was a hypochondriac, but each year, he seemed to be getting that way. He worried about his health a lot, more than most people we knew. He was the kind of person who, when he weighed himself, something he did several times each day, if there was one additional pound, would eat only carrots or raw broccoli until the problem was solved. He was the kind of person who, after brushing, monitored his teeth and gums carefully every night. He was the only person I knew who took Metamucil as a daily drug. He was the kind of guy who loved all-you-can-eat buffets only to complain again and again that he had eaten too much (and, then, he would proceed to stuff himself with carrots). He was always talking about his health in one way or another. He counted his steps, timed his walks, weighed before and after, that kind of thing. That was my dad. He was healthy, and he was health conscious. That part was good. He just talked about it quite a bit.

Dad's worry about health paid off. He was in great shape, better than most. He weighed the same as he had when he'd been in the army sixty years earlier. His marriage was in its 54th year, and he could still wear his wedding suit. I know. Who keeps a wedding suit for 54 years? That was my dad. He always took care of his belongings, particularly his clothes, and especially his shoes.

I confess. I can't exactly explain how, but he sort of managed his way through his first heart bypass surgery. Most of us have a friend or family member who has had this surgery. It is a serious, life-threatening event, but not uncommon these days. Typically, it is performed under emergency circumstances. Most of us are familiar with the scenario. Chest pains. Ambulance called. Family alerted. Emergency bypass surgery. Long recovery.

Well, sometime in his early sixties, Dad was told that he had blockages and needed surgery. What did he do then? He waited until he was sixty-five and on Medicare. Clearly, this is not the kind of thing anyone should be advised to do. No, this is the type of surgery that, if needed and advised, should be done immediately. He had insurance; that was not the problem. I think he just wanted to avoid the deductible. That entire episode remains confusing in all of our minds for any number of reasons.

During the seventeen years that followed his bypass surgery, Dad had a few other medical mishaps, most not too serious. He called one day to say he had floppy foot, a tendon that needed repair after a misstep playing tennis with a neighbor. We had no idea then and still wonder what he was talking about. We hadn't even known he was playing tennis. Anyway, after several months, he was back to normal.

Then, there was the year-long treatment to recover from Arizona valley fever, a fungal infection caught from desert soils (he liked to walk in the desert but claimed he caught the infection after spending days beneath his car clearing debris and repairing damage caused by desert rats building nests). Respectfully, I realize that this can become very serious, that it is no laughing matter. I really do not know how one catches it. However, in his case, I remember the treatment being the worst part of the cure, as he had to drink gallons upon gallons of water to flush his kidneys and be treated with intravenous medication three times a week for months. He told us he felt bloated and was beginning to hate the taste of water. This was discussed in detail during our weekly phone conversations that year.

There were a few other things, like the time we had to take him to the emergency room at the beach because of the damage he did to himself trying to remove a sliver from his foot. He had been digging at it with any implement he could find for days. And there was the aortic aneurism, which really was a big and serious deal, but which, fortunately, was caught in time and surgically removed.

Despite the above, Dad was in great health. He walked daily. He peddled Scottsdale's bike paths, riding 12-15 miles several times each week. I don't want to give him a bad rap, but try to picture your typical eighty-year-old guy enjoying the backside view of thirty-something female joggers. Not simply a flirt, Dad tended to the voyeur.

Dad took great pride in his stomach, toning it with 100 sit-ups each morning and giving a great deal of credit to carrots. Walking the beach at our home in North Carolina or hiking the foothills near his home in the Arizona desert was no problem. Water skiing was an annual ritual when visiting my sister's lake house in Iowa.

Now, I don't want to create any false impressions. While Dad was in good shape, that did not make him an athlete or a jock, of which he was neither. I never practiced batting or threw a football or shot hoops with Dad. He did not know the rules to any of these sports, nor did he play any team sports as a teen, with the exception of a little soccer. His knowledge of golf was limited to watching Tiger Woods on television. Tennis was a late-in-life endeavor. He only took it up because his condo had courts. He found my old tennis racket, a can of balls, and a neighbor who wanted to play. I am certain that he never purchased a can of tennis balls himself. He would have found no reason, as long as the old ones still bounced. It didn't matter anyway, as his tennis career was short lived when he got floppy foot.

Faculty-wise, Dad was in pretty good shape. Eyesight, hearing, brain, all worked well. Faulty opinions? Yes, but no signs of senility, at least none we could see. Mom would know best, as the two spent most of their time together. They were joined at the hip.

Mom and Dad would drive cross country once or twice every year...Arizona to Iowa...Iowa to North Carolina...North Carolina to Florida...back to Arizona. Once in a while, they would drive to California, Oregon, and Montana to visit other family. When they retired and bought a van to drive the country in the early 1980s, we all referred to them as the Van Websters.

As I said, I was puzzled when Dad mentioned he was considering bypass surgery for the second time. Who would entertain the possibility without medical consultation? What were his signs and symptoms? Well, long story short, they left the beach, drove back to Arizona, and a few months later, he went to consult his cardiologist. Dad called last evening and told us he is scheduled for bypass and valve replacement surgery next week. He wants it done before Christmas.

Go figure. That's my dad. He told us that it should be a piece of cake. He will be good for another seventeen years. Good health and all, I'm not sure what to think.

Chapter 3

My Accent

I was surprised to learn I had an accent. I didn't grow up with one, at least one that was mentioned. Now I suddenly realize that, except for when I was a child, wherever I lived, I have always had an accent. I was always considered a foreigner. In some respects, having an accent is like having a sign on your back. It doesn't say kick me. But people do notice. Some ask. Some don't. Some care. I can't say, though, that I was always made to feel like an outcast. I probably did that to myself at times. Anyway, that's how I would hear my accent, somewhere in my head as I imagined how others heard it. Maybe that is another reason why I didn't talk so much. I didn't enjoy the sound of my own voice. It sounded too foreign. Who knows? I can't be certain.

The irony is that this thought never occurred to me before this moment. I have always thought that everyone else had an accent. From my point of view, I always remained the center of my world. I was the same. Everyone else was different. I still believe that today. Perhaps I am a little self-centered. I suspect most of us are a bit that way.

As a child, my language was German, with a distinctive East Prussian twist. To understand the difference, think of the way the same words can be pronounced in different parts of America. Even now, after nearly sixty years in the United States, I still have trouble understanding some people when they speak. I suppose they say the same about me. My daughter-in-law dislikes it when people tell her she has a cute southern accent. I completely understand how she feels. Too many people make assumptions about those who speak differently than they do. Being a foreigner does not make one an alien, at least not the kind from outer space. Rather than make assumptions, perhaps these people should listen to what is being said and not so much to how it is spoken.

I was born in October, 1922, in Preussisch Holland in the German state of East Prussia. The town name derives from early settlers from Holland centuries earlier. To simplify, Preussisch can be shortened to its abbreviation, and most refer to it as Pr. Holland. That's what I do. It certainly is easier to think of it that way.

Most of my official documents say I am from Elbing. Technically, that is true. The hospital was eighteen kilometers away in the much bigger city of Elbing, but our family home was in Pr. Holland. The way I saw it back then, Pr. Holland was the little circle in the center of the universe, at least, my universe. As children, I think that is the way we all imagine the world. Growing up, living in Pr. Holland, I did not have an accent, and I, most definitely, didn't know a foreigner.

Don't search for Elbing, Pr. Holland, and East Prussia on a map, at least not one drawn in this century. None of these places exist anymore. They were erased less than twenty-five years after I was born, when the country boundaries of Europe were changed and the continent re-divided following World War II. That's when the world's powers punished Germany for another of its many terrible transgressions.

According to my birth certificate and baptism records, I was born Gerhard Udo Albert Wobser, after my father (Udo was his nickname) and my adopted grandfather, Carl Albert August Wobser (we called him Grandfather Albert). My name is no longer Gerhard Udo Albert Wobser; why it changed to Jerry Webster is a story for later. In Pr. Holland, when I was a child, everyone called me Gerhard. No one blessed me with a nickname, particularly one as special as Udo.

You might wonder why I refer to Grandfather Albert in English rather than using the German vernacular like *Großvater Albert*. Truth is, sometime in the latter half of 1939, I began dreaming in English and have been dreaming in English ever since. I can still speak German fluently but am not really interested in using many German words. When I am awake, I do all my thinking in English. Dreaming works the same way. Using words like *Tante* or *Onkel* instead of Aunt and Uncle would be as difficult and foreign for me as they might be for you. I left Germany behind many years ago, though, at the time, I was convinced that it had left me.

My sisters loved to tell the story that I was a premature baby, born so very tiny, at 4 ½ pounds, I was able to sleep in a shoebox. As the story goes, I was so small that my parents would keep me in the kitchen warming oven that first winter. Fortunately, someone always took pity. True or not, I remain unbaked and survived. Today, if that were to happen, everyone would be outraged. Funny how parenting has changed. At least my parent's circumstances enabled them to have a warming oven. I can't imagine what would have happened had they used their regular kitchen oven.

I have no memory of my baptism but assume that it must have been a pretty big deal since it took place on Christmas Day in 1922. It was held at the old Lutheran church in Pr. Holland. I know little about how baptisms work, then or now. But, at the time, I imagine the competition would have been quite big on that particular day.

With the exception of Mother, all of us had been baptized as Lutherans: Grandfather Albert, Grandmother Marie, Father, my sisters, and me. Mother was raised in a household that followed Jewish customs. Her ancestry was Jewish, but like many Jews in Western Europe, her family had adopted the culture of their non-Jewish neighbors. Some might say they had assimilated. When she married Father, she abandoned her Jewish upbringing. She chose to follow Father's Lutheran faith, and that is the way our family was raised. None of us felt any connection with the Jewish faith or considered ourselves Jews.

I have always been thankful that some of Mother's rituals were retained and I was circumcised shortly after birth. There was no ceremony for this noteworthy event, rather a whispered conversation between Mother and doctor; my future health was the primary concern. Admittedly, I have been grateful to Mother ever since. I remember being startled to observe the distinct difference when I and the other eight-year-old boys, all uncircumcised, showered before swimming lessons. That was the first time I thought of myself as being a curiosity. That was the first time I ever considered the idea that I might be different.

By all accounts, our family, the Wobsers, was one of the more prominent and successful, some say the most, in our small town of Pr. Holland. However, all wealth is relative. Bragging rights aside, we may have been big fish, but it was a very small pond. As a child, how would I have known? Children don't measure the world that way. Children measure with simple equations, like who is circumcised and who is not.

The surgery...

When Dad called with the news of his upcoming operation, of course Ginger and I were concerned. This was major surgery, one with significant risks. He was not as young as he once was. Fit or not, any surgery was a worry.

He explained it as simply a minor matter, something to get done, the sooner the better. I can't say that he was thinking about extending his life. This was about improving it. He was thinking about making certain that he would be otherwise healthy and able throughout the life that he would live. To Dad, it was the right choice; the quality of his life mattered.

I admit, at the time, I never thought his decision might be selfish. With the advice of his doctor, this was his choice to make for himself. I was sure that he and Mom had given it a great deal of thought and consideration. He never made any decision without regard for her feelings. I believe he was always that way. Now I am not so certain that it was not a little selfish. Anytime a choice is made, others are affected by the outcome, even if they are supportive. He never suggested that the cardiologist considered the surgery an immediate concern – a matter of life or death or a situation that required emergency intervention. But, no matter what, he made his choice.

I have never needed to make a decision like this for myself. My hip replacement surgeries were pretty simple, and both had a great outcome. I never stopped to consider the risks. As far as I was concerned, there weren't any risks other than the standard warnings, the kind found on medicine labels. I admit to not generally reading this kind of fine print. Now I wonder if the same was true for Dad when he chose to have the bypass surgery. Had he really considered what could happen?

Chapter 4

East Prussia

*O*rdinarily, I enjoy my daydreams more than my night dreams. My daydreams are usually fantasies, and I will admit to having more than my fair share of wonderful fantasies. My night dreams are more serious. They take on a darker tone. They usually end suddenly. Day or night, my dreams are seldom filled with world history and facts. If they were, I am quite certain this dream would end and I would sleep. Today, I have no idea what kind of dream I am having. I don't know if it is day or night. I have no idea if the surgery has started, or whether it is over.

There was an early and abrupt end to my formal education. I know very little about world history. I can't recite dates, the names of kings, or the order of events, but I can tell you this: World War II was not Germany's first transgression and misguided adventure. There is a past that was repeated. Germany had been punished before, after World War I, which ended four years before I was born. That was when East Prussia was separated by the Polish Corridor from mainland Germany. Then, Poland gained its independence. Before that, Prussia had been one of the major powers of Europe and the world.

At the youngest age in school, we learned to memorize East Prussia's history: the greatness of Germany and the penalties the world imposed. Our hearts and minds were filled with patriotic thoughts. Our flag was a solemn symbol. Children are taught similar lessons about their homelands regardless of where they live. We did not pass judgment. We were not asked to think. We were instructed to memorize and to accept what we were told. I still remember the class lesson. We recited it by heart.

The kingdom of Prussia dates back to the 13th century.

In 1871, the German states united to create the German Empire. The kingdom of Prussia became the leading state of the German Empire.

In 1920, after World War I, the Treaty of Versailles gave West Prussia to Poland. East Prussia remained part of Germany separated from mainland Germany by Polish lands.

Our family, for generations going as far back as anyone knew, had always been proud Germans, loyal to the core. East Prussia was part of Germany, and Germany was our homeland. We served and defended our nation. We celebrated our flag. We stood when we sang the national anthem. Patriotism was in our blood. Everyone I knew felt exactly the same way. We had no reason to believe otherwise. I was raised to be a German. We were all Germans.

The week before...

Ginger's first instinct was that I should hop on a plane and spend a few days with Mom and Dad to help them through the surgery. She knows me well. Dad vetoed that idea. My sister Joanie was already planning to fly out to Arizona. Mom and Dad had both been resistant, but Joanie insisted. Joanie was the one who would always be there. She would watch out for them. That is the kind of person she is. Every day, I am reminded of how fortunate I am to have a sister like Joanie, always caring, always considerate.

I admit that there are times when my sister and I don't see things the same. There are moments when she makes me irritable, intrudes on my space, and gets on my nerves (I am sure that she feels the same about me). There are even times when I am disagreeable for no reason at all. I suppose it is better that she lives in Iowa and we live in North Carolina. It gives us a buffer and keeps us apart so we can better enjoy the time we spend with one another. But I need to say this. On matters of family, my sister is perfect, often better than that. And, when she reads this, she should smile, and her eyes should tear. She knows exactly how lucky I am.

Dad told me it would be better if Ginger and I waited several weeks to visit. We should come once he got out of the hospital and was done with rehab. That's when he would enjoy our company more. They didn't want us to change our plans for a two-week Christmas trip to Europe. He and Mom would have plenty of help. There was nothing we could do or add. Medicare would allow him to spend a few weeks at the rehabilitation center before going home. That would be easier for Mom. He would need to get his strength back. He wanted us to live our lives and have a good time. We should come to Arizona after the first of the year, after we returned from our vacation. That way, everyone would have something to look forward to.

In retrospect, I suppose Dad gave me the convenient answer I wanted to hear. It's possible that I am not quite as caring and considerate as Joanie. I try, but she always succeeds.

Chapter 5

My Story

As I said, Mela and the kids always want me to talk more. Mela wants the kids to know my life story, every detail, what I felt, who I am. That is how Mela is, always wanting to know more. My daughter-in-law Ginger gets it. Sometimes Mela wants to get into your personal space, to ask a few more questions than politely should be asked. It's not that she is disrespectful; she means well. It's just her nature. But that is not how I am. Not all of us like crowded spaces. I get tired of talking. I become bored with the sound of my own voice. Everyone lives a life. Stories happen to everyone, and everyone is special and unique in their own way. I just never have thought that my story was that unusual or interesting to anyone but myself. Who wants to be burdened with my memories?

It's not that I don't spend time remembering the past. We all do. And there are times I enjoy reliving my life. But it is something that I tend to leave for my dreams, both day and night. Some may say that is selfish. I think not. It is important that my children spend their time living their lives, not remembering mine. That's my priority. Time is not infinite, and our brains can only handle so much clutter. It's okay to be a little selfish. The past is the past. I want the next generation to have their turn and to enjoy their time.

I suppose there is one story I should tell. It is about fate. I believe that there are some things that happen in life that seem to be guided by an invisible hand. They have no explanation. Please don't misunderstand. I'm not interested in a discussion about higher powers. I already know what I believe and leave it to others to debate that question. I am suggesting, however, that despite all the choices one might make, the plans, the wants, the desires, the right turns, the left, some things just happen for the strangest of reasons. They are not random. They fit some larger picture, one that we might not totally understand. At times, certain things happen suddenly, like when the wind shifts direction, and when they are least expected. Some may call it destiny, that moment that, no matter what, was supposed to occur. The first few decades of my life took many twists and turns. Now I believe they were intended to all lead to the exact same place. Call it fate or call it destiny. That is what happened to me.

The thing of it is that to get to that point, to dream of that moment, to tell you what happened, I have to relive all that happened before. I don't have the words, nor do I pretend to be a storyteller. There are many others blessed with that talent. It's just that in order to tell you this story, I have to explain my past.

Chapter 6

My Sisters

As a child, I never lacked for love. Not everyone is that lucky. My three sisters were much older, already in their teens when I was born. I was their darling little Gerhard, the doll they could dress in fancy clothes, the infant they could mother. I was the little prince at their parties. I was their sweet child. It was always that way.

Gertrude, or Trude, was twelve years older. There was no question, she was the boss. Trude was smart, claimed to know everything and how to do anything. We never disputed. She was the most serious, felt the most responsible, and was always in charge. If there were decisions to be made, everyone, at least my sisters and I, deferred to Trude. Trude did the talking. She left little space for much else. Don't misunderstand. Trude was kinder than you might imagine. She had feelings, and she cared. I don't want to give the wrong impression. To put it another way, she was simply the oldest sister, top of the heap, first in the pecking order, front of the line. We all gave her a very wide berth. From Trude, I learned to listen. I really had no other choice.

Charlotte was the middle sister, the one we called Lotte. Being the middle sister in any family can be very challenging. It can be frustrating. Lotte coped very well. Lotte didn't care about too many little things, like jealousies and who got what. She didn't sweat the small stuff. She always enjoyed the moment. She was happy with who she was. The most fun loving and spirited, Lotte was the life of the party. Everyone followed her. If you were near her, you would laugh. Like Trude, she talked a lot. All three of my sisters did. Sometimes when they chattered, I would be reminded of the chickens at the farm. Unlike Trude, with Lotte, talk was seldom serious. She told the best stories. She had the most boyfriends and girlfriends. Lotte also had the most patience. With me, she took the time to explain things in a way that I could understand. And she always would stop and answer my questions, no matter how many. Lotte was eleven years older. Lotte taught me to laugh, to smile, to be cheerful, and to never take myself too seriously, no matter what.

The youngest was Ilse. I have always known I loved her the most. Everyone loved Ilse. Ilse was ten years older. Ilse was the one who cared for others. Ilse was the one who frowned, not a frown of judgment, but a frown of concern. She would offer advice, but only when asked. She was always worried about something. She would never hurt a fly. Ilse was the one I ran to when I fell and scraped my knee, when I was sad, when I cried. Ilse was the most sensitive. At first, you wouldn't notice, but her feelings could get hurt easily. I always thought that Ilse worked the hardest, that she was usually trying to catch up to her sisters. She would even run to catch up when they walked. Ilse was funny too. But she was funny in a different sort of way. Ilse often found herself in humorous situations, like the time she packed a raw egg in her lunch thinking it had been boiled or the time she accidently swallowed a marble. And, when Ilse told her stories, she always knew how to laugh at herself. Ilse understood my emotions. Even when I was much older, Ilse knew how to wipe away my tears.

Each of my sisters was different; Trude was respected, Lotte was adored, and Ilse was loved. What they had in common was that all three were smart, very smart. I know that because following in their footsteps was not always easy. They were all achievers. They were motivated. Mother must have been like that too. At times, being the youngest is a good thing. At times, being the youngest is a bad thing. I had big shoes to fill.

To remember them now, and the memories of my childhood, brings up long forgotten emotions, deep and quiet. I can't say honestly that I think of them often anymore. That is the way of life. We move forward a step at a time. I don't know that we forget, but we don't always remember. Life goes on. But, when I do think of them, when I picture these young girls growing to be women, when we lived in East Prussia, when our lives were undamaged, the thought silences me for moments on end.

There once was a beautiful, large oil painting of my three sisters dressed in their Sunday best as they stood side by side. It hung in our dining room overlooking the table. Although it was destroyed that night in November, 1938, along with most everything else we owned, I can still see their portrait clearly: their happiness, their expectations, their charm, and the look in their eyes. How could they have known then what I know now?

Now, as I feel and imagine our resemblance, I can see the vast difference carved by the decade gap in our ages. As a group, they were always older. I, by myself, was always younger. All three were born a year apart, shortly after Mother and Father were married, before the Great War and the Russian invasion of East Prussia. They were small children, years before I was born, when Father was called to the army and sent off to war. They knew the grandparents I remember only through stories.

Trude, Lotte, and Ilse were their own best friends and their own worst enemies. I was so startled when they fought with each other, afraid that they would never make up. But they always did. Despite their differences, their allegiance was to each other. They were the first to each other's defense. When they came of age and left home, I was left behind. That's when I became an only child.

The girls grew up when our parents were young, still climbing their ladder of success. They remember the struggles, when not everything seemed so assured and easy, when there was still a sense of uncertainty and unknown. When I grew up, our household was prosperous, confident, older, and wiser. I presumed that it had always been that way. That's all I ever knew.

As children, they shared a nanny, a governess. When I was a child, I had three. They watched me, watched over me, guarded me, protected me, taught me, fed me, and hugged me.

No, I never lacked for love. My family always had their arms wrapped around me. As a child, I was made to feel special. I could do no wrong. My future was certain. I was their prince.

The night before...

I called Dad the night before surgery. I was in the car on the way home from another soon-to-be-forgotten Whalehead Club meeting at the county courthouse. The one-hour drive would give me plenty of time to visit. It must have been about nine pm, seven o'clock in their time zone. Mom answered on the third ring, as usual, and passed the phone to Dad.

Our conversation was brief; they were already in bed, already asleep. Dad said they had set the clock for three o'clock in the morning and needed to be at the hospital by five. Joanie had arrived from Iowa safely and would sit with Mom. Surgery was set for seven, and he expected to be awake by afternoon. One of them would call me. I love you. Bye.

I should have thought more. I wish I had called him earlier that day. I wasn't busy. I always looked forward to my phone conversations with Dad. Growing up, I can't say that we talked much. He was pretty quiet, and I was generally not that interested. Other than the routine, I hardly remember any significant conversation. Mom was the one I talked to. She had all the questions. She had all the opinions. But that changed as I grew older, after I left home, married, and settled into my own life. That was when Dad and I became closer and found our connections, when monthly phone calls became weekly conversations. We both enjoyed these visits. We rarely talked about anything important, but with time, we learned how to converse, something we both valued.

This call was shorter than usual and not particularly memorable. Tonight, there was no time for conversation. They needed their sleep.

Chapter 7

The Farm in Crossen

Throughout my childhood, the farm in Crossen was better than any place I knew. Even now, my early memories of the farm are pleasant and comforting. Father purchased it in 1918 and added neighboring acreage and the meadow the following year. Our family owned the farm from before I was born until we left East Prussia twenty years later. Then, our departure was abrupt and forced. There was no turning back, and we never saw the farm again. Only crumbled remains exist today. All I was left with were images and my imagination. These I keep. They belong to me.

At the beginning, the farm was only a business. With time, it became something more, a home where we spent weekends, a spot for gatherings of friends, for cherished family moments. For Mother and Father, the farm was for privacy and relaxation. My sisters loved the animals. For me, it was a place to run and play, to invite my friends, a place for birthdays, hayrides in warm weather, sleigh rides in cold. When I picture the farm of my childhood, the images are vivid and fresh: the colors, the smells, the sounds, the grasses and grains, the quiet, the birds, the sunrise, the dew, the fresh scent of rain.

Years later, shortly after I turned twelve, we would move there. The farm became different then. We were isolated, shunned, and often ignored. Then, I remember the farm as gray and stark. When it became our home, we looked at the farm through a different lens. My memories clash and fill with another set of emotions. As a child, the farm in Crossen was a place of happiness. As a teen, I was reminded of loneliness.

Crossen, the village, was a small scattering of farms as old as the ages. When we lived there, nearby excavations were underway to understand its prehistoric past. Stone buildings, some crumbling, dotted the landscape. Straight, narrow dirt roads, one day dry and dusty, the next, wet and muddy, crisscrossed the fields. Crossen was a place where the few families knew each other, but little more. Each was content leaving the others alone.

The farm was only a few kilometers from our home in Pr. Holland, less than fifteen minutes away. We would travel there by automobile, by foot, bicycle, and occasionally by horse. Yet the distance was deceiving; the farm in Crossen was a world apart.

I never learned the circumstances that caused Father to acquire the farm. It may have been an opportune moment, the result of someone's misfortune, or the time for his business to expand. It could have been both. It could have been neither. What I do know is that, at heart, Father always thought of himself as a *Landwirt,* a farmer. The farm became his pride and joy. Although his day-to-day business was selling farm equipment, livestock, and grain, Father was always drawn to Crossen. Father loved his farm.

Our farm had woodlands, meadows, and more than two hundred acres of fields. We raised potatoes, wheat, oats, beets, rye, and barley. Like many farms in East Prussia, we even had bees. For me, the bees held a special fascination. In the middle of one field, there were many brightly colored wooden boxes filled with their hives. A mishap when I was five taught me quickly to stay away, but my interest continued, only then from a distance. The farmhands would tend to the bees, and we always had their honey on the breakfast table. I admit, while I enjoy honey, to this day, I remain terribly fearful of bees, a misfortune my son and grandson seem to have inherited.

By age seven, I had become proficient with spelling and counting, and I polished these skills by taking careful inventory of the livestock: 12 horses, 28 milk cows, 1 bull, 39 calves, and 26 sheep. I recall that the singular bull caused me a great deal of concern and confusion. But my worry about the bull's loneliness was quickly replaced by Father's illuminating explanation, which I found more confusing and even more concerning. Ever since, I have been sympathetic to cows.

As they refused to stay still, the chickens were difficult to count and, friends or not, at age seven, I avoided the smell of the chicken coops. Knowing that Father was not a pig farmer, and that we never raised pigs, was always a source of happiness. You can be sure that I would have avoided the pigs. They would not have been counted.

Near the barn was a small pond with an assortment of ducks and geese. To this day, I cannot explain why, as a child, I was terrified of the ducks and geese, perhaps from an earlier encounter. My memory fails me. Afraid to get close enough, their inventory remains unrecorded. Fortunately, I have long since conquered my duck and geese anxieties, but my strong dislike for chicken coops continues to this day.

The barn was full of mysterious farm equipment, and for me, it was a favorite place to explore. There were machines for threshing, milking, grinding, and churning. There were plows of various types, a hay wagon, and another wagon for moving all sorts of supplies and for carting firewood. Saddles and equipment lined the walls of the barn. Two horse-drawn buggies were always parked nearby. I am sure that the barn was very old.

The silos were full of grain. At an early age, I was taught that the silos were dangerous and off-limits. The hayloft was always the best spot to hide when we played childhood games. When I was older, I continued to frequent the hayloft. Then, it became my hideaway, a place where I could build things, experiment, and repair equipment – hobbies that would always hold my interest and in which I showed an early aptitude. The hayloft became a place where my loneliness didn't matter. I was occupied with my things. I was left alone.

Winter heat was supplied by wood-burning fireplaces, all meals were prepared over wood-burning stoves, and wood supplied the heat for our baths. There were stacks of wood everywhere, and Father took great pride in his ability to chop wood, although I always thought he took more pride in encouraging others to do the work.

We would ride to the meadow for wood in the horse-pulled cart. At the farm, there were always horses to hitch, cows to milk, chickens to feed, sheep to shear, crops to sow, crops to plant. At the farm, I learned to shoot, to hunt, to skin, to pluck. There was always work to be done and much to learn. Apart from my few odd fears, I found life on the farm to be a grand adventure.

There were gardens for flowers and gardens for vegetables. Father loved the gardens and took great pride in carefully measuring the growth of every plant, a habit I adopted in later years. There was even a small orchard with apple and pear trees. Behind the barn, there was a small building where the workers could stay. The first floor had a bunk room, a large table where the farmhands ate, and a kitchen. On the second floor, there was a small apartment where our farm foreman and his wife, the farm cook and housekeeper, lived. They worked for us for many years, as long as they could, until we were told by the German authorities that we could no longer employ workers. And, even then, they continued to stay; they remained as friends and helped us operate the farm.

Our family's farmhouse was warm and welcoming, with the scent of freshly baked bread usually filling the air and large verandas front and back. Before we had electricity, kerosene lamps were used to illuminate at night. The lamps were seldom lit, only for family gatherings, when everyone stayed up late and watched the stars. Most days, dinner was served mid-afternoon. By evening, we were all exhausted. We slept and rose following the sun's rise and fall.

Now I realize that Father, for much of the time, could be called a gentleman farmer. He met with the foreman weekly to check on the farm's operation. Farmhands were hired to help. In busy seasons, temporary workers passing through would be added to the payroll. Until things changed, he didn't tend the land, raise the crops, or breed the animals. Later, our circumstance became different. Then came the time when Mother, he, and I were to do most of the work. No matter what, though, he did love the farm. Father always loved everything about the farm.

As I grew older, I learned that the farm was part of our family's business, not just for fun. The farm was expected to produce crops and livestock that would be sold for a profit. I am certain that it did. Father never told me otherwise, and I know he was a successful businessman.

Food was always plentiful in our household. Most everything we ate came from the farm, whether we were in Crossen or at home in Pr. Holland. Mother would plan the meals and tell the cook what supplies should be gathered. Mid-week, Father's driver would collect whatever was needed. We always had fresh eggs, fresh milk, butchered meats, poultry, and fresh vegetables and fruits. There was even a small smokehouse where meats were smoked and sausages cured. No matter how difficult times became, we never lacked for food.

The horses were part of the family. We all learned to ride, and we each had our own. My oldest sister, Trude, loved the horses the most. Solo was her favorite. Our dachshund Ludo (named after Father) would follow wherever she rode. After Trude left for boarding school in Elbing, I will never forget the time that Ludo followed Trude's scent to the hall closet and chewed on her riding clothes.

Ilse's favorites were the calves. Each year, father gave her one of her own. Ilse would stay up all night when any animal was in bad health. She would become upset whenever an animal was butchered or had to be put down. Joanie has inherited many of these same emotions. I'm sure she always thought they came from Mela. I wonder if she understands that they came from Ilse. Ilse was the one who was sentimental.

After Ruth was born in 1933, my sister Trude, with Walter and the baby, would drive to the farm from Elbing most Sunday afternoons for dinner. The drive was not far, much less than an hour. Ruth would get so excited when we hitched up the horses for a ride. Her hands would clap. Ruth loved being put on the back of one of the old horses, being led in circles by the barn. When she was a few years older, she and I would climb to my workroom in the hayloft. With paper, string, sticks, and paste made of flour and water, I would build her kites we would fly together in the fields.

Many family parties and gatherings were held at Crossen. The house was large with rooms for everyone. There were sixteen chairs in the dining room, and the table opened to fit all. I know that because it became my responsibility to re-assemble the table leaves when it was pulled open. There was also a large parlor for sitting and a study where Father had his desk and safe. On the porch behind the kitchen was a large table where we could eat or play card games. And there were an assortment of chairs in the back where we could all sit. Tall broad shade trees lined the backyard. One, in particular, was my favorite. It was perfect for climbing. Another was popular since it held the swing.

My sister Ilse married Arthur at the farm in 1937. We all laughed when Ruth, the four-year-old flower girl, proudly kissed her Aunt Ilse and gave her a bouquet of flowers. The following year, we celebrated Ruth's fifth birthday. My sisters were all there: Ilse and Arthur from Berlin with their newborn, Frank; Trude, Walter, and Ruth from Elbing; and Lotte from Spreenhagen. The sun was shining. It was a beautiful day. None of us knew that the day would be the last we would spend all together. It was August of 1938, only a few months before all was taken, all was lost, and all was shattered. Then, our lives would never be the same again.

Day 1...

While I wait for news from Arizona from Joanie or Mom, I should tell a bit about my mother. She is at the hospital worrying about Dad and will have to deal with his recovery over the coming weeks and months.

I think anyone who has met my mom, Mela, would agree that she is an interesting human being. Of course, we all are in one way or another, but in certain respects, Mom breaks that mold. Again, I don't suggest that she is better or best, I am just suggesting that she has a rather distinctive personality. And, unlike Dad, with his generally reserved qualities, Mela seldom holds back. She is not afraid to venture her opinions. She is informed and well read, and rather enjoys contradiction. It makes the conversation continue. The thing about Mom is that she loves conversation.

Mom is six years older than Dad, but I never knew it when I was young. It was a minor fact she chose to hide from other family, the result being that my misinformation was quite late in being corrected. I missed her fiftieth birthday by several years, something we corrected by the time she turned eighty. From a child's point of view, parents usually appear about the same age, somewhere between being old and older. I was more upset that I had been intentionally misled. As to her age, I could not tell the difference.

I won't dwell on Mela here, other than to introduce her. This story is not about Mom. It is about Dad, who is in surgery. Nobody has called me with an update for hours. I assume the operation is going well.

Like Dad, Mom was an immigrant, actually a refugee. At age twenty-two, in September of 1938, Mom and her three brothers arrived in the United States from their hometown of Naples, Italy. Penniless, they each brought one suitcase, and the scant little

English they knew could only be understood by their small group of four.

With world events quickly unraveling and war in the making, thankfully, Mom's father's brother Uncle Ludwig, a dermatologist at Lennox Hill Hospital in New York, guaranteed passage, making it possible for the four to obtain visas to come to the United States.

Mom's parents, my grandparents, stayed behind in Naples operating the family pensione until mid-1941, when they, too, with Uncle Ludwig's help, were able to leave for safer grounds. Quota restrictions prevented them from immigrating to the United States at first, and they spent most of the war years in Cuba before gaining permission to come to America, where they rejoined their family.

It is easy to see, by the way everyone ran for their lives avoiding the terrible fates that awaited them, how important Uncle Ludwig was to the family. And, for most, he was there when their ships arrived, the first to greet them to their new home in America. These were only a few of the many lives that Uncle Ludwig saved with his kind and generous support. Uncle Ludwig will forever be a family legend, revered and remembered.

America was the shining beacon for Mom's family. And that is the telescope that she used to view it. Mom fell in love with America, for all its endless possibilities, for all its opportunities. Mela saw America as the ultimate melting pot, a place like no other, where everyone had their chance, provided they earned it.

Learning English, becoming a naturalized citizen, Mom embraced America and raised Joanie and me to be as American as we could be. There was no question that English would be the language spoken in our home.

With all her heart, Mom believed in opportunity for everyone and privilege for no one. She put her children first, and her faith and trust in the American dream. Of Jewish descent, she was never raised to practice her religion. She never attended a synagogue, but was ferociously proud of her heritage.

Mom ran the household, was a great mother, and a wonderful mate to my father. Dad was the provider, but Mom ran the show. Nobody questioned her position in the family order. Mela was eighty-eight years old when Dad decided to have his bypass operation. She was a good eighty-eight, still playing bridge, still driving, reading all the time, as opinionated as ever; her politics were liberal. Recycling was her passion; everything had a future use. As long as I have known her, she remained curious as a cat.

Who else would think to ask a nine-year-old if he believed in reincarnation, or God, or abortion, the death penalty, sex before marriage, assisted suicide, or even marriage for that matter? That's how Mom was, a bit unusual. She liked to stir the pot.

Chapter 8

My Father Udo

Father was born Ludwig Dorn on August 19, 1881, in Berlin. His birth parents were Agnes Rachael Dorn and Louis Casparius, and he was the child of what apparently was a short-term romance between two university students. History fails to record any other relevant details.

Today, Father might be called illegitimate or worse, but at the end of the nineteenth century in Germany, children born out of wedlock were not altogether unusual. Then, abortion was outlawed, and birth control was mostly a matter of self-discipline. Many marriages were arranged by parents, and not necessarily based upon mutual attraction. Whatever the circumstance, Father was adopted shortly after birth, unaffected by any social stigma that may have been attached, and was raised in a loving household with devoted and supportive parents. As best I know, he had a normal childhood.

As Father's birthparents, Agnes and Louis, remained unmarried, Father's surname became his mother's, Dorn, in accord with German law, unless the father chose to intercede. From what I gather,

Grandfather Louis Casparius was not too interested in whether young Ludwig carried the Casparius name.

Three items Grandfather Louis did pass on were the dark curly looks, a penchant for all things with numbers, and a strong attraction to the opposite sex. Apparently, Louis Casparius was studying to become an engineer of some sort. Father evidently inherited the Casparius gift for mathematics and numbers. He certainly did not inherit Grandmother Dorn's musical talents. Although his birth mother was an accomplished pianist, my father could never carry a tune. And, yes, he did consider himself to be somewhat of a ladies' man. Flirting was a lifelong talent Father excelled at.

It seems entirely possible that these characteristics would pass to me. Apparently, I have a knack for working with numbers and absolutely cannot sing, much less carry a tune; the only thing musical about me is that I have an uncanny ability to whistle. And, like my father, my sisters and I were born with dark, curly hair, as were our children. Also, it does seem that the apple does not fall far from the tree. I, too, enjoy being in the company of women. Mela reminds me of this often. She claims that when it comes to the etiquette of proper interactions with the opposite sex, I remain untutored. I am my father. Clearly, some Casparius blood flows in my veins.

Grandmother Agnes was quite young when Father was born, a month more than twenty years. Whatever the reason, the young Agnes Dorn and not-so-interested Louis Casparius gave Father up for adoption. Father always thought that to be one of the great fortunes of his life.

In a curious twist of fate, the mother of the midwife who delivered Father ended up with the infant. Even in my daydreams, I find this confusing. All I can conclude was that upon delivery, the midwife, Elise Priewer Gorges, handed the newborn baby, Ludwig, to her mother, Marie Priewer Wobser. That is what Father claims and what his birth certificate confirms. And, apparently, this was all done with the permission and cooperation of young Agnes Dorn and the disinterested Louis Casparius. There is no disputing that this was good luck for Father, as he dearly loved and was dearly loved by his adopted parents, Albert and Marie Wobser, who whisked him away five hours by train to a small village near Friedeberg Neumark, Prussia, where they lived on a small farm.

The Wobsers found the name Ludwig a bit formal for a newborn child, and the name was quickly shortened to the nickname Udo. So Father transitioned from being born Ludwig Dorn to becoming Udo Wobser. And that's how we knew him. That's how everyone knew him. When I grew up, Father was Udo to all.

Father once told me that some of the legal formalities may have been missed in the adoption process. Years later, when he was inducted into the Prussian Army, he found himself back to being identified as Ludwig Dorn, an issue sorted out and corrected in an attorney's office in Wurzen after the Great War. Following his discharge from the army, in early 1918, he became Udo Wobser for the second time in his life.

My grandparents, Albert and Marie, were very caring, decent, and respectable people. They opened their farm near Friedeberg Neumark to foster children, and Father grew up in a lively and happy household. Of their many foster children, Udo was the only child the Wobsers adopted. I was never told why. Stepmother Marie's daughter, the midwife, was the product of an earlier marriage. I suppose what that technically means is that Father's stepsister, through adoption, was also the midwife who delivered him at birth. Father loved telling that story!

Father always said that he had many brothers when he grew up. Actually, Udo did have an assortment of foster brothers who lived at varying times in the household. Most were never adopted by any other family and left home only when they came of age. Father told us he never felt that he was an only child. The only foster brother we met and knew was Walter Falk. He became Uncle Walter to us.

Grandmother Marie remains a bit of a mystery, although Father always spoke kindly of her. I believe she was deeply religious. Neither Trude, Lotte, Ilse, nor I knew Grandmother Marie. She died in the first decade of the century, before my sisters and I were born. I cannot recall ever seeing her picture.

Grandfather Albert, on the other hand, was well known to my sisters. He was clearly a family favorite, though I have only dim recollections. I am told he was a frequent visitor despite the fifteen-hour train ride from Friedeberg Neumark to our home. It was a long journey, and the wait as he changed trains in Danzig must have been tiring in his advancing age.

My sisters loved Grandfather Albert dearly. The little I remember is a very old man with a limp. He suffered from an injury incurred during the Austro-Prussian War of 1866. I am not certain if my memory is from pictures, stories, or actual events. He died when I was about eight, in 1930, at the age of eighty-seven, so he must have been born in 1843.

Father once told me that he and Mother had wanted Grandfather to move to Pr. Holland to live with our family when he became too old to travel. But he refused. Instead, they moved him from his village farm to a small house in Friedeberg Neumark and hired a housekeeper to keep watch. Father suggested that I do that for him someday so he could watch his grandchildren grow up. I always thought it odd that he never mentioned what he wanted me to do with Mother, but I assume that was an oversight.

As a child, Father's foster brother, Walter Falk, became his closest friend. Years later, Uncle Walter moved to Pr. Holland and worked for Father, helping him with his business. Eventually he bought the business from Father. That was when we moved to the farm and Father was told he should no longer keep the business in his name. I never learned what became of Uncle Walter. At the end, Father and he had some kind of falling out over money that Uncle Walter was unable or unwilling to pay. We left him behind when we left East Prussia.

Walter Falk was one of many we knew who were left behind in East Prussia never to be heard from again. Sadly, that was when so many we knew were glad to see us leave.

Chapter 9

God-fearing Family

Father always said he was raised in a church-going, God-fearing family. The Wobsers were devout Lutherans, and as a child, Father went to church every Sunday. Shortly after his birth, he was baptized, and when he was twelve, he was confirmed in the Lutheran church. When I was twelve, Mother and Father insisted I do the same, as had my sisters. Father told me that he was informed by his faith. He always hoped that my sisters and I would not forget our religion when we raised our own families.

At age seventeen, Father took the five-hour train trip from Friedeberg Neumark back to Berlin to meet his birth mother. I have no idea whether his adopted parents encouraged him to do so or whether his birth mother had in some way kept contact. I have no idea who arranged their get-together or why they did at that particular moment. Regardless of circumstance, Father told me that this was when he learned, for certain, that he had been adopted. He had always had suspicions. His adoptive parents, Albert and Marie, chose not to tell him as a child.

This strikes me as rather remarkable. It could be that, since there were foster children in the house, they wanted Udo to know he was different from them. I don't know how I would have felt if I had learned something like that when I was seventeen. I never asked Father how he reacted when he was told this.

By the time Father became acquainted with his birth mother, my grandmother, Agnes Dorn, had married a man named Ferdinand Baruch, and they had two children of their own. My sister Ilse once told me that the Baruch children never knew the real story. Birth mother Agnes took great pains to introduce Father as their cousin. Apparently, there was quite a bit of family resemblance between Father and his half-sister. I have never seen pictures. That family connection was severed long ago when the children moved to America.

There was other news that may have surprised Father. I don't know, and he never said. He learned from his birth mother that both she and his father were Jewish, a fact clearly noted on the birth certificate, which he had never seen until then. Years later, when Father told me this story, I understood that this information had little meaning for him. It changed nothing in his life. With regard to religion, he was a Lutheran. He had been raised as a Lutheran. He was committed to his faith. His birth parents may have been Jewish, but he was not. He had even been baptized. In terms of ancestry, there was no denying his Jewish roots, but it had little to do with him.

This relationship with his birth mother seems to have continued from that point forward. My sisters told me that when they were young, Grandmother Agnes would visit each year with her daughter, Lucie Margarette, Father's half-sister. They would take the overnight train ride from Berlin.

For reasons not shared, my sisters did not like Grandmother Agnes and her daughter. Who knows why we develop these ideas as small children? My sister Ilse once told me that Grandmother Agnes was "a real pain in the neck." Although I never met her, because my sisters felt that way, I adopted their attitude, fair or not. Sometimes that's the way we think as children, and sometimes it lasts a lifetime.

Chapter 10

Walter Stange

As best I can tell, Father was not the best student. School could not keep his attention. When it became time for the university, he was passed over. He was influenced by his foster brothers, who had all left home when they were old enough to pursue occupations that did not require advanced education. His adoptive parents, the Wobsers, were not educated people. Grandfather Albert had always worked with his hands, and education had never been that important. They were farmers. Of course, the times were quite different in the late 1890s. University education was mostly reserved for students pursuing professions such as medicine or the law. Training for other fields was done through apprenticeships.

Grandfather Albert had a brother who lived near Drahnsfeld, Germany, who offered to make some arrangements for Father. So, at age eighteen, Father left home, took the train to Drahnsfeld, and became a retail apprentice for the German postal service. From what Father told me, that was like being a sales clerk in a store. He would learn business and how to be a businessman.

Within a few months, Father concluded that he was not suited for life in Drahnsfeld and particularly not postal work. He had other interests. He wanted to go to a larger city. He had always lived in a small town. He was young and energetic and wanted to experience life. Father's next stop was Berlin. It was a place with exciting opportunities for someone with his recently acquired business skills.

By this time, Father had acquired many new talents. Although he told me how and when he left his home with Grandfather Albert and Grandmother Marie, Father never spoke to me about his time in Berlin. Apparently, that was not shared with anyone that I know. It shall forever remain a mystery and a closely held family secret. It clearly was not a story for my little ears.

Many years later, I learned that Father's Casparius bloodlines may have contributed. The leaves did not fall far from the tree. Udo fathered a son during his stay in Berlin, a son with a great resemblance to me, although I could never recognize it when we met. Perhaps I was a little jealous of someone intruding on my place as the favored son. That would be entirely possible.

I know little about my half-brother Walter Stange. He was twenty years older. I was six when I first learned that I had a half-brother. Apparently, this knowledge came as quite a surprise to our entire family when it first became known in 1928. During a visit to Berlin, Father entered a butcher shop to see someone. Mother and my sister Ilse followed and found Father speaking to a young man who bore a great likeness to Father. That was when Father introduced them to his son, Walter Stange.

My sister Trude came to know him well, and Walter Stange was a help to Trude and her family at various times. Walter lived his entire life in Berlin. I understand that, before I was born, Father offered to adopt Walter, to make him part of our family, but the offer was never accepted. I know none of the details.

What I do know is that sometime following the birth of his son, Walter Stange, in 1902, Father hopped on a train to Pr. Holland, a 24-hour ride from Berlin. Whether he was chased, followed, or pursuing opportunity, I will never know. All I am certain of is that twenty years later, Pr. Holland was where my life was to begin.

Day 1, Afternoon...

My sister, Joanie, called mid-afternoon. Dad was out of surgery. He was still sleeping. The doctors said that the surgery went well. It took several hours. He was resting comfortably.

Mom got on the line. She told me that she was okay. Dad was in the recovery room. She was glad Joanie was there with her. She wanted to know how we were. They were going to go get a bite to eat. There was nothing to worry about. All was fine. We will call you later.

We cried a bit. These are the moments that exhaust emotions. We were all relieved.

Chapter 11

Preussisch Holland

As much as we enjoyed our weekends at the farm in Crossen, our family home was in Pr. Holland. That is where I went to school. That is where I went to church. That is where Father's business was located. That is where I spent my childhood. Pr. Holland was the town where we lived.

Father always claimed that, despite its 800-year heritage, the train station on Bahnhofstrasse is what put Pr. Holland on the map. I suppose he was right but always thought that seemed an odd thing to say. In school, I had been taught that Dutch colonists had founded Pr. Holland and that Pr. Holland was older than most maps. Since we lived in Pr. Holland because Father had gotten off the train at the station in 1902, I am sure it was on the map by then.

Pr. Holland was old, much older than any town or city in America. It was founded by settlers imported from Holland by the Teutonic Order in the late thirteenth century. Originally, Pr. Holland was a walled city. Many of the old East Prussian towns had surrounding walls. The walls would define town boundaries and fortify the town from potential threats. Often, towered entrances would be used for toll collection. When I grew up, all that remained of the walls were the two towers, the Steintor by the market and Muhlentor on the other side of town.

Slightly larger than a village, Pr. Holland was a typical East Prussian small town with a population of several thousand. Elbing, eighteen kilometers away, was the big city. That's where the hospital was, where the doctors were, where the university was, where the large factories were, where the big department stores were, where the ferry to the beaches on the Baltic was, where the ships arrived connecting us to the rest of the world.

Elbing was surrounded by many small towns and villages, and Pr. Holland was much like the others, perhaps a bit larger. When I grew up, most families did not have automobiles. People stayed in their towns and villages, often for their entire lives. There was little reason to venture very far from where one lived. The weekly markets and small stores provided most things one would need. Although we owned automobiles and Father went there often for business, our family seldom traveled to Elbing for anything else. Most everything we wanted could be found in Pr. Holland.

Similar to small-town life anywhere, I thought we knew everyone in town and everyone in town knew us. Of course, that is an exaggeration. I know better now, but from my childhood perspective, it certainly seemed true. Safety and security were never an issue. Crime was non-existent. Adults kept a watchful eye on all the town's children. I always knew that if I broke any rule, no matter how insignificant, my parents would know before I got home. It was that kind of small German town. Few rules were broken. People followed the rules. Years later, I would learn that even if the rules were not just, most people did nothing to object. Everyone would follow the rules. It was easier that way. That might not be right, but that is what happens.

Having grown up in Pr. Holland, each of my sisters had many friends. They must have been popular because, whenever they returned to visit, our house would be full. Most people knew us by name or by sight, and we knew most families in much the same way. Mother and Father were well liked and respected, and because I was related, many people knew me too. I was always told that our family was regarded as one of the leading families in town. My sister Trude loved to boast about this.

Father enjoyed people. He was always friendly, stopping people on the street to visit. Perhaps that was one reason why he was such a good salesman and his business was so successful. Mother would always tell me that Father knew how to talk. He often participated in town events and meetings. He told me that was important. Pr. Holland was our town and we needed to be involved. Our opinion mattered. We were part of the community.

My sisters would tell me that, because I was a Wobser, I had to act a certain way. I never understood exactly what they meant. Mostly it seemed that they were playing a game to make me behave. Or maybe they were concerned that I would do something to embarrass them with their friends. In those days, children behaved. I did have to act in a certain way. Children did not get in trouble. Our parents did the talking. As children, we listened. Those were the rules.

In school, we studied the map of Europe and learned that, from our small train station in Pr. Holland, one could connect to other train stations throughout Germany and go almost everywhere in Europe. I must have been about nine at the time and recall asking myself why anyone would ever have to leave Germany. Didn't we have everything anyone might need? Why would anybody need to leave the best country in the world? At least, that's what I thought.

Trains from Danzig to Koenigsberg and back passed through the station on Bahnhofstrasse several times each day. The train station was always filled with commotion and excitement. Porters were moving luggage on large carts, big boxcars were being unloaded, families were waiting for loved ones to arrive, others were waving farewell. But, again, those things, seen through the eyes of a child, might appear different as an adult. All I can really say is that the station was busy whenever I was there. I am sure that it wasn't busy all the time. Pr. Holland was still a small town.

Near the train station was the market, and on market day, once a week, farmers and merchants would fill their stands with an assortment of items. On other days, the same farmers and merchants would visit other nearby town markets. Each town would have their own market day. On one end of the market would be fresh flowers, fresh vegetables, breads, baked goods, fruits, cheeses, poultry, and meats. On the opposite end, a variety of other items would be for sale – clothing, shoes, pots and pans, books, furniture, everything imaginable.

When I was very young, I would go to the market with Mother or one of my sisters. As most of our food came from the farm, we seldom shopped for food at the market. However, Mother liked fresh flowers, and we would often walk to the market, look at everything, and bring home a bunch of fresh-cut flowers.

Mother always liked to look but rarely bought anything other than flowers at the market. She told me that the things we must buy should be purchased from the good stores in town owned by people we knew. That was something I never understood when I was little. The market seemed to sell the same items that were for sale in the stores. Mother would always say we do not waste our money; we worked too hard to get it. I was taught to be very careful about what is bought at the market.

That is a difference between Mela and me. Mela loves to shop sales. She always looks for the bargains and deals. I was not raised that way. I was taught that you get what you pay for. In Naples, where Mela was raised, they haggled for prices at the market. When I was raised, our family purchased nothing at the markets. Mother never trusted the market. Be cautious and frugal. The things you must buy should be made to last a lifetime. I suppose things are done differently in Italy than in Germany. Mela and I have that difference. I wonder if the kids notice.

Steinhorsstrasse was just beyond the market. The train station was on one side, and Steinhorsstrasse was on the other. This was the commercial street where the shops were located. At street level, each building had large glass windows trimmed so we could see the items for sale. There was the butcher, the shoemaker, the dressmaker, the tailor, two dry goods stores, the druggist, even a department store. Everything we needed could be found in the shops behind those glass windows. Above each shop were apartments. Usually, that is where the families of the shop owners lived. Many of my schoolmates lived there, and I spent many childhood hours playing with friends in the small park at the far end of Steinhorsstrasse.

Father's business was around the corner on Poststrasse. I remember my sister Trude, so grown up and important, working there for Father. She helped manage the office before she married Walter and moved to Elbing. When I was little, Mother would always remind me not to disturb her because she was being paid to work. Father owned several other buildings on Poststrasse. Most of these, he purchased in the early 1900s as his business was starting to grow. His office was in one building above the large warehouse where he kept much of the farm equipment that was for sale. In another building, there was a large garage where he kept two of our automobiles. That is where father's chauffeur worked. His job was to maintain the automobiles and to drive us wherever we needed to go. The other buildings were mostly used for storage.

Further down the street were the two old churches, St. Bartholomew and St. Georges. St. Georges was where I was christened, where we went to church on Sunday mornings, and where my sister Trude and Walter were married when I was nine. That was the first wedding I ever attended. I was so excited. Trude was wearing a veil all decorated with myrtle. My nanny got so angry at me for picking stems from the veil, but I was worried that Trude would be scratched from all the thorns. They tell me I was that kind of child. I worried about many things.

St. Georges was the center of much of our life. Most of our family friends attended services there each week. Later, that was where my friends and I would go for confirmation classes. When I joined scouts, St. Georges was where our monthly meetings were held. My sisters were always busy participating in youth group activities at St. Georges when they grew up.

Near the churches were the ruins of the old castle, mostly stone columns and rubble that were exciting to explore. There was the old tower, but that was walled off. By looking at it, you would never know that it had been an actual castle in its day. In school, we studied the castle and learned that it was built at the end of the twelfth century.

On the far end of Steinhorsstrasse was the synagogue, and near that were the Jewish cemetery and the hill where we rode our sleds in winter. I was never inside the synagogue but was told that it was quite old, built in 1860. There were only a few families in Pr. Holland who attended the synagogue. I know my parent's friends, the Lessers, did. I think the Aris family, the Rosenbergs, and one of my schoolmates went there too. Mother once told me that there were fewer than a dozen Jewish families in Pr. Holland, not enough for the synagogue to have its own rabbi. The synagogue was set afire by the Nazis and destroyed on Kristallnacht in November of 1938 along with most of the synagogues throughout Germany.

Our house was just a few blocks away, on the south side of town, where most of the houses were located. We lived at Bahnhofstrasse 9. Wherever you lived in Pr. Holland, you could walk to everything. Like I said, we lived in a small town.

During the final days of World War II, most of the remaining German population in Pr. Holland fled, fearing for their lives, and of those who stayed, few survived. That was when the Russian Army retaliated for Germany's atrocities and ravaged much of East Prussia. The devastation in Pr. Holland was complete. Following the war, the East Prussian lands were taken from Germany, and the area was repopulated with Polish immigrants. I'm certain that I would not recognize my childhood surroundings. Most were destroyed and fail to exist. The people and the places are different. Little remains the same.

Today, Elbing is named Elblag, Pr. Holland is named Paslek, and East Prussia is now Poland. German was our language then. Now they speak Polish.

Day 1, afternoon...

Today, I find it difficult to get much done around here. I have work to do but can't concentrate for long. I don't want to miss the call from Joanie or Mom. They must be beat. It has been a very long day for the two of them. They started early this morning.

It's hard to sit still. When I do, my thoughts turn to Dad. When I was a kid, Mom used to subscribe to the Reader's Digest. One of the sections was titled something like, "My Most Unforgettable Character." If the magazine is still published, I'm sure that section remains. It was always well read.

They should write an article about Dad. He will always be one of the most unforgettable characters I will ever know. I'll never forget the first time I introduced Ginger to my parents. We were living in Washington, D.C., at the time and flew to northern Wisconsin near Hayward, where Mom and Dad kept a small cabin on a lake.

Since we were dating, impressions were important. I wanted Ginger to like my parents. I wanted my parents to fall in love with Ginger. I knew she was the one. I hoped she felt the same about me.

We were only there for a few days, a long weekend. The first day, a Saturday, we spent much of our time on the lake. At lunchtime, we took the boat across to a small resort known for its burgers. After a great lunch, I drove the boat on the return. Dad wanted to water-ski, something we all enjoyed. The lake was absolutely perfect for skiing. I knew he wanted to show off for Ginger. That would be his style.

Ginger, Mom, and I were visiting as we pulled Dad across the lake. At one point, we heard him holler. We hadn't paid too much attention to him, just a quick glance every minute or two. Simultaneously, we all swung our heads around in his direction.

There was Dad. He had a big smile on his face. He was holding the ski rope with one arm, the other he held in the air. In his hand, he was holding his swimming trunks. So much for first impressions.

To this day, I have no idea how he had managed to take his trunks off while he was on one ski. We caught the image on film. The moment was priceless. For Ginger, it was telling. The large poster, labeled "Ski Wisconsin," would be his gift that Christmas.

It was forty years ago that my dad streaked the lake. If given the chance, I bet he would try to do it today. Ginger married me anyways. That's Dad. He is one of a kind.

Chapter 12

The Beach at Kahlberg

For as long as I can remember, our family spent summer holidays on the Baltic Sea at the beach in Kahlberg, often for as long as a month. When I grew up, Kahlberg was a crowded summer resort with a long, sandy beach and two-mile promenade lined with changing rooms, boathouses, cafes, and fancy hotels. It is much the same today, only with a different name. Now it is called Krynica Morska.

Mother's sister and my cousins from Leisnig would join us. We would stay in a big house, large enough for both families. At Kahlberg, there were many families we knew, and we were with children of all ages. Everyone returned year after year. We spent our days playing on the beach and exploring our surroundings. I formed a lifelong friendship with my cousin Heinz. He was two years older and always the leader of our adventures, sometimes to my disadvantage. I also remember one time his sisters were there, and my sisters too. They were all much older than Heinz and me. They had grown up spending summer vacations together at Kahlberg. I was too young to remember.

By day, we combed the beaches for amber and seashells, built immense sand castles, hunted for hidden treasures, and swam in the cold Baltic waters. The shallow waters along the inland side of the island were perfect for searching for sea life like clams and crabs. Sun-drenched and worn, we always managed to return home for the evening meal. We ran as a group, and just like at home, the older kids kept a careful eye on the younger ones.

When we visit Ginger and Ralph on North Carolina's Outer Banks, I am reminded of my summers at the beach in Kahlberg. Like the Outer Banks, the Vistula Split is a barrier island. The Frishe Haff, similar to the Currituck and Albemarle Sounds, is a freshwater inland sea separating the coastal island from the mainland. There were no bridges to connect the island to the mainland. To get to Kahlberg, we had to go by boat. The barrier island is about fifty kilometers long and three kilometers wide. Much of it is heavily wooded with large pine trees. It has large, shifting sand dunes, and wide, glorious beaches.

The trip to Kahlberg was always an adventure. First, we would go by automobile to either Elbing or Tolkemit. From Tolkemit, we could take the steamship Tolkemit. If we left from Elbing, we would take one of three steamers. I can't remember their names. Our excitement always grew as we waited at the pier for the steamer to arrive. The pier would fill with steamer trunks and suitcases. Nobody travelled light in those days. All the adults would dress up for the boat to Kahlberg, even though it was not a very long trip.

From Elbing, the first several kilometers would be calm and gentle water as we glided along the Elbing River. Sometimes, the calm waters would change quickly to large waves when we crossed the Frishe Haff. Invariably, someone, mostly me, got seasick. Motion sickness, whether on a boat or in an automobile, was another characteristic of my childhood.

When the water was not too rough, we could stand by the railings and feed bread to the seagulls following closely behind. As we spotted the lighthouse, in the most knowledgeable fashion, we would inform the adults that we were halfway to our destination. We all knew the way there. I was always excited.

I still can smell the pine needles when the boat arrived. After the boat docked on the south side of the village and we stepped onto the island, all the children, me included, would race up the sandy hill. It was overgrown with large pine trees, and the path was softly cushioned with pine needles. Our eyes would widen at the sight of the Baltic Sea, so immensely blue and white, as we crossed the top of the dune. I loved the salt air, the warm sun. I remember how I cried the first time I dipped my head under water and the saltwater stung my eyes. These things never change.

Some years, Mother and Aunt Trude brought their housekeepers and nannies to manage the household while they spent their days at the spa. And, one or two times, Father and Uncle Adolf would join us, but that memory is dim. All I remember is Father teaching me to catch crabs. I screamed when his finger was caught in a crab's pincer. Mother thought it was funny. I was concerned about Father. I don't think Father stayed the entire time we were there; he always needed to return to his work. Parents faded into the background. We were on holiday. We avoided the adults and spent our time with our friends.

I know the kids and grandkids think I'm strange when I make my annual attempt to stand on my head at the beach in North Carolina. They don't know that is a habit from my childhood. They hide their heads in embarrassment. They laugh and say I am showing off, too old to act like that. They wonder what others will think; they get concerned that my swimming trunks will fall down when I turn upside down. But I don't care. We all played that way on the beach in

Kahlberg. In my head I am still a child at the beach. Who wants their childhood to end?

When we visit North Carolina, Mela and I enjoy spending our entire time on the beach, sitting, watching, walking, and searching for treasures hidden in the sand. And, when the waters are right, we swim in the ocean, floating on the waves for hours. I love these times. I feel like I am touching an old and special memory. Mela tells me the same. It reminds her of her childhood when she and her brothers swam in the Bay of Naples. We don't want these memories to stop. Why should they?

Day 1, evening...

Joanie called again at ten pm our time to give us an update. Dad was now out of recovery but in intensive care and still sleeping. She said he was mumbling about all sorts of things in his sleep, nothing she could understand. He was even talking in German sometimes. Mom had been able to make out a few words, but little made sense. I learned that Joanie and Mom had one disagreement. Mom had wanted to spend the night at the hospital but had been convinced to go back to the condo for the evening. Joanie thought Mom was getting pretty nervous and irritable. I bet Mom felt the same about Joanie. They would get some rest and come back first thing in the morning. Dad was well cared for. The hospital would call if anything came up overnight. It was easy to tell that it had been a very long day for both.

Ginger and I stayed up late that night. I needed to talk, and she was a good listener. I am older now. Parents are a bit less invincible than they were before. This whole episode is affecting me more than I expected. I guess it was a long day for all of us.

Chapter 13

Jewish Blood

Mother told me that her family, the Helfts, was Jewish, that they followed Jewish customs and I had a little Jewish blood in me. I must have been very little at the time. I did not understand what this meant. When I asked, Mother's answer was that it was a bit like being a Lutheran except, when she was young, her family celebrated different holidays and they went to a different church. I really did not think any more about that. It did not seem very significant, and it certainly didn't change anything that affected me. I was concerned about the blood, though, not that it was Jewish, just the idea of blood. I thought about that for a long time.

When you are young, questions are often answered with these childlike explanations. They leave lasting impressions and sometimes misinform. Mother often said that, with me, things went in one ear and out the other. Maybe she was right. Before I was ten or twelve, I don't recall that we talked about her family's Jewishness and her Jewish upbringing more than once or twice. And when we did, her standard answer was we don't go to the synagogue. The Wobser family goes to the Lutheran church, and we celebrate Christmas. Even though her family was Jewish, she told me she had changed and had given that up. She was no longer Jewish. She had become a Lutheran just like the rest of us.

We did speak about religion when I was a bit older, particularly when I had to practice for my confirmation classes. But, as to her Jewish faith or heritage, I know little. I know she believed in God, that she prayed, and that she went to same church that I went to. That is about it.

Years later, it turned out the Jewish blood did make a difference. Then, it had little to do with religion or what we believed. That was when the Nazis defined being Jewish as a race and we all struggled to understand what it meant. Then, it changed the rest of our lives.

Chapter 14

The Helft Family

The Helft family lived in Wurzen, a German town of about 12,000, located on the River Mulde, and on the old train line between Leipzig and Dresden. Wurzen is in Saxony, the area of Germany that bordered Prussia at that time. Before the Berlin Wall fell, Wurzen would have been in East Germany. It is 300 years older than Pr. Holland, quite a bit larger, and more of a trading than farming center. The Helft's second daughter, my mother, Alice, was born in Wurzen on April 9, 1887. There were four children in her family, three girls and one boy.

My grandfather, Ludwig Helft, Louis to his friends and neighbors, Opa Helft to his grandchildren, owned and operated a popular department store near the Marketplatz in Wurzen. The store was large, occupying two floors of a building on a busy street corner. Opa's store sold a wide assortment of goods: furniture, linens, glassware, pots and pans, pillows, blankets, utensils, clothes, and the like. The front had big glass windows with large bays where items were displayed to the townspeople as they walked by. The street corner was a gathering spot, and Louis, the shopkeeper, was well known in Wurzen.

Opa also owned a few businesses along the back alleys where some of the items sold in his store were produced. These were housed in small buildings where a handful of people would work. He also traveled to Leipzig and Berlin frequently to add inventory to his store.

Mother loved and admired her father very much. Louis Helft was widely regarded and well liked. Mother claimed that Opa was one of the town's most important and successful businessmen, a *Geschaftsmann,* and the Helfts were a well-to-do Wurzen family. The family's position in Wurzen was very important to Mother. She would remind me that I was a Helft too. She was raised with high expectations, and she expected the same from me. At times, I found that expectation troubling. As a child, I worried about Mother's approval, sometimes too much. She was tough. I wonder what Mother was like when she was my age.

My grandmother Jenny Helft came from the Frank family. She was Opa's first wife and the mother of three of the four Helft children. Grandmother Jenny died young of breast cancer, at age thirty-five, in 1895, when Mother was only eight years old.

Mother never told me much about Grandmother Jenny except that she was very beautiful and very strict. Mother said that since Grandmother Jenny died so young, she did not have many memories of her mother. I can't imagine what it must have been like, at age eight, to watch your mother get sick and die. It must have been very sad. That would have been very difficult for me.

I was told that Opa worked long hours keeping the store open. Knowing that his children needed more parenting than a nanny could provide, Mother said he put an ad in the paper to search for a new wife and remarried within a year or two. That was the way many marriages were handled then, either advertised or arranged. With his second wife, Mother's stepmother, Rosa, Mother's little sister, Jenny, was born in 1898. She was named after Grandmother Jenny. Mother never said much about her stepmother. I don't remember her. I have only seen pictures. She died before my sisters and I were born.

These years were difficult. Between 1895 and 1898, Opa's parents, Ernestine and Philipp, both passed away. They were my great-grandparents and lived in the town of Bernburg, also in Saxony, about one hundred kilometers from Wurzen. Mother told me Opa was always taking the train to Bernburg to check on his parents and to make sure they were well cared for. That was her only memory of my great grandparents.

My sister Lotte once told me that many generations of the Helft family lived in the Bernburg area, and we had a number of distant cousins there. Some spelled the family name as Helfft with two f's. I never thought that mattered much since, when Mother married Father, she became a Wobser, which is what I was. Lotte felt otherwise. She knew a great deal about family. Mother and Father even had a family tree that Lotte had drawn. Years later, when I left Germany, they gave it to me to preserve for my family.

Mother's older sister was Aunt Trude. My oldest sister, Trude, was named after her. Aunt Trude was only a year older than Mother and her closest friend. Most times, Mother was very serious, but not when she was around Aunt Trude. They laughed all the time whenever they were together. Uncle Alfred, Mother's brother, was four years younger. He served in the German Army and was wounded in World War I. Mother never told me what he was like as a child.

Chapter 15

Cousins, Aunts, and Uncles

$\mathcal{L}$earning the names of my first cousins and who was an aunt and who was an uncle is confusing for a child. That has not changed. It is as true for my grandchildren today as it was for me when I was growing up. On the train to and from Wurzen, my sisters would make me practice and recite everyone's names. How families fit together is not the kind of thing I thought about very much. Whenever they did this, my first instinct was to pretend I was getting motion sickness. Then, they would stay far away. I was far more interested in my friends and in looking out the train window than reciting the names of my aunts and uncles.

My aunts and uncles became aunts and uncles because my parents told me to call them Tante or Onkel. My cousins became cousins when I was told they were my cousins. I had no idea what it really meant to be a cousin. Now I still get confused, and I confess to having little interest. Don't misunderstand. The people interest me, just not the labels. Most were old when I was young. Most were gone by the time I was at an age to remember. I just knew they were my family.

Mother's sister, Aunt Trude, was married to Uncle Adolf. He died in 1934, and I know little about him. They had four children, Erna, Leni, Ruth, and Heinz. Cousins Erna, Leni, and Ruth were about the same age as my sisters. I never knew them well. Cousin Ruth died when she was 10, just a few years after I was born. Erna and Leni were already away at the university when I was a small child. My sisters were friends with them, as they were all about the same age.

Heinz was two years older than me. He was interesting. I knew him well, and we became lifelong friends. Older kids can be a bit superior. Heinz was like that, sometimes telling me what to do and how to act. Still, I liked him. I was a little impressed because of his age. He knew or claimed he knew things that I had not yet learned. He was very smart. As a child, sometimes I found myself in trouble because of Heinz. I still remember how upset Mother was when Heinz and I found the bamboo poles in the basement and he tried to teach me to fish using food we took from the kitchen. Sometimes I followed him more than I should have.

I wonder if, in some ways, there was a little bit of competition and jealousy between Mother and her sister, Aunt Trude. It was all unsaid. It was just a sense I had, the kind of thing like who was happier, who was wealthier, and who married better, those types of comparisons. I'm not sure. I think that may have been true. Mother never talked about it. At times, I felt that comparison between Heinz and me when we talked about our families. Who had the better car? Who was more successful? That kind of thing. Mother and Aunt Trude were so close in age that it was entirely possible.

After Opa died, Heinz and I were given grandfather's pocket watch and gold chain. Actually, because he was older and more responsible, Heinz was given the watch, and I was given the chain. It is a story and connection we cherished as children. I still have the chain. It is at home in my dresser drawer. It is one of the few possessions that I have from my childhood. I hid it from the Nazis when I left Germany and have always kept it close. I imagine Heinz still has the watch, or maybe the Germans confiscated it when he left. I wonder if he remembers.

Mother's brother Alfred married Aunt Hilda. Her family, the Hartmanns, lived in Wurzen too. They only had one child, my cousin Inge. Like Heinz, Inge was close in age, only four years younger. Whenever Inge's family visited, it was my responsibility to make sure she enjoyed herself. I remember Mother telling me that I needed to learn to be the host. I liked Inge very much.

Inge was so tiny, even when she grew older. And she was very sweet, particularly when she got her own way. I remember she used to cry when she was told she couldn't do something. Mother once told me that she thought Aunt Hilda doted on her too much and that Inge was spoiled. I didn't say a word. I didn't want Mother to think I was spoiled. Spoiled or not, Inge was fun to be around.

Mother's youngest sister, Jenny, married but never had children, so there were no more first cousins. That left me with five on Mother's side and none from Father. Heinz and Inge were the two first cousins I knew best. They were my favorites. When Mother mentioned cousins, they were the ones that I thought of. We just did not see Inge as often as I saw my cousin Heinz. And Heinz was a boy. As a child, that made a difference too.

Chapter 16

Funerals

Opa Helft, my grandfather, died in 1932. The entire family attended his funeral: my parents, my sisters, my aunts and uncles, my cousins. His was the second funeral I ever attended. The first was for Grandfather Albert in Friedeberg Neumark when I was eight; the second for Opa when I was ten.

I had nightmares after Opa's funeral. When I went to Grandfather Albert's funeral, he was placed into a heavy, well-built coffin they put into the ground. That made sense. The coffin would protect Grandfather Albert from anything that lived underground. I'm sure one of my sisters had explained everything. I don't know. That funeral did not give me nightmares.

With Opa, it was much different. Mother told me he was wrapped in linens, something they called a shroud. This was a Jewish custom. And the coffin was not as strong-looking. It was completely made of wood, like a pine box, and it did not give him the protection I was expecting. That upset me. I was worried about Opa. I was afraid of what might happen to him. The ground is full of snakes. I had nightmares about snakes.

The following year, we returned to Wurzen and put flowers on Opa's grave. That was the first time I saw a tombstone with a name of someone I knew. At least we could remember where he was buried, although I could not understand why that was so important. I couldn't imagine we would retrieve him from underground. There was the old cemetery in Pr. Holland and even an older small cemetery on the farm in Crossen, but I never knew anyone buried there. Father told me not to walk on the graves at the farm. Even though we did not know the people buried there, we needed to give them respect. I would not have walked there anyway. I couldn't imagine all those people underground living with snakes. I was terribly afraid of snakes. It still gives me the creeps.

Our family is different from many when it comes to the topic of funerals. Neither Mela nor I are too interested in the ritual. I suppose it is because we didn't spend our lives near the towns where we grew up. Both family and friends are widely scattered. I really would not want them to spend money to attend my funeral. Mela has convinced me that cremation is best and that tombstones do not last forever. She believes that the Earth is not large enough to bury all the people that die. As for paying respects, we both believe that we need to pay more attention to the living. Visit me before I die. We can enjoy one another's company. A funeral is a rather one-sided affair.

For me, there will be no funeral, no coffin, and no tombstone. I hope my grandchildren will thank me. There will also be no snakes to worry about.

Day 2, morning...

It was early when they called; I don't remember the time. Both sounded relieved and excited. Dad was awake. All was well. He smiled when they got to the hospital this morning. He gave them the thumbs up. The breathing apparatus had made his throat sore, and he was unable to speak. But he nodded in answer to their questions. He was tired and needed his rest. He was doing okay, just a little battered and sore from the surgery.

The nurses planned to get him to sit up in the afternoon. Until then, Mom and Joanie would sit and watch him snore. They would call later. I could talk to Dad when they called.

A lifetime had taught me to hear the emotion in Mom's voice. I knew her worry. I knew her relief. The worst was over. The rest would be easy. Tonight Joanie might take Mom to the casino for an hour. There was little they could do at the hospital, and Mom needed a change of scenery. Joanie was planning to return to Iowa in the morning. She had Christmas to prepare for. Her kids, Abram and Micah, would be home from college. We were on the road to recovery. We were all thrilled.

Chapter 17

Aunt Hilda and Inge

When Opa Helft died in 1932, Uncle Alfred and Aunt Hilda took over operating the department store in Wurzen. Mother told me that Aunt Hilda needed to work there too because Uncle Alfred had suffered injuries in World War I and his health was not so good. She said he had limitations. I never knew what that meant. As long as I could remember, Uncle Alfred had been working at the store with Opa. He had started shortly after returning from the war in 1918.

I always thought Aunt Hilda was a bit strange. Mother said she was unhappy. I guessed she was angry because she had to work in the store. Mother explained that Aunt Hilda had been an only child and expected that her life would be better. She had grown up in a very privileged world. Father said it was because of Uncle Alfred. I didn't understand that. He was always friendly and nice with me. He had told me stories about what it was like in the Great War. Aunt Hilda was the odd one. I never thought she cared too much about me even when I spent time with her daughter, Inge. That didn't make sense since she was my aunt. She was very friendly with my sisters. I don't think she liked Father very much either. I heard her say he worked with his hands. I never knew what she meant by that.

Mother felt bad for my cousin Inge because both her parents were at the store so much. Inge was left alone with her nanny. Maybe that is one of the reasons Inge was spoiled and accustomed to getting her own way. Since Mother felt sorry for her, I always felt a little sorry for Inge too.

Inge must have been nine years old when her father started to get really sick. That was in 1935, just after we moved to the farm. Inge was sent to stay with us for several weeks that year. He had been sick the previous year but had improved. She had stayed with us then. This year, I learned that he was getting worse. I remember how homesick and upset Inge was. She cried all the time. She told me that she loved her father very much. He was kind. Her mother was strict.

It must have been about two years later, when Inge was eleven, that her father, Uncle Alfred, died. For someone so spoiled, Inge had a tough life. She had such a sweet smile and had such a cheery way about her. I only saw Inge once or twice after her father died. A few years later, immediately after Kristallnacht in 1938, Aunt Hilda sent Inge away to Brussels to a home for girls. She wanted Inge to be safely away from Germany. The evening of November 9, 1938, in Wurzen had been very bad. They feared for their lives. The Nazis had burned and looted their store. Everything that Opa Helft had built was destroyed.

Chapter 18

Family Values

For my first three years, my sisters were my nannies. Then, much of my world changed as they left for boarding schools, one after the other. By the time I was six, all three sisters were out of the house. I really did not know them well. We were almost a generation apart. Much of what I know came from stories Mother and Father told, and when my sisters were home on holiday or for family celebrations. Our difference in age made our time together brief and our relationships distant. To them, I was a child, and to me, they were old. When I was still learning to talk and make sense of my surroundings, they were grown and ready to embrace their individual adventures.

My family was independent and strong-willed, always prepared for whatever came along. Everyone was self-confident and competent. In those respects, Mother and Father were very much alike and my sisters much the same. The Wobsers were a serious, hardworking family. I doubt we were particularly unique but am convinced that our success and good fortune grew from these traits.

Self reliance, integrity, and respect for others were values that were always stressed. From a young age, my sisters and I were taught to be skilled at whatever we set out to do. We were not risk takers. Instead, we learned to calculate risks and rewards, and to act accordingly. I suppose another way to describe much of this is to say that we were taught to be rational, not arrogant, but sometimes a little overly self-confident. Too much bravado is not a good thing. Mela reminds me that my side of the family has more than our share. Me? It helped that I liked to listen. I learned a lot while they all talked.

Education came first, before chores and absolutely before hugs or affection. Mother ruled firm and insisted we excel. We would be prepared for the world. In my case, I still believe she pushed too hard. But I was the last child, she was in charge, and I never rebelled. In matters of home, my father deferred. As to Mother, when it came to matters of me, patience was not one of her virtues. Mother was a stern taskmaster.

Mother and her sister were raised in much the same way. Their education was never curtailed or limited because they were girls. In fact, Opa Helft always pushed them to further their education. I don't know if it was because their mother was so ill when they were young or because Opa was too busy running the store to cope and parent. Perhaps Opa thought that the schools in Wurzen were not good enough. Whatever the reason, they were sent away to boarding school early in life. They rounded out their education by attending finishing schools, where they were taught languages, music, art, philosophy, and history. They both received very good liberal arts educations.

Weimar, Germany, was home to many private boarding schools for girls. Mother never told me which one they attended. They benefitted, as they grew older, when the nineteenth-century limitations on higher learning for girls were being done away with in Germany. I have always thought Father to be street-smart and Mother to be book-smart. This was a tough combination, and I could never get away with too much.

The importance of a quality education for girls must have struck a chord with Mother and Aunt Trude, as both made certain that their daughters were well prepared for their worlds with education and skills. They also pushed the boys hard too. But the girls were born first.

The first to leave our home was my sister Trude, who was sent off to boarding school in Elbing when she was fourteen. She studied business. When she returned, before she was married, she was employed by father as his business manager. Next to leave home was Lotte, who was off to Leipzig to get her teaching credentials and to pursue a career as a home economics teacher in the German school system. Finally, there was Ilse, who made her way to the Deaconess hospital, where she studied nursing. Both of Aunt Trude's daughters, Leni and Erna, went on to study medicine. Leni was unable to finish. She chose to help Aunt Trude manage the family business after Uncle Adolf died. Erna became a practicing physician.

As my sisters left, our home emptied quickly. For a very brief time, I had the run of the house, but in very short order, a nanny was hired. Again, I was being told what to do. I missed my sisters. My days of being the little prince were over. Now it was Mother, Father, me, and the nanny.

Day 2, mid-afternoon...

Something is not right. Dad is not recovering from surgery as he should. Joanie said that he seems confused. He seems to have his long-term memory, but short-term is a struggle. I am not sure what that means. They will send him for a CAT scan in a little while. We won't learn the test results until tomorrow. Dad is still in intensive care.

Joanie is concerned and wants to be certain Mom and Dad are alright. She plans to delay her trip home a few days, at least until Dad is released from the hospital. Mom is holding up quite well. She has a book and several crossword puzzles and says she is fine sitting at the hospital. At eighty-eight, she is amazing. She told Joanie there is no reason to worry. There is nothing they can do. It is up to Dad. She is sure he will be okay.

Sitting there is stressful. They wait and wait for something to happen. It has been a drain on their energy and emotions. They were both expecting to see some improvement today, and it was hard when they realized that wasn't the case. Hopefully, tomorrow will be better. They will go back to the condo. She wants Mom to get some sleep. I'm not sure what to think. I want to know what the doctors say.

Chapter 19

Mother and Father's Marriage

When Father arrived in Pr. Holland at the age of twenty-one in 1902, he went to work for the Aris family business buying and selling farmer's crops and supplying farmers with seeds and equipment. Apparently, he was good at his work. Mother said that Udo Wobser had become known as man who knew how to manage and get things done. Father made a name for himself. During this first decade of the new century, he grew to become a respected member of the Pr. Holland business community.

He travelled frequently to the farms in the area and learned to do business with merchants in nearby villages and towns. At first, he would travel by horse, but he quickly acquired an automobile and mastered its operation. Father had a lifelong love for automobiles. I don't remember a time when we owned fewer than two or three automobiles, a rarity in the 1920s.

In 1903, he joined the Prussian Army. I don't know if he enlisted, was drafted, or simply registered. I do know that this didn't interfere with his work. He was able to report for training and maneuvers whenever required.

Sometime around 1905, Udo Wobser started his own agricultural business selling to farmers whatever they needed, and buying and selling the grains they harvested. That was when he purchased the building at Poststrasse 9 to store his equipment. As the business grew, his first employee was his foster brother, Walter Falk, who left Friedeberg Neumark and joined Father in Pr. Holland.

I've only heard stories about how Mother met Father, how a young woman from Wurzen met a young man living four hundred kilometers away in Pr. Holland. My cousin Heinz, who always claimed to know much, told me that Opa Helft put an ad in the newspaper searching for an eligible suitor for his unmarried twenty-year-old daughter. My sister Ilse told me that Mother saw a newspaper story about Pr. Holland's new rising entrepreneur and asked her father if he knew how they could be introduced.

Since I was about ten years old, when I heard these competing claims, I neglected to ask my parents for the real story, and my sisters had no other knowledge to offer. So it appears that this is a story left for speculation. Whatever the case, it seems accurate to say that Grandfather Louis asked someone to investigate Udo to see if he was a suitable mate for his daughter. I have no idea whether there was any type of courtship, but apparently, all parties agreed with the terms of the arrangement, although there is some question as to whether the investigator was ever paid for his work.

Some Jewish families reject the notion of marrying outside the faith. Since Father's birthparents were both Jewish, I suppose he may have claimed his Jewish credentials, and it may have been a factor in Opa Helft's approval. That seems unlikely, though, given Father's religious beliefs and Mother's decision to abandon a Jewish household and to join her new husband in a Lutheran life.

In any event, my parents were married in Wurzen on April 9, 1909. The wedding party was held in Wurzen at her parents' home, and it was certain they approved. A generous dowry from Opa made it possible for them to purchase our family home on Bahnhofstrasse in Pr. Holland. Nine months and eleven days after the wedding, their first child was born. Gertrude (Trude) was followed in quick succession by Charlotte (Lotte) and Ilse. By 1912, Udo and Alice found themselves busy parents with three little girls under the age of three.

Their lives were apparently much less chaotic and more stable by the time I showed up on the scene ten years later.

Chapter 20

World War I

World War I, the Great War, quickly changed family life for the Wobser household. The assassination of Austria's Archduke Franz Ferdinand in June of 1914 triggered a series of events creating a global world war centered in Europe. And, by the time it ended in November of 1918, more than 15 million people had lost their lives.

First, Mother's brother, Alfred, and brother-in-law, Joseph, were drafted. Then, when Russia's first and second armies invaded Prussia in August of 1914, Father was called to serve as well. I understand that some of father's military service was limited to serving as a guard at the prisoner camp in Pr. Holland, which kept him close to the family. But there were more dangerous assignments that were only alluded to and never discussed. In any event, the times were perilous and must have been difficult for all. While Father was away, Mother and the three young girls were forced to cope on their own.

For several weeks during the Russian invasion, Mother and the girls moved in with the grandparents in Wurzen to escape the more immediate war zone. Although they definitely felt the danger, fortunately, war never came to Pr. Holland. When they returned to Pr.

Holland, Mother found herself in charge of running both the business and the home during Father's absence.

Apparently, Mother excelled at managing the family business, which blossomed during the time she held the reins, some say more successfully than when Father was in charge. All I know is that Mother, whatever the task, was regarded by all as sharp, shrewd, and competent. Father loved telling stories about Mother's success. She had a knack for wining and dining the customers. Each of my sisters clearly inherited Mother's winning ways. I am not saying they were manipulative. I'm just suggesting they were adept at getting things done in their own way.

For Father, age and postings eased much of the war burden. He was already thirty-three years old when World War I started. Our immediate family survived intact, unblemished, and undamaged. But both Uncle Alfred and Uncle Joseph returned home with war injuries that would shorten their lives. The disruption of war would always be remembered. Father had a lifelong disgust for war. Nonetheless, he was very proud that he had fulfilled his patriotic duty and served as a soldier for his country.

By 1918, normal family life resumed in the Wobser household, and the family quietly and quickly prospered. To expand the business, Father acquired more land and buildings on Poststrasse and purchased the farm in Crossen. By 1922, when I was born, the family was well settled. Mother and Father had attained middle age and were living the good life. Father was forty-one, Mother was thirty-five. The business continued to grow. They acquired another farm, a dairy, and a cheese factory. The girls, 10, 11, and 12, were busily engaged with their own lives.

I have no clue whether my arrival was a surprise or planned, but the family seemed thrilled, and if there was any objection, I was not made aware. I entered a family that was happy, prosperous, and successful. And I was their darling boy.

Day 3...

Today, our phone calls are more frequent, every hour or two. Either I call them or they call me. We are checking on one another. This is a different type of family crisis, one unlike any we have had before.

I am having second thoughts. I worry about Mom. Dad is well taken care of. Maybe I should be in Arizona. I know that is not entirely sensible. There is nothing I can do there except be with Mom and Joanie. I can't change whatever is going on. Joanie is strong and supportive. I am glad she is taking charge. There is little I can add. They don't need me for hugs. We all know we love each other. But, sometimes, moral support helps. Maybe I need theirs.

They are back at the condo now, having spent the day at the hospital. In our last conversation, Joanie said it was a very difficult day. There was some good news and some worrisome news. The good news is that Dad definitely appears physically and mentally better than yesterday. He knows who they are and seems to understand for the most part what is going on. He is calm and not in pain.

The concern is the CAT scan they took yesterday afternoon. According to the neurologist, it indicates that he had a stroke. It is in the right hemisphere of his brain. This is the area that affects vision, and Dad seems to be having trouble seeing. Most of the time, he keeps his eyes closed. But, when he does open them, he doesn't focus or seem to track well. Joanie is vague about whether he is talking. When I ask, she says, "Sort of." Nobody can tell us what this means for the future. All we can do now is wait and hope he improves.

I realize that I haven't been able to say a word to Dad since the night before the surgery. There hasn't been the right moment to put the phone by his ear. I need to talk to Joan and Mom about our upcoming European trip. Should Ginger and I cancel? It doesn't seem right to go. I know what Mom and Dad would want us to do. They have always been clear about those kinds of things. They would insist that we live our life. Still, I am mixed. Let's see what happens. We have a week to decide.

Chapter 21

Our Household in the 1920s

World War I was over. Germany was to pay a big price during the decade that followed. Life for many Germans became very difficult, particularly those in larger cities. The reparations the world extracted placed an enormous burden on the German economy. Unemployment was extreme. To solve the problem of paying their war debts, Germany began printing more money. The result was an unimaginable catastrophe. Hyperinflation set in. A loaf of bread costing a few Reichsmarks in the morning could cost 100 Reichsmarks by evening and 1000 Reichsmarks by week's end.

Fortunes were lost. People were angry. Fingers were pointed. Politicians railed. Blame was placed. The uncertain seeds of the future were already being strewn.

I don't recall any of this. I've read stories but don't remember. Perhaps it was because of where we lived, in East Prussia, in an agricultural area, away from the big cities. Or maybe it was because we grew all our own food on the farm. Perhaps it was because father's business was successful. Probably it was because Father and Mother shielded me from this because I was a child. I don't know. We never talked about these problems. The adults dealt with these issues. They didn't include me in these discussions. All this happened before I was ten.

I do know this: Father's money was in his land and properties during these times. The modest fortune he had accumulated was tied up in his holdings and not sitting as savings in a bank where its value would disappear. This was a stroke of good luck or maybe his genius. While many watched their savings evaporate as currency was revalued, Father actually benefitted financially from these times. Land bought at pre-inflation prices later could be sold at post-inflation prices. The same held true for grain and livestock. And, when times became better, the dairy, the cheese factory, and the second farm were sold for profit.

What I remember as a child was always being well fed. I never remember lacking for anything. And I certainly don't remember being sad. The first ten years of my life went by in an instant. I was surrounded by my sisters, my parents, my grandparents, aunts and uncles, and cousins. We were a family united by closeness and caring. The distances and differences never interfered. We saw each other frequently and knew each other well. The Wobser family never lacked for company, whether at the farm or in town. We had friends and family.

Many people were part of our daily life. At the farm in Crossen, there were four: the foreman, the housekeeper, and two farmhands. At Father's business, there were three salesmen, two others in the office, and the chauffeur. At our home, there was a housekeeper, my nanny, the cook, and a maid.

Later, I realized that these were all paid employees. As a child, I never thought that way. I never considered that they were the hired help. I saw them as family, and all treated me as their own. Now I am sure it was never that simple, though I believe that Mother and Father were always fair with their employees and treated them well.

The workers at the farm were always teaching me new things. Father's driver taught me all about automobiles. The cook always had a special treat waiting in the kitchen. It may have been more complicated than the way it appeared. From my perspective, everything was perfect. They were my friends.

Of course, even good fortune has a beginning, and every beginning has an end. But that was a lesson to be learned later. I had no knowledge of that then.

Chapter 22

Our Home in Pr. Holland

When my sisters left home, the house in Pr. Holland became eerily empty. I suppose, by town standards, our house would have been considered large. When the three girls left, it echoed of silence.

I was more than a bit frightened by the basement. It seemed to go on forever and was always dark and foreboding. There was a room with a billiards table that sat unused; a room for storage filled with steamer trunks, luggage, Christmas decorations, and such; a second kitchen with a large baking oven; a room lined with shelves filled with canned goods; a shop room where all the tools were kept. There was a furnace room that had unfamiliar noises and where I was convinced danger lurked. There was a laundry room filled with two large tubs, drying racks, a clothes wringer, and an assortment of equipment for ironing and pressing our clothes. Two things in the basement that always captured my imagination and experiments were the laundry chute, which ran from the upstairs bedrooms to the laundry, and the dumbwaiter that connected the basement kitchen with the main kitchen on the first floor. By the time I was seven years old, I had already learned, firsthand, that neither the family dog nor the family cat shared my fascination with either the laundry chute or the dumbwaiter. Both stayed far away when I was lurking nearby.

The main floor had a large kitchen, a parlor, a sitting room, a dining room, a small library, and a large study that Father used as his office. There was even another room I was allowed to use for my train set. I never knew what that room was really for. We just called it the train room. I could use the train room for all kinds of things, like my science projects, and not just trains. For reasons not to be shared, as they might illustrate my darker nature, the dog and cat avoided the train room too.

There was a large radio in the parlor where we could listen to the news from Berlin. There was a telephone in Father's study. We would gather there for family telephone calls. We also had a telephone at the farm in Crossen and another at Father's business. Late in the evening, the study was where Father would usually sit and read the newspaper.

On the second floor, there were bedrooms, six in all. There was a room for each of us children, a room for my parents, and a room for the nanny. Of course, when the girls left home, three of these rooms sat empty.

The attic was another place I tried to avoid. It was used for storage. We kept our winter clothes there in summer and our summer clothes there in winter. The attic was large and dark, and I cannot remember a time that I was not afraid to go up there. One time, there was a bat in the attic, and Mother had to chase it with a broom. Whenever I had to go to the attic, I was certain that the bat had invited all of its friends to live there too.

Adjacent to the house was a two-car garage. Father kept the Brennabor in the garage. I don't remember what else was in the garage, but it was full. He kept the other two automobiles, the Opel and the Butz, at his business. They were used mostly for work.

Lights, electricity, and heat, I always took for granted. I cannot remember a time when we didn't have these conveniences. Our baths had indoor plumbing, and we had ice boxes and stoves. I think most everyone living in town had telephones, but I can't be certain. I was told telephone service came into our area years before I was born, not long after the turn of the century.

Today, I realize what a privileged life we had in Pr. Holland. Then, I must have assumed that everyone lived that way. At least, I thought they did. I am not sure that I ever paid attention to the difference. Later, it became clear that others noticed.

Chapter 23

Mother, Father, and I

Father was a proud man. He often said that we should be grateful for the good German life we lived. Mother always told me to sit up straight and work hard. My mother was strict and very serious. But she could be funny, and when she laughed, she had a good laugh.

Our home life seldom varied except when we had company, visited others, or when the sisters came home, particularly, my sister Lotte. She always invited her friends. The house did not echo in silence when Lotte was at home. But, when it was just Mother, Father, and me, the house would be pretty quiet. Sometimes it was too quiet.

Mother managed the family. She was in charge of our home and the help; father was in charge of the business and the farm. Mother was mostly home; father was mostly away, either at his business or with his driver, travelling for business. Saturday afternoons and Sundays were the exception. Father worked on Saturday mornings, but the remainder of the weekend was typically spent at the farm. Generally, we came back into town on Sunday mornings for church, but other than that, Sundays were spent at the farm. After Ruth was born, Trude, Walter, and Ruth would come to dinner on Sunday afternoons.

Every once in a while, Father would take me fishing. He loved to fish. When we were on holiday at the beach in Kahlberg, he would take me to the pier so we could go crabbing. In Crossen or Pr. Holland, we would take the car, drive to a pond, and fish. Even when he was away on business, he liked to carry his fishing equipment. He told me that he would often stop at a lake and fish when he had spare time. When Father and I fished, Mother would often join us, and we would pack a picnic.

During the week, I seldom saw my father. He normally worked late, and usually, I was upstairs in my room or in bed by the time he came home. Later, when we moved to the farm and he no longer owned his business, everything changed. But, when we lived in Pr. Holland, Mother would wait for him for dinner. I would eat earlier, and Mother would always sit and visit with me during my dinner. I remember that mostly we talked in serious tones. She tended to treat me like I was older than my age. I imagine that was because she was used to talking to my sisters.

Chapter 24

Going to School

For me, school began in 1928, the year I turned six. This was a major event in my life. Some of the children in Pr. Holland started with kindergarten one year earlier, but since I had a nanny, there was no need to go to kindergarten. I learned quickly that, in my family, school was serious business. That was a tough lesson for a six-year-old then, just as I am sure it is these days.

I remember how excited I was. After spending most of my first years with adults, it was a welcome change to spend my days with kids my own size and age. At first, I was a bit of loner. We all were loners those first few days. It took me time to adjust to this new experience. Once I realized that we were all a bit lost and finding our way, I got used to everything and made many new friends. It turned out that I had met many of the kids while sledding the previous winter. Without our winter caps and masks, it took us all a bit to figure that out.

The school wasn't far, just a few blocks from where we lived. Until I was considered capable and old enough to walk there and back on my own, Mother would walk with me each morning. And she would be in the schoolyard each afternoon to make certain I returned home without delay. I resisted, but Mother and Father were very protective. I became one of the oldest students to require a chaperone to and from school each day. I remember being embarrassed to have Mother as an escort. I imagine it is the same way now for kids.

One memory that sticks is that, most days, I wore a sailor suit to school – in warm weather with short pants and in cold weather with long. There were no school uniforms. Most boys, at least in the early grades, chose to wear sailor suits, and I did the same. Nobody wanted to be different. We all wanted to be part of the crowd.

Once given the freedom to walk to school on my own, I quickly learned the shortcuts and where all the other kids lived. Of course, we all suffered the refrain that homework came first. Within a day or two, I quickly learned the consequence of not telling Mother to whose house I was going. That never happened again.

What I remember most, though, is Mother's constant reminder. It was her job to run the home, Father's job was to run the business, and my job was to go to school. Period. No ifs, ands, or buts. There was no room for discussion.

Day 4...

Today's reports have been better. Dad is still in intensive care. Seems he slept fairly well last night and was more comfortable today. The doctor took his chest tube out this afternoon, which really helped.

Mom said he has been taken off oxygen support as well and he is eating more. She told me he isn't too excited about hospital food. She said one of the items today was pureed cottage bread. I have no clue what that could be. According to her, it really didn't look particularly enticing.

Dad had his eyes open more and whispered a little, but his throat is very scratchy. They could hardly hear what he was saying. I think what she was telling me was that he was trying to talk. She sees improvement, but he still sleeps a lot. The big concern at this point is his vision. He doesn't seem to see out of his left eye, but he does see on the right side. When he looks at them, he doesn't seem to focus very well.

They still have a difficult time understanding what he is trying to say when he talks. He seems to understand them. He nods his head when they ask him questions. Sometimes Mom wonders if he really does understand or whether she and Joanie are just hoping that he does. It is difficult to have any kind of conversation. Tomorrow, when I call, she will try to hold the phone to his ear. Mom thinks that will be good for him.

I asked Mom how she was holding up. She said she was fine, a bit tired. She became silent for a moment, then: This is life, there is nothing we can do but hope. Mom told me she was concerned about Joanie. Joanie needed to go home and be with her family. That was more important. She asked that I speak with Joanie and tell her. Mom said she would take care of Dad. That was her responsibility. Joanie should be with Marv. That was Joan's responsibility. Mom asked about Zak, Stacy, and Ryan. She asked about Ginger. She told me she needed to hear about cheerful and good things. She said that the hospital was a lousy place to be. Sad and gray is depressing.

As we were about to end our conversation, Mom asked about our trip. She had been to Prague and Vienna, but that was more than 80 years ago, when she was a small child. Did I know that Grandma's old friend, Otto, had been the chief architect of Prague? Would we go to any concerts in Prague? Is that where we would meet up with Manfred and Marianne? Would we see the Boys Choir when we are in Vienna? Were we going to Budapest? Would we see the fireworks on New Year's Eve in Salzburg? Where else were we going? I hesitated. Go and have a great time. It was our turn. Don't worry. She would take care of Dad. Give my love to Ginger. That was my Mom. Always asking a million questions.

Chapter 25

The Parakeets

*B*eing six brought other responsibilities. Mother thought I was old enough to take care of the pet parakeets, aptly named for my parents, Alice and Udo. One was blue, the other was green. I have long forgotten which was which. I don't know why I was given this wonderful task. It seemed exciting the first week. By week two, the excitement started to dim. By week three, I knew I had been had. Parakeet care became a much disliked chore.

The birds belonged to my sister Ilse. But she had left, and the birds had stayed. It was quickly clear that my life would have been better if Ilse had taken the birds when she had left home. They made a mess and reminded me of the chicken coops at the farm.

Regardless of the circumstance, Mother believed that it was time to teach me responsibility. I can still recite her instructions. Each morning, I was to remove the cloth that covered the cage. Then, I was to feed the birds. Each evening, before I went to bed, I was to put the cloth back on the cage. Doing these steps in the proper order was important. Parakeets do not eat in the dark. Every Saturday, I was to clean the cage. And, never, no matter what, was I to leave the cage door open. Do not tempt the cat.

My excitement turned to unhappiness, and then, it turned even worse, particularly on Saturday's when Mother would insist that the cage be cleaned before I could do anything else. To this day, I blame Ilse for leaving her birds behind.

It was only a few months when panic erupted one Saturday morning. During cleaning, Alice flew the coop. The cat, the cook, my nanny, Mother, and I spent several anxious minutes in pursuit of Alice. Father, hearing commotion from within the house, came in from outside to see if he could help. When he opened the door, Alice seized the moment and was never to be heard from again. Of course, we were all distraught, and we never told Ilse.

I remain unsure of the exact nature of Udo's illness, but sometime later, Mother solemnly explained that Udo had died, most certainly of a broken heart. As for me? Finally, I found a use for the dumbwaiter. It could be part of the funeral.

I have never had a love of parakeets, and it did not turn out well when the kids had parakeets years later. I will let them tell that story.

Chapter 26

Expectations

I went to the elementary school, the *Volkschule*, for the first four years of my education. Classes included learning to read and write and music and religious instruction. Mother also insisted that I take extra classes in mathematics and science. These were optional, and parents had to pay for them. They were not part of the basic educational program.

Childhood then was not altogether different from childhood now. There were birthday parties for friends, overnight sleepovers, and play dates. The boys avoided the girls until we were old enough to know better. Recess was always the most popular class. There were school trips and class projects.

I must have been about five when Father taught me to ride a bicycle. From that time forward, my bicycle and I were inseparable. And, much like the snow sled, my horizons expanded. Unlike today, safety was not so much the issue. There were very few automobiles in Pr. Holland. At that time, in 1927, most were probably owned by Father. The roads were cobbled in the center of town. All the other streets were dirt and dusty when the air was dry, muddy when it rained.

There were no traffic signals, crosswalks, or stop signs. The biggest obstacles were the horse-drawn buggies and whatever the horses may have left on the roads.

One of my greatest worries was the exam to be taken upon the completion of the fourth year at the *Volkschule*. Throughout Germany, ten-year-olds were required to take this exam. We all worried and prepared for months. Those who did well would go to the *Mittelschule* to prepare for the *Gymnasium* and then the university. Failure would mean remaining in the *Volkschule* for the next several years and perhaps a career that required more hands than brains, not to mention a certain amount of ridicule from others.

There was never a question of what was expected of me. By ten, I had become accustomed to a good life and wanted more of it. Mother was very clear. I knew that I had to do well in order for this world to continue. Failure was not an option, nor was average. I was expected to be at the top of my class.

Chapter 27

Latin and Greek

op of the class or not, I moved on to attend St. Georges, the middle school that was adjacent to the church. The classes were difficult, far harder than what I had experienced thus far. I struggled with Latin and Greek. I did well in mathematics, taking courses in algebra, geometry, and calculus. I also enjoyed the science courses. I didn't like history. Religion was always part of the curriculum. Father told me I had inherited his mathematical ability. I told Mother that I wanted to become an electrical engineer. Of course, that was not the first career I had identified. Prior to that, I had expressed an interest in any number of occupations: farm foreman, automobile mechanic, train conductor, milkman, and soldier.

My curiosity for how things worked became a hobby, and the train room and the hayloft became my hideouts. I spent hours upon hours taking things apart and trying to assemble them back together, sometimes with success and, other times, with failure. As long as I kept up with my studies, Mother and Father would encourage these experiments. I remember using my chemistry set to make soap, putting everything imaginable under the lens of my microscope, assembling a crystal set radio, and building anything that involved wheels. I am sure if I could have located our two old parakeets, they would have been objects of my research.

I loved all things mechanical and all things science, and have ever since: the cars in the garage, the machinery at the farm, and my projects in the train room.

When I was nine or ten, scouting became a big part of my life, and I joined the boy's youth group through the church. These youth groups were very much part of German culture. We met weekly and learned about various scouting projects, not dissimilar to the way scouting is in America still to this day. We would earn badges, recite oaths, wear uniforms, learn to tie knots, and do good deeds. Nearly all of my friends from school were part of our group. Each spring and fall, we would go for an overnight outing. There must have been 30 boys in our club. We would go camping, go hiking, build bonfires, cook meals, tell stories, and sing.

All in all, I was a pretty normal kid with a pretty normal childhood. I had close friends. We did things together. These were good times. Unfortunately, good times don't always last.

Chapter 28

Murder in Pr. Holland

*I*t was close to nine when an event happened in Pr. Holland that stunned and shocked us all. Father came home that evening very upset. He said that an eighteen-year-old boy, a clerk in a store in the center of town, had been attacked by a gang and was not expected to live.

Crime was unheard of in Pr. Holland. Nobody locked their doors. We did not have a town jail, only the old prisoner-of-war camp that dated back to World War I and was never used. Nothing like this had ever occurred in Pr. Holland, as far as anyone remembered.

The attack gained nationwide attention. It was reported in the Berlin newspaper. It was reported on the radio.

Arthur Knopf has been stabbed by Hitlerist high-school students in the town of Preussisch-Holland, in East Prussia, while they were going through the streets in demonstration. Knopf is in a critical condition and is not expected to live. On being arrested, the students said that they stabbed him because they don't like Jews.

Jewish Telegraphic Agency, Berlin, March 18, 1931

This certainly caught our attention. Mother turned to me with a look of alarm. Father said not to worry. It had nothing to do with our family. We didn't even know the Knopf family.

That incident in 1931 was when I first learned that there was a long history in Germany of hating the Jews. Some people held strong feelings about Jews, blaming them for everything imaginable that was wrong, much stronger than the stuff that was playground banter.

This was the first time I learned that there were people who thought Jews were their enemy. I had heard kids say many things about Jews. Kids talked about the Poles in much the say way. But I never thought that meant anything. This was harmless conversation. That was just the way some of my friends talked. Some kids make fun of others. They were just repeating what they heard others say. Cruel and stupid? Of course. Dangerous? No. Now I know better. Now I know that it was dangerous. Behavior like that can never be tolerated and can never be condoned. Then, when I was nine, I had no idea what this kind of talk really meant.

I certainly had no idea why some people would physically harm someone because they were Jewish. To be honest, I had never thought about the possibility. My sense of enemies or opponents was limited to childhood games on the playground or in the backyard. It is difficult to remember what a nine-year-old thinks, but clearly, a nine-year-old thinks more than a parent might know.

From my observations of the synagogue and my church, I knew that a few people were Jewish and most others were not. I knew that my cousin Heinz in Leisnig was Jewish. He had told me he celebrated Hanukah. I knew we celebrated Christmas and that he did not. I remember listening closely, probably because it had something to do with presents. Some things don't change. Kids have their priorities.

By then, I knew that Mother had grown up in a Jewish family. So what? Everyone had parents, and they all grew up in families. This was not something significant. There was never a time that we denied our Jewish ancestry. It was not something avoided. It was simply a topic that rarely came up. It was neither a family secret nor a family discussion. As for religion, we were Lutherans. As for ancestry, we were what we were. Father had always been a Lutheran. Mother had become a Lutheran. My sisters and I were Lutherans. The synagogue held no part of our life, and we didn't follow any Jewish customs or celebrate Jewish holidays. Our religion was not Jewish.

I need to be careful about the impressions I create. Religion was never a bible-thumping theme in our family. Faith was not something we ordinarily spoke about or discussed. We never wore our religion on our sleeves. I suppose, like so many others, we went through the motions and gave lip service to certain beliefs. It is true that we felt informed by our faith and we respected many of its customs and beliefs. I was baptized and confirmed, we attended church services, we typically said grace with our meals, and I was taught to say my prayers. But there were seven days in every week, and church held our attention for only a brief part of one morning. Most of our religion was about caring, kindness, giving, being considerate, and respecting others. I believe our family was like that, and in that regard, we were a very typical German, small-town family.

I can't be certain if the murder that year in Pr. Holland caused Mother and me to have a conversation about hatred and prejudice, but we must have talked about it at that time. Perhaps I wondered whether Mother might be in danger because she had been Jewish. I can't recall if the subject was the sensationalism of there being a murder in our small town or the fact that someone was attacked and killed because they were Jewish. I just know that is when I started to think of things a bit differently. I knew one thing for certain. This had nothing to do with me.

These were the years when Mother and I would visit while I ate dinner, when Father often didn't get home until late in the evening, after I was in my room or in bed. Any conversation about our Jewish roots would have been with Mother. These were not matters Father and I discussed, ever. He had no interest. And, even with Mother, the conversation would have been brief.

Mother would have told me we should be tolerant of everyone. We all have similarities. We all have differences. We respect everyone. Educated people do not act this way. Bad, stupid people had committed this horrible crime. They would be caught, and their punishment would be severe. She would have told me not to worry. Jewish ancestry or not, we were Germans, first and foremost. That's what mattered.

Certainly, the murder would be something that would be talked about among my friends. Nine-year-old kids talked about everything, and we would have all talked about this. It was big news. It happened in our home town. It was in the newspaper and on the radio. We all knew the store where it had happened. The adults all said it was the first murder anyone ever remembered taking place in Pr. Holland.

I am sure each of my friends claimed to know someone who marched in the demonstration, someone involved in the case, or to have special knowledge about a particular fact. We would all listen intently as details were unveiled. We would all voice our opinions.

I am not sure whether we talked about Jews too. We might have. We all knew that Jews were different from us, just like the Poles. That was what everyone said. They went to the synagogue. My friends and I all went to the church. That was common knowledge. I suppose it's possible that one of my friends would have made a disparaging remark about Jews. Kids do tend to repeat what their parents or older siblings say, often without a clue as to what it might mean. I knew enough not to be entirely comfortable with these conversations. But

I had no desire to distance myself from my friends. All the kids ran together as a pack, and I was part of the pack.

It is also entirely possible that I repeated something one of my friends said and my parents heard me. But I doubt it. I had been raised to be polite, and polite people did not make disparaging remarks about anyone. Certainly, that would have triggered a conversation with Mother and, more than likely, been grounds for a mouth washed with soap, something threatened from time to time and that I had successfully avoided.

What didn't really connect for me was that my family fell into the category of the Jews that were in the center of this storm. I thought those were others. Soon, I was to learn that they were us.

Day 5...

Today, I didn't call Mom and Joanie much. I know they are getting tired. There is only so much one can do in this situation. They
called when they returned to the condo for the evening. Dad is
still in intensive care. He is not progressing as rapidly as everyone
had hoped. At this point, we are just taking one day at a time. He
is very frail.

Dad has been in intensive care now for close to a week. It is
clear that everyone is getting worn thin. For me, I have diversions.
I'm sitting out here in North Carolina doing what I do. For Mom
and Joan, each day, they go back to the hospital and sit and hope.
Joanie tells me they are playing Scrabble but not keeping score.
And nobody has any certainty of what the next day might bring.

At least they are sending daily email updates to friends and
family. That eliminates the commotion of too many phone calls.
Joanie tells me the emails have worked out well. Everybody is
being very respectful. I can't imagine what it would be like if they
had to return phone calls each evening.

Mom says Dad still has a sense of humor and isn't in much
pain. They have been telling him about all the cards and emails.
He knows that everyone is thinking of him. I still haven't heard his
voice, so I suspect he is not talking. Sometimes, I wonder if Mom
and Joanie are making his situation appear better when they talk
to me. It is difficult to get a clear idea. I don't know what she
means when she says he has a sense of humor. Does he laugh?

Ginger is urging me to go out for a few days. It is easy to do,
and there is no reason I shouldn't. I guess I have been holding
back to see if I could fill in for Joanie, but she is still there. I would
take my turn, but it doesn't make much sense to me until she
leaves. I know that Joanie feels different than that. If I want to do
so, I need to go soon. With travel time and logistics, a two-day

visit will take four days. Unless we cancel Europe, I should go to Arizona tomorrow. We are talking about cancelling the Europe trip. Mom won't hear of it. She insists we go. It is what Dad would want us to do. They have had their turn; now it's ours. She is stubborn and adamant. We worry about her. We don't need all of this to take her down too.

Mom, again, told me she hopes Joanie will go home. Joanie needs to be with Marv. I know Mom. It's not that she wants Joanie to leave; she just needs some time for herself. She is starting to feel smothered, and when she gets like that, she can become pretty unpleasant. Joanie just wants to make sure Mom can manage. I don't want to see Joanie get her feelings hurt. That's happened before. I know Joanie and how much she wants to help. They will work it out. They always do. But, still, it is difficult. It is easy to see how everyone's nerves are shot.

Chapter 29

Father's Fiftieth Birthday

ertain events are remembered for a lifetime. They are recalled and relived. Father's fiftieth birthday in 1931 was one of those times. A grand party was planned at the farm. My three sisters would be there, as would my cousin Heinz from Leiznig and my cousin Inge from Wurzen. All my aunts and uncles would attend, close family friends too.

When we learned that Trude would marry soon, the party was expanded to become an engagement celebration as well. Trude would marry her boyfriend, Walter, from Elbing. Father had told me he had given permission. Knowing Trude, I was pretty sure that she had told him what to do. Mother and Father were very excited. This was their first daughter to be married.

Everyone dressed up. Mother took me to Elbing to buy new clothes just for the party. It's curious the things one remembers. The day of the party, Father taught me to polish my shoes. He told me that when he hired employees, he always looked at how they took care of their shoes. Men who took care of their shoes were responsible. If they took care of their shoes they would take care of their tools.

Years later, when I hired employees, I always took a quick glance at their shoes too. When I taught Ralph to polish his shoes, I told him the same story.

It was summer, and a large tent was erected. Help was hired to assist our cook prepare the food. The farmhands built a wooden dance floor. Musicians were engaged. Even a fireworks celebration was planned.

At the party, Father stood up, raised his glass of champagne, and made a toast to my sister Trude and to her fiancé, Walter, the soon-to-be newest family member. What I remember most was that it was the first time I ever was given my own glass of champagne.

Father's friend Mr. Lesser stood up and talked about Father, how much he had accomplished in his fifty years, how successful he had become, how he had served his country so well. I remember being proud.

Later, after everyone had eaten, the music started, and everyone danced. First, I had to dance with each of my sisters. Then, I danced with my five-year-old cousin Inge. All she wanted to do was spin in circles. I even danced with my cousin Heinz.

Mrs. Lesser had invited her brother Jarus, who was visiting from Marienberg. My sister Lotte seemed real impressed with Jarus. They danced with each other several times that evening. That must have been the first time they met. I wonder if they had any clue then that they would marry nearly ten years later.

Of course, nine was that age when good can turn to bad in the blink of an eye. Unfortunately, that's what happened to me. Cousin Heinz dared me to drink more champagne. We snuck around and took sips from glasses while the grownups danced. Inge asked me to dance some more. My fun ended just as the tent began to spin. That's when I got sick. Mother got angry. Father laughed and carried me to bed. To this day, I still worry about getting sick when I drink a glass of champagne. I never even got to watch the fireworks that night.

Chapter 30

Being Ten Years Old

Some memories fade, others blur, and a few are crystal clear. The years run together; the events overlap. I had reached my tenth birthday in pretty good shape and with hardly a scratch. Some things I understood, some things were a question, some things I worried about, some things I liked, some things I hated, some days I was bored, some days I was busy. I guess that is the life of most ten year olds, even today.

I knew enough to know that the world was not perfect. Although I had seen a few exceptions, I was generally convinced that it was a good, kind, gentle, caring place. I am sure that is what my parents wanted me to know.

My tenth year passed quickly. Middle school at St. Georges continued to be a challenge, and I found myself feeling the weight of schoolwork. My backpack was always heavily loaded with books.

Trude and Walter were married. Opa Helft died in Wurzen. We attended his funeral. My sister Lotte found a teaching position in a small town on the outskirts of Berlin. Ilse was just about to finish nursing school. Summer seemed over as soon as it started. We rented the house at the beach in Kahlberg for a month with Cousin Heinz's family. Cousin Inge visited for a few weeks. Her father was ill.

We were all engaged with our daily life. I was busy with my homework, my projects, scouting, and my friends from school. Mother had been occupied with the wedding, sorting out her father's death, and keeping the household running. Father was busy with his work and away much.

For me, a personal milestone that year was that I had been allowed to ride my bicycle on my own to the farm in Crossen. I had to ask permission first. But, now, my friends and I could go there and ride the horses. That was a big thing. Again, my universe was expanding.

At ten, I continued to view the world as consisting largely of my own undertakings. Parents were to be respected and to be avoided by any means possible. Being ten was incredible. We possessed most abilities and knew nothing of consequences. Fear, risk, and worry were feelings that were mostly ignored. Being ten was about self.

School was a challenge for ten-year-olds. We had already learned about continents, countries, languages, rivers, and oceans. We knew how to read. We knew how to write. We had mastered numbers. Now we began learning how to assimilate the world around us, about history, biology, more complex mathematics, and national events. Schoolwork required listening to the news on the radio each evening, reading classics, and writing reports. We were assigned projects, given deadlines, and required to give oral presentations in front of our classes. We were finished with memorization and recitation. Now we were expected to think and arrive at conclusions. I found this abrupt and demanding. I was expected to express myself, something I had successfully avoided for much of my ten years.

Listening to the news in Father's study each evening taught me about national events and, in 1932, introduced me to national patriotism. Up until now, my world had been Pr. Holland, the farm in

Crossen, the beach in Kahlberg, and my grandparent's home. Now I was learning about Berlin, about the rising political leader Adolf Hitler, and about my country, Germany.

Again and again, both in school and on the radio, we were told about the enormous price that Germany was forced to pay because of World War I. We were told that it was an unfair burden. The German people were fed up and angry because of the economic conditions that resulted. It was not often that I was able to sit with Father and listen to the news. But, when we did, he told me that he believed that Germany needed new leadership that would stand up to the rest of the world. Germany needed jobs to be created to make life better for Germans. He had served our country. It was time for Germany to serve its citizens.

Now I have learned that there are moments when it is more important to listen to what is left unsaid. Father never warned me of the dangers of Germany or of the tactic of making Jews the scapegoats for all that was wrong. He never warned me about the dangers of Adolf Hitler and his followers. No, Father wanted a strong Germany, with decisive leadership, a Germany that would regain its dominant place in the world. To this day, I am certain he never considered the price that he might be forced to pay or how this might affect our family.

Of course, even though I was being taught to think on my own, I was still a kid of ten. What did I know? I believed what the adults told me, both at home and in school, and they all wanted what was good for Germany. Patriotism flourished.

Chapter 31

1933

1933 was a year filled with major changes. The first was unveiled on New Year's Day when newlyweds Trude and Walter announced they were expecting a child. Mother and Father were thrilled. This would be their first grandchild. At ten, I was still processing where babies came from. Life on the farm had taught me certain basics. I knew this involved something more than a stork and had remembered some of what Father had told me about the bull and the cows, but a more enlightened discussion had not been broached. Uninformed conversations with friends had only added to the mystery. Despite my lack of information, I recall being surprised that I was to become an uncle. Uncles were all old, and I was not.

Continuing my new ritual of listening to the news each evening, I became totally versed in the plans for the Berlin Olympics. Updates were given every few nights. We learned about the stadiums being built, all the construction in Berlin, and the countries that would participate. We memorized the names of German athletes who would compete. This was big news, the kind of news that would be shared among my friends. We all knew that hosting the 1936 Olympics would be a big triumph for Germany, even if it was still three years away.

From the radio that year, America became something more than a place on the world map. I learned that construction of the Golden Gate Bridge in San Francisco had begun that January. I was impressed with this amazing engineering feat, the building of the longest bridge in the world. I imagined a bridge to the Pacific Ocean. I remember spending hours with my train set trying to construct my own miniature version.

We also learned news about Germany and changes within our government. Some of this I remember with clarity. Some I learned later that year in school. And other parts I learned later in life. Now my memory is somewhat fuzzy; events happened so quickly. Most of what we heard on the radio was of distant events happening in Berlin. Living in East Prussia, we were far from Berlin with a swath of Poland between us. Some days, we felt like we lived in the country, like Germany was the mainland and Berlin was the big city. The radio brought us our news. The radio controlled the images we created. We only heard. We didn't see. We could only imagine.

By the end of January, President Hindenburg had appointed Adolf Hitler as Germany's Chancellor. Hitler was a name kids repeated on the playground and at school. With time, we were taught to raise our arm in salute. Everybody saluted. He led the marches in Berlin: to change the government, to restore Germany's greatness, to create more jobs, to give Germans a better life. That's what we were told. He would make Germany great again. It was only later that I learned that his scapegoat for the woes and ills of Germany were the Communists, the gypsies, the least able, and most definitely, the Jews.

Power accumulated quickly, and the detractors were eliminated, like dominoes efficiently falling, one after the other. Father told us that if the Prussian leaders who controlled Germany's government didn't listen to the anger of the crowds in the streets, the Weimar republic would fall and the Nazi's would take power.

The signals and warnings had always been there. We listened to it on the radio. Most of us in Germany were blind to the truth. The harsh reality is that the world hardly noticed. We never considered the consequences. And, at the time, we never believed that the dominos that were to fall would fall upon us. Germany was our home.

I can't recite the chronology or elaborate on the facts. I can't explain the reasons or defend how we lived our lives. What I can tell you is how the events of 1933 sowed the seeds that fundamentally changed our future, that there was little handwringing or emotion, that circumstances were beyond control, that there was no recourse or appeal. I can tell you that events were incremental, that the unbelievable became the believable and, ultimately, the normal. We adapted to the situation before us. That was all we could do. That was the best we could do.

Chapter 32

The 1933 Boycott

April 1, 1933, was a most forgettable day, not sunny or rainy, not hot or cold. It was a Saturday, a day for me to spend time with my friends. That Saturday, the Nazis carried out the first nationwide organized action against Jews: a boycott targeting Jewish-owned businesses. The boycott was an act of revenge. Jews had allegedly circulated stories in the international press damaging Nazi Germany's reputation. It was payback, a warning shot over the bow. The Jews were the victims, and April 1, 1933, became a day we would never forget.

Stormtroopers, members of the brown-shirted paramilitary wing of the Nazi Party, stood menacingly with their arms crossed in front of Jewish-owned businesses. In many instances, the Star of David was painted in yellow and black across doors and windows. Signs were posted saying, "Don't Buy from Jews," and, "The Jews are our Misfortune." Throughout Germany, acts of violence against individual Jews and Jewish property occurred, and the police rarely intervened. The clear message, in Hitler's new Germany, was that Jews did not belong.

There was no significant destruction or violence in Pr. Holland that day. But the few Jewish-owned businesses in town were all targets of the boycott. I will never forget the signs hung at the cobbler's shop near the Marketplatz and the teenagers standing in front of the tailor's shop, creating a nuisance and preventing customers from entering.

We had no idea, no reason to expect that Father's business would become a target, too. There was no forewarning. That morning, along the front of his building, in large red letters, was the message, "Udo Wobser is a Jew."

I speak as an adult now, with the collected wisdom of age and hindsight. I will always remember that Saturday through the eyes and mind of a ten-year-old boy. That was the day Father became known as Udo Wobser, the Jew, no longer simply as Udo Wobser. That was the day I learned that I could be both a Jew and a Lutheran at the same time, that being a Jew was about bloodlines and ancestors, that it was about race, not only religion. That was the day I learned I was still a German, but now I was a German Jew. That was the day I learned that my family was a member of a much larger family, a family that ran generations deep, a family that was viewed with disdain and contempt.

From that date forward, a line had been drawn. It wouldn't matter what we thought, how we had lived, what we believed. Please don't misunderstand. We had never rejected the notion. We simply had never been taught to embrace it. Before April 1, 1933, I never entertained the idea that our family was Jewish, that I was a Jew. It meant nothing to me. If asked the question, I would have answered, "No, I am Lutheran."

Ultimately, the answer was not ours to give. Others told us who we were. Both Mother and Father were descendants of Jews. There was no denying. There was no appeal.

At times, I wonder what Mother and Father really felt that day. Given the choice, how would have they answered the question. Did they consider themselves Jews? Now I know their answer was obvious. Our opinion did not matter. There was no choice. No one asked. The question was not needed; the answer was evident.

In 1933, fewer than six hundred thousand Jews lived in Germany, a fraction of the population, about 1%. Most were proud Germans, citizens of a country that produced great poets, great writers, great musicians, and great artists. Many, more than one hundred thousand German Jews, had served in the German Army during World War I. Many were decorated for bravery. And, many, like our family, did not think of themselves as Jews. Families had assimilated and inter-married. Families had been raised in other religions. We were one of those families.

I have often wondered how they chose Father's business instead of others and why they targeted our family. There were a dozen Jewish families in Pr. Holland. Anyone could go to the synagogue to learn who the Jews in Pr. Holland were. But our family belonged to the church. We did not go to the synagogue. The church had records of our baptisms, confirmations, my sister's wedding, and our pledges. Our family had been part of the church in Pr. Holland for over thirty years.

To my knowledge, no one went door to door asking who was Jewish and who was not. Perhaps Mother or Father or my sisters had discussed our heritage with others. Had Father's success created enemies? Did we live too well? How would I know whether friends of Mother or Father had forsaken their friendship? At age ten, I wouldn't have known these kinds of things. Now I know that town records contained this information. Both my parents' birth certificates clearly stated that Mother and Father were the children of Jewish parents. Now we know that there was a systematic effort underway throughout Germany to identify the Jews.

We never chose to run away from our roots. But I was never taught that we were a proud Jewish family. I was always told we were a proud German family. We never rejected our past. We always respected it for what it was. Father was doing what he had been taught to do since he was a child. Mother had chosen to follow her husband. The harsh reality was that it did not matter what we thought. From that date forward, as far as the Nazi government was concerned, we were Jews.

Day 6...

Joanie called me tonight after Mom went to bed. We talked for a long time. It has been a bit since the two of us talked without Mom in the room. This has been hard on Joanie. She is pretty broken up. I can't imagine the stress she is under. She never expected to be away this long. Christmas is a little more than a week away. Her boys will be home. There is a lot to do. She doesn't want to leave Mom. I reminded her that she needs to go home.

Mostly, she is worried. She is afraid that Dad will not make it. She wanted me to know if I wanted to see Dad, I should come out tomorrow. She said I should prepare myself. He is in pretty bad shape. He is very sick and very frail, much worse than they thought. There has been little change in his condition. Joanie thinks he is slipping away. She is not sure if Mom fully realizes it. Mom is always upbeat and positive. There is never a day without sunshine.

Mom interrupted our conversation. I guess she woke up and heard Joanie on the phone. She got on for a few moments. Mom understood that the two of us wanted to talk. She was glad that we were. She wanted me to know that she is all right. She understands what is going on. She may be old, but she is not fragile. She is a realist. She is well aware of what might happen. Joanie does not need to treat her with kid gloves. She does not want Dad to suffer. Her biggest fear is that if he comes through this, how will he be? Will he be the person he was? What has the stroke done to him? Will he be confined to a chair and just stare out the window? That is what she is afraid of most. Dad would never want that. She knows this. They have talked about that. They know what each other wants.

Mom told me that she and Joanie had brought some of Dad's big band tapes in for him to listen to today. They both thought that he seemed to enjoy the diversion. Mom said that she is worried about Joanie. This is very tough for her. She told me that I needed to be more sensitive to Joanie. Joanie is a big help, but Mom thinks she needs to be back home with her family. That is more important. There is nothing we can do for Dad. She can manage. Joanie does not need to remember Dad this way.

I told Mom that she ought to go back to bed. She needs her energy. She needs her sleep. Then, we spent a few moments all crying on the phone. Everyone is exhausted. She asked about Ginger and told me to tell Ginger that she was doing okay and that she loved her.

As for me...I like to remember our good times. I feel a tinge of guilt but mostly have no regrets. One thing for certain, I feel a bit older.

Chapter 33

The Day After

The weather was warm and sunny on Sunday, April 2, 1933. Life for most was back to normal. The signs and the graffiti were removed. And, over the weeks ahead, the shops and stores were open for business, and customers entered the doors. All over Germany, the targets of April 1 were still neighbors. Many were still friends.

But the stigmas remained. Most of the Jewish population was now known, including the Jews who thought they had assimilated. Though the formality of the Nuremberg laws was still two years away, the Jewish population was being catalogued and marginalized. The Nazis continued to consolidate their power, and the efforts to force the Jews out of Germany continued to grow.

Much of our family life continued as normal. Father went to work each day. I continued to go to school. We continued to go to church. We never changed our religion. Plans were made for our summer holiday. Spring planting took place at the farm. If there were changes that took place in Mother's or Father's lives, I was never made aware of them.

What I noticed immediately was how my classmates at school changed in the way they reacted to me. Before, I was "in." Now I was "out." At that age, school life can be cruel. Someone let the air out of my bicycle tires. I was disinvited to a birthday party for a friend, someone whose birthday party I had gone to every year I could remember; our family had been guests in their house. A parent told my parents that it would be better if I no longer went to scout meetings each week.

I never felt in physical danger; it wasn't like that at all. I was ten years old and could watch out for myself. I just was no longer welcome. I was excluded. I was shunned. It was a very painful time. There was nothing I could do. I can't imagine what Mother and Father must have felt watching this happen to me.

Over the coming weeks and months, Father's business suffered too. It didn't happen overnight. The slowdown happened gradually, a little bit at a time. Father always said that the difference between profit and loss was only a few Reichsmarks. I guess that slowdown took away those few Reichsmarks. Farmers still needed to buy and sell grain and livestock. Farming equipment was still in demand. But the business began to lose some of the ingredients of its success. Customers who had been loyal for more than twenty years went elsewhere. Certain suppliers didn't want to continue their relationships with Father. It was incremental, around the edges, and it began to make the difference between profit and loss. It was a slow and cruel punishment. People did not want us here anymore.

We heard from Aunt Hilda in Wurzen and from Aunt Trude in Leiznig. Everyone seemed to share the same experiences. Business was not as good; kids were not as welcome. There was nothing one could do.

Father refused to blame everything on the Nazis. He said that the Great Depression in America had spread throughout the world and people were angry because it affected their pocketbooks. Grain and farm machinery were not being sold because people did not have enough money. It wasn't just the Jews who were suffering. Many people throughout the country were suffering. The Prussian government in Berlin had been kicked out. Many thought the Nazis were going to fix things.

Father believed that when business picked up, when the Nazis repaired the economy, there would be enough for everyone. Everyone would be happy again, life would return to normal, and no one would be blamed. We were all part of what made Germany great. I wasn't so sure. My immediate concern was what was going on in my school. My life was clearly disturbed. Father always held out hope for Germany. He always believed in his friends. Now I believe he didn't recognize his enemies.

Chapter 34

Summer in Kahlberg

We went on our annual holiday to the beach in Kahlberg that summer. Again, Cousin Heinz's family from Leizng joined us. We spent our days on the beach and our evenings playing board games and cards. Mother even taught me to play Skat. For the first time, I could play with the adults. Mother and Aunt Trude visited the spa during the day. This was their annual ritual. They told us stories and made us all laugh. At Kahlberg, it was like nothing had happened. Everything returned back to normal. Everyone was on vacation.

My sister Trude and Walter came by boat from Elbing and stayed for a few days. Walter had become like an older brother to me. He taught me to dive at the pool. He couldn't stay for long, as he had been promoted to manager at the store where he worked in Elbing. He told Father and me about the new automobile he was about to buy. I remember Father telling him to save his money, that he was about to become a father and would need money to raise a child. Father told me to listen because I would need to know this myself someday.

I had never seen my sister Trude so large. I was afraid she would explode. She always was so slender, but now she was pregnant with the baby. Mother said the baby was due any day. This thought was very troubling. I kept my eyes on Trude all the time. I was worried, and I was excited. I kept bringing her glasses of water. I'm sure I was a pain in the neck.

Things were not the same for Cousin Heinz and me that summer. And, ever since the champagne incident at Father's fiftieth birthday, I had been a little suspicious of the trouble Heinz might cause for me. Actually, our awkwardness had little to do with that. Two years older, Heinz had discovered girls, and he really did not want to be shadowed by his younger cousin. And, again, I was the pain in the neck.

I learned quite a bit from Heinz that summer. Even though he didn't want to associate with me too much during the daytime, he was stuck sharing a room with me at night. Heinz claimed to be quite informed when it came to matters of life, and I learned in detail about how Trude had become pregnant. I was shocked and amazed. Technically, it all made more sense. But I still found it troubling. Of course, now, I possessed new information to share at school in the fall. Perhaps that would get me back into the group of old friends. How could they possibly know these things?

Most of my days were spent with various friends on the beach collecting amber and building immense sand castles and forts. Ten was an age when I had one foot in the camp with the little kids, who I could impress with my knowledge and strength, and the other foot with the older group who would sometimes let me join in when they needed one more player for their soccer game, or when the boys needed someone to deliver secret messages to the girls. I excelled at that role.

If I remember correctly, both my other sisters Ilse and Lotte joined us at the beach in Kahlberg that year. April's events caused our family to be drawn closer together. The significance was not to be underestimated. We all knew things were different. But, mostly, Lotte and Ilse were there because of Trude. Everyone wanted to be the first to hold her child. Ilse even returned to Elbing with Trude for the remainder of the summer. She planned to help care for her sister after the baby was born.

Sometimes long forgotten memories suddenly reappear. I can still picture Mother and Aunt Trude knitting and sewing day and night. Skullcaps, booties, and blankets were in a large pile on the table. They were hemming fabric to make cloth diapers, knitting small sweaters, and sewing small gowns. Even my sisters, each well skilled, joined in the effort. The first grandchild was about to be born. I recall thinking how great this would be. It would be a nice change for someone new to appear on the scene and grab some of the attention. I had been under a spotlight for most of my life. I was ready to relinquish my position.

I spent one more summer at Kahlberg, the following summer, in 1934. But that year wasn't the same. I really don't know why. It might have been the weather, the friends, or just the overall situation. Of all the summers we spent in Kahlberg, my best memories are from the summer of 1933. That summer, I needed to be away from home.

Chapter 35

Moving to Crossen

The family has always claimed the April 1, 1933, Nazi boycott caused Mother, Father, and me to move to the farm in Crossen in 1934; to exit most of our life in Pr. Holland. Now I wonder if the cause and effect were not quite that simple, whether there was more to the story. It was long ago, and I'll never know for certain. It is true that April 1, 1933, marked an abrupt change in our life and we found ourselves cast in a very small and unwelcome minority.

No matter what, I was still in school. I had little choice in that matter. Though I was isolated and my ability to participate in activities outside the classroom had been severely restricted, I still needed my education, and no one, not even the Nazis, were denying my school attendance. Mother's resolve that I receive a good education had only strengthened.

Now there was a new normal, certain rules had been rewritten, and at times, we were uncertain as to how we fit in. There still was a life in Pr. Holland. Father's business continued to operate, certainly not as successfully as it had in previous years, and we still went to the Lutheran church. In fact, I was scheduled to begin confirmation classes at the church. Those doors were still open.

Every situation had its own irony. Father was to be honored by our town's council in the coming year. A celebration was being planned to commemorate the twentieth anniversary of World War I. Father and the seventeen men from Pr. Holland who had served in the army would be commended. A large stone monument listing their names would be unveiled. War veterans throughout Germany, many of whom were Jewish, would be honored. In Pr. Holland, even a parade had been planned. Father and the other veterans would wear their military uniforms as they marched through town. No one would paint graffiti on his business that day.

It was not difficult to be confused by these mixed signals. We all were. None of us were certain as to what the future would bring. Would we be accepted as Germans or rejected as Jews? These mixed signals were particularly hard for Father. He always wanted to believe; he could never accept. For me, in school, the signals were pretty clear. I continued to be an outcast and had little reason to expect that to change.

Despite the turmoil, our lives were regaining a rhythm. I was in my second year at St. Georges and taking courses that would prepare me for the next level. Lotte was in her second year of teaching home economics at a public school outside of Berlin. Ilse had finished her courses at the Deaconess hospital and now would be able to support herself with a career in nursing. In Elbing, my niece Ruth was born and keeping Trude busy. Walter's career was on the rise, assuring their family of a rewarding and prosperous life.

Mother wasn't saying anything to Trude, but she told me she secretly hoped they would have another child. Now that I knew the facts of life, I remember nodding my head knowingly. From Wurzen, we learned that Mother's brother Uncle Alfred's health had improved and that business in the store was picking up. Cousin Inge was starting her first year in school. From Leiznig, we heard that their business was recovering, and there was even talk about expanding. Cousin Heinz would be entering the gymnasium; Cousin Erna had completed the university and was now going on to medical school; and Cousin Lena was in her second year at the university.

It must have been late in 1933, shortly after my eleventh birthday, that Mother asked me what I would think if we moved to the farm in Crossen. I would still attend my school, but our way of life would be quite different. When I asked why, her response was that it would be better for the family. I didn't have a clue as to what that meant.

There was no question that the events of 1933 had taken a toll. Our way of life was changing. Two Jewish families in Pr. Holland had already moved away, one to America, the other to Berlin. It was clear that the Nazis were making it more and more difficult for Jewish families to live in Germany. Jews were being told that they could not work in certain jobs. In some places, Jewish students were being told to leave their universities. There was talk about limiting household help for Jews to make their lives more difficult. From the radio, we learned that, particularly in the larger cities like Berlin, Jewish-owned businesses were closing or being sold and families were leaving Germany to live elsewhere. Although our small town life in Pr. Holland was far removed, we could still see it here. It was the incremental shifts, the way I was treated by classmates at school, the family friendships which drifted away, the customers of Father's who had moved on.

Our roots ran deep in Germany. While Mother and Father had the resources to move away from Germany had they wished, they would have to leave everyone they loved: my sisters, Mother's family, and now, their first grandchild.

Moving from Germany would have been unthinkable, out of the question, an idea that never would have been considered or discussed. There was never a suggestion, at least one that I heard. Although our situation in Pr. Holland had changed significantly, things had calmed down. Mother said that because business was slower, we may have to tighten our belts a bit. Mostly, I needed to stay away from trouble at school. We needed to wait for the economy to improve and for the anger in the streets to disappear. Times would get better.

I look at this differently now. Age has taught me that things are often not as they seem. Obvious answers don't always solve complex questions. 1933 was a difficult year for Mother and Father, stressful and uncertain. With their daughters full grown with lives of their own, Mother and Father may have decided to step back and relax. Father had sold the dairy and the cheese factory. He told me he had made a modest profit. They had saved their money. They had done quite well. They had all that they needed. Father was now 52 years old, past middle age by most standards. For the first time, his business was suffering, and he had reached that point where his enthusiasm waned. I imagine he felt like he was swimming upstream.

Their savings would assure a good life for their remaining years. Mother and Father both loved the farm, and there would always be good food on the table. It was only time before Ilse and Lotte would marry. More grandchildren would be a certainty. The farmhouse was large, and everyone could visit.

I would leave home before long. With the education and skills I would acquire, my opportunities in Pr. Holland would be limited. The political situation made that even more apparent. They would encourage me to follow my dreams, to build my own career, and that certainly would not be in Pr. Holland, not in these times. The family business would not be suited for me whether I would want it or not.

The same week Mother spoke to me about moving to the farm, Father told me that he had some concerns about Mother's health. She had gained a considerable amount of weight during the last few years. It was harder and harder for her to get around. I didn't say anything, but I remember thinking that he had gained a lot of weight too. The house in Pr. Holland was too large, had too many stairs and too many rooms. Although we had plenty of help to run the house and farm, Father felt it was too much, much more than we needed. And, if we could no longer keep household help, he wasn't sure what we would do. Perhaps it would be better if we were to move to the farm in Crossen.

I am not sure if there was one single reason for the decision to move from Pr. Holland to the farm in Crossen. Family lore has it that we were forced to move because of the Nazis. As I recall my conversations with Mother and Father, I think that is too simple an explanation. That may have been partly true, but I do not believe it was entirely the reason.

That winter, between 1933 and 1934, Mother and Father organized our move to the farm. Father leased our home in Pr. Holland to another family. His foster brother Walter Falk already owned a one-third share of the business. Now he would take over the business and become its owner. With Aryan ownership and a new name, the problem of Jewish ownership would be eliminated. Monthly income from the lease of the house and payments from Walter Falk would assure a comfortable retirement at the farm in Crossen. In a few short years, I would be away to a university, perhaps even away from Germany. Father was convinced we could wait out the storm.

By the summer of 1934 and our annual holiday at the beach in Kahlberg, our home was in Crossen. We had moved from Pr. Holland. We could live a quiet life undisturbed by the events going on in Berlin. I could ride my bicycle to and from school, even walk or be driven if necessary. I would finish my education. Our life would be simpler. Trude, Walter, and Ruth could visit every Sunday. We could all help operate the farm. To put it another way, we had adapted. Father had retired, and we moved to the farm.

Day 7...

I jumped in the car about five am and drove the two hours to Norfolk to catch my flight to Phoenix. I would have to fly to Atlanta and change planes. My layover in Atlanta would be a few hours. I would arrive in Arizona about two pm. The change in time zones really helped going this direction.

The day gave me plenty of time to think and reflect. I could even drown my cares at the Atlanta airport, but that didn't really seem necessary or a good idea. I did think about Mom and Dad and the interesting life they have had together. They both had lost much of their youth but had managed to make up for it as adults. In many ways, while I had grown older, they had grown younger. Sometimes our paths intersected. There were moments when it seemed that we all were the same age.

One of those times was when Ginger and I visited them in Rockford sometime in the 1980s. I can't remember the exact year, but I know that we would have still been in our late thirties. We couldn't have been older.

Dad explained that he had been doing some "agricultural" research. He was a tool and die maker by trade, so this had absolutely nothing to do with his work. Turns out he had been given some marijuana seeds and was seeing if he could grow a few plants. Note: Many years earlier, when I was in college, I had introduced them to marijuana. It had been Mom's idea. She'd wanted to try it. This was a short-lived fad for me. I became grown and responsible. Smoking with my folks cured me of the intrigue. It had not been part of my life since then.

Dad had harvested his crop and purchased a used cigarette roller from the second-hand store. He didn't want to roll his joints by hand. Mom had suggested that they produce filtered joints. They both agreed this approach would be better for their health.

Was this a surprise? Not really. He had hinted for months. Bottom-line? Ginger and I spent the evening with Mom and Dad at their basement bar sipping martinis and sampling their new-found pleasure. Beyond that, the details get blurry.

Our enjoyment was a one-time thing. Knowing them, I suspect they continued this form of evening entertainment for a few months before it came to a sudden and unfortunate end.

Dad had been growing his plants beneath an indoor staircase where they would go unnoticed. He had carved out the space, even installing plant lights to encourage growth. Each day, he took and recorded meticulous measurements. He mixed a special fertilizer and was amazed at his success. Their harvest was for personal use and plentiful.

When he was away for business for a few days, he left Mom in charge of the daily watering. Mom claims it was an accident, that she had used the wrong container. She did not know it was carpet cleaning solution. Dad claimed that it was intentional, that she wanted to end the experiment. He argued that he had clearly labeled the correct container, which had been left in the garage. In any case, the plants had not survived. His growing days were over. He had no more seeds. At least, that was the last I ever heard of this story. With Dad, you can never be sure.

Joanie and Mom met me at the airport. It was a relief to see them, and I think they both felt the same. We drove straight to the hospital.

Chapter 36

Transition

We had to adapt. We had little choice. I adapted to the way things were at school. I was eleven turning twelve. At my age, without the laughter and banter among classmates and on the playground, school became dull and boring. Little was left except classes and homework. Before our world changed, I was active in school activities, excited to be with my friends, looking forward to field trips, and raising my hand in class. Now I kept my head down and avoided most encounters. I did not go where I was not welcome. I was excluded, not invited, and mostly told to stay away. It was a tough time for me. I did the best I could.

There was an occasional schoolyard fight; sometimes my nose was bloodied, and sometimes I held my own. I quickly learned the easiest and safest approach was to mind my own business and stay out of the way, to be an introvert. Mother would say, *Spiele nicht mit Feuer,* don't play with fire.

Some friends stayed friendly, and there was one teacher who tried to look out for me, but the reality was that there were only two camps, mine, and theirs. Mine was singular and solitary. Theirs had numbers, muscle, and approval. Anyone trying to stand with me ran the risk of guilt by association. Intimidation ran deep and wide. By then, I was the only Jewish student in my school of several hundred.

That first year of living on the farm marked a big change for me. Physically, I was changing, getting stronger, growing taller, discovering things about my body that I was previously unacquainted with. I missed being with my friends, being able to talk about these things, to learn what is often unsaid, to understand what is normal and natural. We all need others to help unravel these early teen mysteries. I had no one my age. Mother and Father were not substitutes for friends. Ever since, I have believed I missed an important part of growing into adulthood. Mela accuses me of trying to make up for it at times.

We also had to adjust to daily life on the farm. Spending weekends at the farm was one thing, a respite from daily life in town. Now the farm became our home. It was a big change. We were physically removed from neighbors and from the energy of everyday town life. I would go to school, return home, and seldom make stops along the way.

Farm life offered a repetition, newness, and a continuity that was good for each of us. There were chores to be done, hard work to distract, and animals to befriend. There was space to be left alone. It was quiet and away. There were no encounters with old friends, which could be difficult. At the farm, there were no forced smiles, no taunts, or insults. There was no animosity.

I think Father struggled more than Mother and me. I think he was surprised. Retiring to the farm should have been the sunniest and happiest days of his life. But Udo Wobser had always been a man on the go, the man in charge, respected, and successful. He found the adjustment difficult. He no longer went to work.

I suppose, in many ways, Father found this retirement forced, not entirely his choice. Retirement came sooner than he had ever imagined. He was isolated. Lifelong friends had deserted him. Father always enjoyed being with people. It wasn't easy for him. Some days, he told us he felt unwelcome in his homeland. He said he felt he let us down.

I could see the restlessness in Father. He would be up before sunrise attacking whatever needed to be done, telling himself that he could conquer. But, by day's end, you could see the defeat in his eyes. He was a proud man, but he was tired. There were days Mother and I watched him age with frustration.

Eventually, Father found his way. But I never thought he was the same. As I spent more time with him, I could see that he was older. Maybe because I had grown and was nearly as tall, I realized that Father was not as physically imposing as I'd once thought. I suddenly noticed his hair had turned gray and his shoulders sloped. His enthusiasm evaporated. We recognized that something important to his life had gone missing. He could still provide for his family, but somehow, he could not provide for himself. At times, he was difficult with Mother and me, never physical, but certainly verbal. Mother and I shared that burden.

Mother made the adjustment easily. At least, that's what I thought. She, like Father, stayed busy at all times. But she was able to do so with humor and purpose. For Mother, there was always something to be made for her grandchild: scarves, mittens, and sweaters. She would be busy in the kitchen canning and preserving vegetables from the garden. Mother baked wonderful breads and cakes. I had never seen her do these things before. We always had kitchen help in our household, but now Mother took part. We ate well and much. They both added pounds.

Like a rock, Mother showed an inner strength that we all relied upon. She took things in stride, as they were. What she could change, she would. And what would not change, well, that was the way it was.

I'm not sure Father would have survived these times and the years ahead if it were not for Mother. Father worried; Mother could not be bothered with worry.

It is too easy to overanalyze. Mela and the kids always laugh at me when I think too much about myself, but I can see that Mother and Father are both inside me. I hope what shows is the better of both, yet I know that is not always the case. When I appraise myself honestly, I know that my moments of depressed silence and worry are from Father. Yet from Father came my inventiveness, ability to think things through, and certainty. I hope I have some of Mother's calm and resolve.

Evenings, we sat in the parlor and listened to the news from Berlin. As the Nazis consolidated their power, it seemed that new decrees were issued daily. Jews were being marginalized, treated like second-class citizens, and pressured to leave Germany. My sisters were always a worry. Mother and Father talked about them all the time. Sitting there in the country, with the fireplace burning and the silence of the farm at night, even Berlin seemed very remote. We needed it to be far away.

Today, I can see that the move to the farm was good for us, but the transition was difficult and took time. It was the right choice at the right moment. There really was no other place for us to go. For Mother and Father, farm life did ease the pressure of other issues. For me, I learned a bit about self-reliance. With Mother and Father's help, I learned how to survive, to live within myself without close friends, how to be a bit of a loner. I would need to know these things in the years that followed.

Chapter 37

Showing Affection

I cannot remember a time when I saw Mother or Father show any real affection to one another. I never saw them hug. I never saw them embrace or kiss or even hold hands. Perhaps that was the German way. Perhaps their upbringing didn't allow it. Perhaps it was something they hid from their children, or this was something that had been lost with time. I don't know. We never spoke about these things. Even though there was no outward demonstration, I was always convinced that they cared very much for one another.

I wished that my parents had shown more affection. I needed some certainty in those times of uncertainty. I believe that it is important for a child to see parents express their affection and love for one another. I don't believe it should be left to fairy tales. I have always tried to show my affection for Mela in front of the kids. Perhaps sometimes too much, but it is because I missed seeing that as a child.

I always think of Mother and Father as one with the other. I suppose they loved each other, but I don't really know. What I do know is that they built a life together, raised a family together, and shared a common set of values. Did they have a good and happy marriage?

Children rarely know the truth. I guess we all assume certain things about our parents. But the reality is that they are the only ones that know for certain. They are entitled to their privacy. I wonder how the kids view Mela and my marriage. Some truths are never spoken.

Now, as I say these things, I realize that when we moved to the farm in Crossen, it was the first time I saw Mother and Father spend so much time together. Father had always been working. Mother had always been busy. Of course, they would be together at parties and family events. But, at those times, there were many other people around. I imagine my sisters would have known more. Mother and Father were younger when they were children. My sisters remembered different things. I never asked them if they thought Mother and Father were happy with one another. All I knew was that they shared the same household.

Chapter 38

Jewish Restrictions

*L*iving on the farm in Crossen, we were far removed from much of what was happening in Germany. It was clear that the pressure on Jews to leave Germany was rapidly increasing. Each day brought a new restriction. Jews were treated with disdain. Life for German Jews was quickly deteriorating.

By 1935, Hitler was in complete control. The Nuremburg laws had been issued defining who was a Jew based upon ancestry. Mixed marriages, like the marriage of Trude and Walter, were no longer allowed. Our lineage was certain; there was never a question. But many others learned that they, too, were to be categorized. Jews had become the scourge of Germany.

Already Jewish students were excluded from exams in medicine, dentistry, pharmacy, and law, and Jews were excluded from military service. Now new decrees were issued. Jews no longer were allowed to vote, benefit payments to large Jewish families stopped, Jews were banned from parks, restaurants, and swimming pools, Jews were not allowed to own typewriters, Jewish civil servants were dismissed, and many Jewish students were removed from German schools and universities. There were more bans than I can possibly recite. The list seemed endless.

What was distant became reality when we received word that my sister Lotte had been removed from her job. She was told by the school officials that there was no choice. Because she was Jewish, her position was terminated. Jews were prohibited from teaching in public schools.

I can't recall a time that I have seen Father more upset and angry. This was his daughter. This was his country. What right did they have?

Mother must have kept her anger bottled up inside because she remained calm. When I asked her why she reacted this way, she told me that she was so relieved that it was nothing worse. She told me that Lotte would find another job. Under no circumstance did she want her daughter working for people who found Jews offensive. Lotte was better than that.

These were difficult times. The old order was quickly changing. The Nazis were constantly issuing new orders to diminish the role of German Jews in daily German life. It was a slow, grinding process. Each day, there was something new we were forced to swallow. Like many, Father still hoped and believed that our normal life would return. Governments had failed in the past in Germany. This government could fail too. Even though we did not understand, we still were patriotic. I know I repeat myself. Jewish ancestry may have been in his blood, but more than anything else, Father was a proud German. I think what hurt Father the most when Lotte lost her teaching position was that he realized that his country had betrayed him.

Mother and Aunt Trude went quickly to work to resolve Lotte's situation. They had a childhood friend who lived in Berlin. Her husband had just died, and she was in need of a nanny for her two children. That's how Lotte went to work for the Braunsberg family, owners of a large German textile company. The following year, Lotte wanted to take the Braunsberg children, Hugo and Rosie, to the opening ceremonies of the 1936 Olympics in Berlin. They didn't go. No tickets were available. The only Jews allowed in the stadium were competitors. And, even for these few athletes, it was only the result of international controversy and protest.

Chapter 39

1936 Olympics

The 1936 Olympics in Berlin gave pause to the deteriorating situation around us. The Nazi government was on the big stage, and they wanted to impress the world with their behavior. I spent hours by the radio listening to the Olympics. Throughout Germany, everyone listened.

Nazi Germany used the 1936 Olympic Games to promote an image of a new, strong, and united Germany while hiding what was really going on. Anti-Jewish signs were temporarily removed. Newspapers silenced their harsh rhetoric. Foreign spectators and journalists were shown a peaceful, tolerant Germany. To appease international opinion, German authorities allowed Jewish fencer Helene Mayer to represent Germany. She won a silver medal and, like all other German medalists, gave the Nazi salute during the medal ceremony. No other Jewish athlete competed for Germany. If I remember correctly, nine Jews, mostly from Hungary, won medals. Nothing was said on the radio about the boycott or the controversies surrounding the Olympics that year. As far as we knew, the Olympics were a tremendous success.

By now, Ilse was living in Berlin too. Her nursing training served her well, and she was able to find work. And we received word that Ilse had a suitor. Mother told me that another marriage was being planned. Ilse would marry Arthur Behrend, originally of Koenigsberg, but now living in Berlin. They would be married here at the farm next year. We would have a big family party. Ilse was even hoping Arthur's cousins from Naples, Italy, might come. Everyone would be invited.

By any standard, Arthur was an interesting man, so unlike any of our other family members. Whereas Father had always been a robust, industrious entrepreneur with a mechanical mind and street smarts, and my brother-in-law Walter was quick-witted and a man in charge of his own destiny, Arthur could not have been more different. He was a well-educated musician, a trained vocalist. He was an artist who tried to make his career from his art. He actually sang in the chorus for a local radio station in Berlin. It wasn't that he had a disdain for work; he just wasn't made for getting his hands dirty. An only child, he had been raised for the good life by a doting mother. Father liked him enormously from the moment he met him. We all did. He was always kind to my sister Ilse. We always said that Arthur lived in his own world.

Day 7, afternoon...

When they greeted me at the airport, they both looked tired and drained, Mom especially. And, at the hospital, Joanie was right. I did need to prepare myself to see Dad. He was stretched out on a bed in intensive care. He was pale and gaunt. He was wearing wrist restraints to keep his arms to either side of the bed. The wrists immediately caught my attention. Nobody had said anything about having to restrain him.

Both Mom and Joan looked at me and shook their heads. Mom said Dad had been restless at night, pulling out his tubes and trying to get out of bed. They take the restraints off when we are here but usually put them back on after we leave.

I held Dad's hands, hoping for some recognition or some gentle squeeze. Nothing. They were warm but lifeless. How long has he been like this? Joanie said for the last few days. I remember staring in silence, choking back my tears. That was all I could do. My throat would not allow me to speak.

Chapter 40

Hitler Youth

In October of 1936, I turned fourteen. By fall, the Olympics were over, and Germany continued to march to the beat of its own drummer. The respite provided by the Olympics was past, and the internal war against the Jews continued. Externally, it was clear that Germany had plans underway to expand its borders. Violating the Treaty of Versailles, Germany was flexing its muscles. Actually, Germany had been secretly engaged in rebuilding its armed forces for a number of years. When the Nazis came to power, these efforts rapidly increased. Even before the Olympics, Germany had reinstituted the military draft with a goal of expanding the German Army to more than five hundred thousand men. Hitler was determined to rebuild the German empire in Europe.

While these military matters did not directly affect me, efforts by the Nazi Party to recruit Germany's youth certainly did. The Nazis intended to win the hearts and minds of young people. They did so through the Hitler Youth groups and by taking control of the German school system. The Hitler Youth was premised on the belief that the future of Nazi Germany was its children.

Originally, the Hitler Youth was intended to train boys to enter the Stormtroopers. The murder of the eighteen-year-old Jewish clerk in Pr. Holland in 1931 stemmed from a demonstration by a similar Nazi youth gang fed with anti-Jewish propaganda. Stormtroopers and members of the Hitler Youth helped lead the 1933 boycott against Jewish businesses. There was no question that the graffiti on Father's business in 1933 was painted by members of a Nazi youth gang. These were gangs of thugs organized by the Nazi party. These were planned and orchestrated events.

Maybe I was too young to see this before. Maybe I was too sheltered. Perhaps it was a secret kept because we were Jewish or suspected to be. Perhaps my parents had hidden this reality from me. I don't really know. I am not certain that my parents saw this either. Did any of us recognize what was really going on? Now these brazen acts were all out in the open, right in front of our eyes. They were no longer secret. They were taking place all around us: in Pr. Holland, in Berlin, throughout Germany.

In December of 1936, all German Aryan males between the ages of ten and eighteen were required to join the Hitler Youth and to prepare for service as soldiers in the armed forces and the SS. Germany had a long history of encouraging youth groups. Health, exercise, and outdoor activities were part of German culture from a young age. Now all existing youth groups were merged and consolidated into the Hitler Youth, including my old scouting group. After-school meetings and weekend camping trips sponsored by the Hitler Youth trained my classmates to become faithful to the Nazi party.

Teachers and educators were part of the Nazi vision. Teachers joined the Nazi party in greater numbers than any other profession. By 1936, the Nazi regime had purged the public school system of teachers deemed to be Jews or to be politically unreliable. That's why my sister Lotte was terminated from her teaching position.

In both the classroom and in Hitler Youth, instruction aimed to produce race-conscious, obedient, self-sacrificing Germans who would be willing to die for Hitler and Germany. Devotion to Adolf Hitler was a key component of Hitler Youth training. My classmates swore allegiance to Hitler. They pledged to serve the nation and its leader as future soldiers. Teachers in my school led classes teaching love for Hitler, obedience to state authority, militarism, racism, and anti-Semitism.

As a Jew, obviously, I was excluded. Everyone I went to school with was included.

I was miserable. I can't find the words to convey the extent of my misery. I was fourteen years old. I went to school. All of my classmates in school were being taught to hate me, to hate everything about me and my family. My classmates were listening to their teachers. This would continue for my remaining time in school.

Mela and Joanie often ask me to talk about these years. I resist. What more can I say? I have nothing more to tell. Who would want to keep and share these memories?

Chapter 41

Hatred

I was the same person yesterday as I am today. There are days I repeat that sentence to myself over and over because it does describe my life and the situation my family was thrust into. Nothing about us changed. Everything around us changed. We were never the enemy. We did nothing to cause this. Yet ours was not a case of mistaken identity. None of this occurred by accident. All that occurred happened by intention. How could religion and ancestry make these distinctions?

We must have been numb. At times, I stare at my hands and wonder what must have gone through our minds. I draw a blank. I can't remember. I can't imagine how my parents must have felt, how confused they must have been. Were they angry? Were they afraid? What were their expectations? What were their hopes? And my sisters? We were just one family at this one point in time. We were not alone. This was occurring throughout Germany, in the big cities and in the small towns. And the sad truth is that this type of hatred happens throughout the world even today. They call it ethnic cleansing. There was no way to resist. All we could do was adapt and survive.

There are many tragedies in my story. The world is full of stories of tragedy. My story is not singular. It is not unique. This has happened to too many, not only the Jews. In many respects, my family's story hardly deserves this attention given what others have gone through. Now the thought that haunts is how history repeats, over and over again, how it never learns. The world is full of people suffering from numbness. All that has changed are the names and the places. Entire cultures are being erased. Some horrors never stop.

Sometimes I resist speaking about these moments because there is too much to say. I know that sounds odd, but try to understand. Nothing about these times makes any sense. Nothing. Putting it to words only makes it sound too simple.

Chapter 42

Arthur and Ilse's Wedding

Ilse and Arthur's wedding in 1937 was a welcome change to a cloudy year. This time, the party was small and intimate, just the immediate family: my sisters, Ruth and Walter, my parents, and me. Four-year-old Ruth kept us entertained. Ilse looked beautiful, Arthur did too. We forgot our misery. It was a happy occasion.

At first, we thought the party would be larger, but things had been tough in Wurzen. Cousin Inge's father, Uncle Alfred, had succumbed to his illness. It was not unexpected, but the suffering was prolonged. Aunt Hilda and Inge were sorting out their future. No choices were easy. The word from Leiznig was that they, too, were busy. Erna had completed medical school and was doing her residency in Switzerland. Heinz had found a way into the university in Cottbus. Leni was helping Aunt Trude manage the business, which was struggling at present. Arthur's cousins in Naples declined the invitation. They were conserving their resources. They hoped to leave for America soon.

We held the wedding ceremony in the dining room at the farm. It was winter, too cold to be outdoors. Even our church was off limits. It wasn't that we were banished; we just were no longer welcome.

Germany had issued strict laws prohibiting mixed marriages. There had been a question with Ilse and Arthur. Arthur, too, had been raised a Lutheran. And his Jewish ancestry was not quite as clear and a bit more denied. His parents were no longer alive. Old records needed to be found. They needed to both prove they were Jewish. The cousins in Naples had helped with that.

Our family time together was short, only two days. Everyone was busy. Lotte had taken a new job. She was teaching home economics at Gut Winkel, a training camp in Spreenhagen. She was preparing young Jewish adults for emigration to Palestine. Both Arthur and Ilse had responsibilities in Berlin. Their time for celebration was limited.

I rode with Walter when we drove Ilse and Arthur to the train station for their return to Berlin. On the way back to Crossen, it was our turn to visit. I always enjoyed my time alone with Walter. Though he was much older, I never felt our twenty-year difference. He treated me as if we were the same age, particularly when Trude was not nearby. At fourteen, I was beginning to resent my oldest sister, Trude, who acted too much a mother at times.

With Walter, there was closeness. He listened, something Trude seldom took the time to do. My days had been difficult, and I needed his friendship. With Walter, I could talk about anything. When I needed advice, I could ask. He could be serious. He could be funny. He always knew jokes. Walter was a good father to Ruth. She hugged him all the time. You could always see how close they were. She was different when she was with Trude.

Father always thought highly of Walter. Father often said he was a man bound to do things with his life; he was smart and ambitious, and he was principled and not afraid of hard work. From Mother, I knew that Walter was not Jewish. She thought it important to know now that we were more conscious of what being Jewish really meant.

I imagine that, at my age, I had little sense of propriety, of what is personal, or the questions one was permitted to ask. Aware that Trude and Walter would no longer have been allowed to marry, I asked Walter that question. He reminded me that when they were married, Trude did not consider herself Jewish either. None of us really did. She had never told him. Our family had never said. Walter had not known. They had married in the Lutheran church. And then he told me he didn't care if we were Jews or not. He loved my sister; that was all that mattered to him. Throughout his life, Walter remained a good man. He always stayed true to his word.

Day 8...

First thing this morning, we went back to the hospital. I will never forget. As we were walking through the corridor, a Mexican woman stopped us. She had seen Joanie and Mom walk by her husband's room every day for the past week. He had been very ill but now was on the road to recovery. They would leave the hospital later in the day. She wanted to hug Mom and Joanie. She felt bad for them. They looked so tired and sad. What a kind moment. I held back my tears.

That morning, I sat with Dad. Joanie took Mom out to run some errands. They wanted to give me some time alone with him. I tried to talk to him a little. I found that difficult, and I stopped. I had no idea what to say. I didn't know how to talk to someone who didn't talk back, who didn't acknowledge my presence. Before they left, Joanie had urged me to talk so he could hear the sound of my voice. She was convinced that he could hear and would find it comforting. I wasn't sure she was right. I tried, but the words would not come out of my mouth. Maybe it wasn't that I didn't know what to say. Perhaps I was just too overcome to speak.

I know that my emotions in this situation are not unique. My experience was rather ordinary. Ginger had been through this multiple times with her family. So had most of my friends. Yet these emotions surprised me. I knew what to expect. There is a natural order to life. It's just that I had never seen my father helpless. He had always been there when I needed him. He was the one who had put his arms around me when we were riding that sled. He was always, and now he wasn't. All I could think was that it was not my father lying in that bed. This was someone old and gray. Dad was never like that. This was not my father, at least, the one whom I had known. Mom and Joanie still had hope. I'm not sure that I did anymore. And, if I had any hope, I was no longer certain what I hoped for.

Mom, Joanie, and I spent the afternoon and evening together. That was about all we could do. As Mom asked, I pulled Joanie aside and told her she needed to go home. We hugged. She would in a few days. She would be home for Christmas, but now she wanted to help Mom.

I told Joan that I had seen no life in Dad, no recognition, nothing. Joanie said that she and Mom had seen him respond. Sometimes they would talk to him, and he would wiggle his toes. I found myself wishing I could be a better cheerleader. There are times I wish I could do better.

Chapter 43

Good from Bad

$\mathcal{I}$ have always found it odd how good can come from bad. But, when I consider my own life, I would have to say that has been true for me. Often, good things have resulted from bad situations. Although those years at the farm in Crossen were lonelier than I can imagine, my days were shared with my parents. This was a gift of time few children ever receive.

Clearly, there were moments when our situation was far less than perfect, when we suffered each other's presence, and when the farm seemed so small that there was nowhere to hide. And there were times when there were words spoken out of anger and frustration, words that should never have been said. Yet now I find that a lifetime filters memories, and I am left with only those I cherish.

The three of us, Mother, Father, and I, spent many hours together. We worked together, shared our meals together, and passed much our free time together. I was able to learn parts of Mother and Father that my sisters never saw. I was able to know them well. In my case, good really did come from bad.

As I have recounted my memories, I hope I have described them as they were. There is little to be gained by repeating, exaggerating, or minimizing what has been said. The truth is that the details of these lives mean little today. While significant to me, their lives are only interesting to a few.

I can only add one or two thoughts. While we were together, Mother and Father became more than the sum of their parts. Together, they were coaches, teachers, and mentors. They were my biggest fans. Despite the difficult times, they both opened up and shared their lives, their hopes, their fears, their frustrations, and their dreams.

The frustration for my father was particularly immense. And the unrelenting frustrations and disappointments would only continue and never stop. Others throughout Germany would suffer similar fates. The rewards of his lifetime were disappearing before his eyes. I never saw him cry, never saw him weep, rarely saw him angry, never saw him frightened. Then, and still now, just like when I rode the sled down the hill in Pr. Holland, he was the father who put his arms around me. He made sure I was safe and protected. He kept me from danger. When I looked at his eyes, I knew he was sad, that life was no longer his to control. I knew he was defeated. Yet, no matter what, he refused to allow me to feel that I had lost. He refused to allow me to share his defeat.

As their child, all I can offer is that my parent's love has sustained me for a lifetime. I hope someday my children will be able to say the same. That would be the best reward.

Chapter 44

Gut Winkel

Mother and Father had no idea what to do with me by August of 1938. Continuing my education was no longer an option. I had finished the middle school in early summer. Actually, the German school system was finished with me and was glad to show me the door. While we searched everywhere, there was no school we could find that would make room at the next level. My cousin Heinz had been more successful. We had struck out. Nazi restrictions had eliminated any right that I had to attend school. Spaces were available for Jews on an extremely limited basis.

Neither Mother nor Father nor I had ever considered the possibility that my formal education would end with the eighth grade at age fifteen. We were frustrated and disappointed. My future, once a bright certainty, was now far from being known.

The central question at each evening's meal became what to do with me. Sitting at the farm would not be the long-range plan. The expectation had always been that I would complete my high-school education and go on to the university to prepare for a professional career in the real world. But expectations were one thing and realities another.

It would take many years before I realized how much of my childhood and adolescence I missed. I didn't know it then. I had no idea what I lost. Years later, when our kids were in high school, I learned this firsthand. And, when I did, it was a difficult time for me. I never told Mela or Ralph or Joan about my depression and despair. It was real. It was painful. And, with time, it passed. I certainly was not prepared for those feelings.

German schools were not altogether different from American schools. There was a significant social element, parties, dances, clubs, girlfriends, boyfriends, and so forth. I knew my sisters had those experiences because they talked about them. For many, the teenage years are a time to test the limits, to experiment, and even break some rules. I was denied those moments, all of them. As a teenager, I never had the romances, the heartbreaks, the friendships, or the camaraderie. As an adult, in my own way, I needed to manufacture these for myself, and I have always been grateful to Mela for being my partner. She has always understood, and I know that has not been easy.

When the subject of my future came up, honestly, I can't say that I was disappointed that I was finished with school. I was elated and happy to close out that chapter of my life. As I said before, school was miserable. My classmates despised me. My teachers didn't feel I belonged in their classrooms. Mother had pushed me pretty hard. Classes in Latin and Greek became very tiresome. I was excused from much and excluded from more. Perhaps, if circumstances had been different, had I been able to experience a normal school life, I would have looked at this time in a more positive way. But, given my situation, I wanted to be as far as I could from school.

My attitude towards school colored our dinner conversations. Mother and Father were dead set that I continue my education. I was not. And, at times, harmony turned to acrimony. Our frustrations would mount. The doors were closed, and we were stuck. There was no place to go. I had no idea where I belonged.

It was my sister Lotte's suggestion that I return to Gut Winkel with her after Ruth's fifth birthday party. She knew that summer holidays were ending, others would be in school, and I had no place to go. She could see that Mother and Father were deeply disappointed. She knew this was not a healthy situation. Lotte was the one who told Mother and Father I should leave Crossen and that I needed something in my life, a purpose, an interest, and a way to move forward.

Gut Winkel was a Jewish training center located in Spreenhagen, a small town outside of Berlin. Lotte had moved to Spreenhagen earlier in the year when she began her new job as a home economics teacher. The Braunsberg children in Berlin had grown too old to need a nanny. Hertha Braunsberg recommended Lotte to center director, Martin Gerson. The Braunsberg family had been generous supporters of Gut Winkel and other Hashara camps located throughout Germany.

As the Nazis came to power, Gut Winkel and similar camps were established to help prepare Jewish youth for emigration to Palestine. The Nazis allowed these training centers to exist because they shared a common interest. The Nazis wanted Jews out of Germany, and these training centers provided young Jews with the agricultural and technical skills that they needed in order to leave. Gut Winkel, in particular, prepared young Zionists for kibbutz life in Palestine. Typically, Gut Winkel would house forty to fifty young men and women who would stay in the camp for three to six months.

Although my sister Lotte had been part of my life since my very first day, we never had spent much time together, at least time when I could hold up my end of a conversation. By the time I was four years old, she had already left for school. During the years that followed, she returned for holidays and family events. Yet these were short visits, not the time to get to know someone well. I had formed impressions and had been told the family stories of her childhood, but the three months we spent together at Gut Winkel were when I really got to know my sister.

Lotte was a member of the small Gut Winkel faculty, and I was not permitted to stay with her in the teacher's housing. Instead, Lotte arranged for me to enroll as a camp trainee. This was the best thing that could have happened.

I lived in the men's dorm with the other trainees and participated in all of the training activities. Finally, I was with other young people who could be friends. I was a bit younger than most, but not by much, and that did not seem to make a difference. I was accepted as part of the group. And, as time would permit, I finally was able to get to know my sister Lotte now as a friend.

Today, I know what a special and unique experience I had at Gut Winkel. By most estimates, fewer than twelve hundred young Jews went through training at one of the Hashara camps during this time, and I was fortunate to share this experience. Few stories remain, as these camps were shut down only a short time later. During my time at Gut Winkel, I believe I grew up and matured. I made friends. I learned many skills. The friends were long forgotten, but the skills would serve me well in coming years.

I am sure I considered whether I, too, wanted to begin a new life in Palestine. I must have considered whether I wanted to embrace the Jewish faith. I have long forgotten the exact reasons why I chose to reject either notion. At fifteen, sometimes reasons are not an explanation. I did learn that Lotte had made her decisions. At some future time, she would leave Germany and live a Jewish life in Palestine. I know how she agonized when making these choices.

Most of the young men and women who received training at Gut Winkel during the time I was there left for Palestine and escaped the Holocaust. Many became leaders in the future of Israel.

I left Gut Winkel and returned to Crossen in time for my sixteenth birthday in late October. Trude, Walter, and Ruth joined us for a quiet dinner. We wore silly hats to make Ruth laugh. Sitting at the table that evening, I felt grown up. I knew I had changed and that Mother and Father recognized this too.

Day 8, evening...

Mom and I stayed up late talking. It was something we both needed to do. Mom spoke about mercy deaths and assisted suicide. She emphasized that there would be no heroic measures to save Dad. They had made that decision long ago, and she felt comfortable with that. She wanted the same. I had no doubt.

Assisted suicide was one of those topics that had always been talked about in the abstract, a conversation we had off and on probably for close to 50 years. She had always been an advocate. To her, it had always been a simple issue. As is her custom, she wanted to know how I felt. This time, before I could respond, she answered her own question. She was no longer so sure. She told me she had never considered hope before. Hope changed the entire equation. She said she had not given up hope. Love was different. She would always choose what was best for Dad. That was love. But hope? Hope was about what she wanted.

She talked about life support, something she had rejected in idle conversation in the past. She admitted that everything is different when it happens to you. She was not ready to give up on Dad. Then, she changed the conversation. Tomorrow would be a new day.

That's my mom. Most of my friends have been in this surreal world at one time or another. All of us have parents. Generations pass. We are not unique. Now it is our family's turn.

Chapter 45

Kristallnacht

November 9, 1938, started out as a pretty typical day at the farm. Father and I rose early, ate a hearty breakfast, and then went to work. We were rebuilding the stone walls that surrounded the fields. Several walls had collapsed. Deterioration and rainy weather had taken their toll. The walls were hundreds of years old and had been rebuilt any number of times.

I can't imagine the amount of work it took to originally create the walls. Farmers must have first cleared the fields of trees, a backbreaking task given the tools at hand. Then, they would comb the fields for fieldstone, hauling the stones in wheeled carts to the sides. Even then, they were not done. Before planting, they would have to search for the smaller stones and remove these from the fields. It had been the work of many lifetimes.

On the edges of the fields, they would stack the fieldstones in just the correct way so the walls would fall into themselves and remain upright. No mortar was used, only gravity and genius. When one field was completed, they would move on to the next. It was a time-tested art used to surround farmland all over Europe for thousands of years.

Fortunately for Father and me, previous occupants had accomplished most of the difficult work. The fields were cleared of trees, and the fieldstones lay by the side of the fields. Some walls had fallen flat. We only needed to restack the stones that had collapsed. Still hard and tedious work, it paled compared to the original task.

November was warm that year, and by midday, we were both exhausted and hungry. It was the kind of work that made you feel healthy, that gave you a sense of accomplishment, where you could see something get done. But it certainly was not gentle work. We would sleep well that evening.

As we sat down in the kitchen for our midday meal with Mother, the phone rang. I remember getting up and answering it. It was Aunt Trude from Leiznig. She asked to speak to Mother. The phone was used so much differently than it is used today. People did not call to visit. Visiting was done in person. If that was not possible, then long chatty letters would be exchanged back and forth for much that needed to be said. Phone calls were expensive, placed for very specific reasons, and usually brought bad news. They were always brief.

Mother remained on the phone with Aunt Trude for quite some time, far longer than typical. When she returned to the table, she acted confused. She told us something was going on in Cottbus, where my cousin Heinz went to the university. The synagogue was on fire, and a Jewish-owned department store had been looted. Piles of books from the synagogue were being burned. Nobody knew why or what was going on. There was little information. No one could explain. Aunt Trude was very disturbed. She was worried about Heinz. She said that an older man, a friendly Nazi party member, had advised Heinz and a friend to leave Cottbus for the day. They were driving back to Leiznig. Heinz thought they should go to Hamburg, that it would be safer there, because it was near the international seaport. There were many rumors. Heinz had heard that Hitler was planning a visit to Cottbus, to inspect several military airports that had just been built. Perhaps this was a Nazi show of strength in advance of his visit.

The times were so different from the way they are now. There was no twenty-four-hour news coverage, no internet, no television, and no way to learn any additional information. That is all we knew. Nothing new would be known for hours, and perhaps even days. Worry would serve no purpose. Discussing would reveal no answers. Mother returned to what she had been doing. Father and I went back to our work rebuilding the stone walls. That was no more that we could do.

Later that evening, about seven pm, the dog barked. I remember telling Mother that there must be a fox in the yard. It was not unusual. After dark, a fox might pass through the yard, eyeing the chickens, setting the dog to bark. Opening the back door and giving a shout would usually send it away. One or two would try again tomorrow.

`I had just gotten up to go out back to check on the chickens when we heard heavy footsteps on the porch. Then, there was a loud pounding on the door. It was unusual to have unexpected visitors at the farm anytime, and particularly in the evening. Father went to the door.

As long as I live, I will never forget that moment when Father opened the door. There were seven men dressed in SS uniforms. They told Father that he, Mother, and I must go with them immediately. This was an order, a command, much more than an instruction. It was clear that this was not a conversation, not a discussion. Protesting or failing to comply was out of the question. We took nothing with us. We were marched out of our house and told to get into one of their vehicles. The entire exchange, from the time they knocked on our door, took moments, hardly more than a blink of an eye.

No one said a word. In silence, we rode the few kilometers into town. These men were known to us. Two were our neighbors; others had been Father's business customers; another had been Lotte's boyfriend in school; one was a World War I veteran who had marched in the parade with Father only a few years before. They had once been our friends. I had played with their children.

We were driven to a building at the army prison compound on the far side of town. This was the same compound where prisoners of war had been kept. Father had guarded the compound as a soldier during World War I.

We were taken to a room where we joined about twenty others. We knew some but not all. There were the Jewish families living in Pr. Holland, the families that attended the synagogue. Father and the other men were led away. We were left with the mothers and children. We were scared. We were terrified. We were told nothing. We had no idea what was happening. People were crying. It was just that sudden.

It was several hours before a German officer came to speak to us. We were told we would not be harmed. We would be released to go to our homes in the morning. There were important matters that needed to be discussed with our husbands and fathers. No questions would be answered. None could be asked.

No one slept that night. How could we? We did not know what to do. Early the next morning, we were told we could leave. The men would not be released, at least, not now. Mother and I walked back to the farm in Crossen. We left Father and the other men behind. I can't remember Mother and me speaking one word as we walked home. We could not imagine what words to use.

It was when we reached the house that Mother first wept. She was always so strong. I had never seen her cry before. I was sick with worry about Father, in shock over the events of the past twelve hours.

What had just happened? Now, as we climbed the steps of our front porch, all we could do was shake our heads in disbelief.

Glass was scattered everywhere, windows were broken, plates and dishes were shattered, furniture crushed, family pictures ripped from walls. Everything that was perfect when we left only a few hours earlier was now destroyed. The prized family heirloom, the oil painting of my three sisters so prominently displayed in the dining room, was ripped to shreds. The dining table, whose leaves I had carefully tended for family parties, was now bits of tinder. The glass cabinet and the porcelain figurines that had followed Mother since birth were now just broken shards. The good china and wine goblets, passed through generations and used only on rare occasions, lay in fragments on the floor.

It hardly seemed possible that less than a day had passed since Father and I were rebuilding the stone walls along the fields. Everything that was, was no longer. All we could do was weep and wait. We were alone. We were helpless.

Now, as I reflect, I wonder who can do this to another? How could a God allow these events, this hurt, to happen over and over? We were only one family, but what happened to us happened to family after family. This was not a random event. This was not an accident of nature. We did nothing to provoke this. No, this was done with the intention to harm. Even as I write these words, cruelties such as this happen again and again and again. The possessions never matter, but the lives certainly do. How can this be?

When Joanie and Mela ask me to talk about these times, I don't think they understand my bitterness and my hatred. These are thoughts I do not want to share. I do not want to remember these moments. I do not want my family to relive my memories. I want this out of my brain, out of my head, out of my mind. What have we really learned from history? Only that it repeats. That is the single truth. I want my children to think better.

We were fortunate that day. All we lost were our possessions and some pride. Many others throughout Germany were less fortunate. Word was passed that Father and the other men were alive. We still had no idea what was going on. Our radio had been destroyed. Our phone line had been cut. We had no news. We were isolated.

Trude and Walter must have heard about events in Pr. Holland because they arrived by midday. I am not sure how they learned about us. Had this happened to them too? They shared our disbelief. Mother and I were sitting on the front porch holding our heads when they arrived. Five-year-old Ruth was so distraught.

Trude took charge and enlisted Ruth and Mother to begin with the cleanup. Walter took me to the prison camp to learn about the status of Father. I will never forget how important Walter was that day. He went to the guards and demanded to know what was going on. If it was not for Walter, I don't know what I would have done. Trude too. That day we needed her to take charge.

As the day wore on, we learned that ours was not an isolated event. The destruction of Jewish homes and businesses had happened throughout Germany. Synagogues were destroyed. Books were burned. Men were being jailed and put into camps. We learned that November 9 was not the only day. These actions had begun before and would continue for days. The Nazi government wanted all the Jews in Germany to leave. Germany was being cleansed. Hitler was washing the Jewish blood from Germany. We had all been put on notice.

Every day, for the next ten days, I walked to the prison camp to see Father and to bring him his meals. I thought he was broken and battered, but he seemed to brighten each time I came to visit. Every day, we talked with one another. For four years, our family had withstood an adversity that remains still hard to comprehend and not one of our choosing. Father and I had become very close, but never closer than those ten days.

Oddly, other than that first day and night, I remember little of Mother during this time. We must have eaten together. We must have spoken a great deal. I don't recall very much. My thoughts were with Father.

Mother put her energies into learning about the welfare of the rest of our family. We learned that Lotte was okay. Nothing had occurred at Gut Winkel. The Nazis were still favoring the camp as a mechanism to send Jews out of Germany. The camp was no threat to the Nazis.

Ilse and Arthur had a difficult time in Berlin. Ilse was at work the evening of November 9 when everything took place. She had seen fires burning but was unaffected. When she came home, she had found Frank under the care of a neighbor and Arthur missing. Apparently, the Gestapo had come for Arthur and taken him away. After a several-day search, she located him. Later, I learned that Arthur was arrested that night and sent to Sachsenhausen, the Nazi concentration camp in Oranienburg, thirty-five kilometers north of Berlin. They had kept Arthur there for several weeks. The punishments must have been severe. He lost fifty pounds during his confinement and was only released because Ilse obtained a fake ticket showing that he would leave for South America. I never learned what other price either had to pay.

When Trude and Walter returned to Elbing after helping Mother and me, they found their apartment ransacked. Fortunately, the destruction was minor. Walter was being harassed for having married a Jew. They wanted no mixed marriages in their neighborhood.

The news from Wurzen was equally troubling. The family store had been destroyed. Hilda was giving up. There was no way she could continue. Plans were being made to send Inge away, as soon as possible, to Brussels, if possible. She would be safer there. Aunt Hilde had her own plans. At the earliest possible moment, she would try to leave for England to set up a new life for herself and Inge.

From Leiznig, we learned that Aunt Trude was trying to recover what she could from the family business. My cousin Heinz had found his way to Berlin, where he was staying with an uncle. Cousin Leni and her husband were also in Berlin trying to obtain permission to leave for Australia. Cousin Erna had already moved to Belgium.

Mother told me that as soon as we could get our affairs in order, we would move to Berlin. We could stay with Ilse and Arthur while we figured out what would be next. Everything was very confusing. We needed to worry about having enough money. That could be uncertain and would certainly affect our plans.

First things first. We needed Father to be released from prison. And, before we left East Prussia, we would need to see about Trude, Walter, and Ruth. What about their future?

Chapter 46

Ultimatums

We were told that Father would be released after documents were prepared and signed transferring all properties the family owned to new Aryan owners. If everything was signed over, he would be released unharmed. These would be very one-sided negotiations. The buyers would set the price. Father would be forced to sell the farm, the house in Pr. Holland, and the properties that were leased to Walter Falk for his old business. The authorities had a complete list of everything. Earlier in the year, all Jews had been required to submit this information to government officials. In addition, Father would have to agree that our family would leave Crossen and Pr. Holland within 30 days and never return.

These were not conditions. They were ultimatums. Once met, Father would be free to leave prison. Father was never told that any monies paid under this forced sale would be put into a bank account frozen by the Nazi regime, that his access would be limited, and that, when he would leave Germany, these funds would be forfeited. Any other bank accounts that he held were also frozen and forfeited.

Father was fifty-seven years old, too old, and too weakened to start over again. This was his entire life's savings, his entire life's work. Everything that he owned was being taken away. Everything he had worked for was lost. I can't imagine what he felt. I only knew that he was helpless.

Later, we talked about what this meant. He told me that what he owned and accumulated didn't matter. He still had his family. We still had our future. Go forward. You can't look back. It will destroy you if you do.

I know. Outlook is everything. And rationalization can be a very poor excuse. That day, Father gave me the gift of a lifetime. Until then, his possessions had always been significant; material gain was what my sisters and I always were taught to strive for. We had always bought the best things, worn the best clothes, driven the newest car; everything always had to be the best, the greatest, the most. Ever since that day, I have seen the world through a different prism. Life is not quite so crystal clear. I'm not certain that I have taught my son this lesson so well. Some things have to be learned in their own way. I am sure that he will learn one day. Then, I hope he passes this lesson along to the next generations.

Chapter 47

Never to Return

Ten days after he was put into prison, Father was let go. He was weary and worn but appeared otherwise undamaged. The large laceration on his forehead would eventually heal. He seemed glad to be out in the sunlight and said he was looking forward to sleeping in his own bed. He never told us what had happened. When Mother asked, he refused to answer, just shaking his head. We were overjoyed with his release, but dazed by our situation. No one celebrated; all we could do was sigh with relief.

The following day, Walter Falk came to visit. Father's foster brother had a problem. Father had been forced to sell the buildings on Poststrasse where the business was housed. The new owners had already met with Walter to discuss the terms of his lease. Walter would be able to continue to lease the buildings and operate the business. However, there was one condition. Walter could no longer make any payments to Udo Wobser for the purchase of his business. If Walter refused, the lease would be terminated and the business ruined. When Walter had bought out Father and Mother's shares in 1935, he had agreed to make monthly payments to our family for the next fifteen years. Father and Mother relied on this monthly income.

Walter told Father he had no choice. The payments would stop. It was either him or us. He must have no further association with the Wobser family. Added to the events of the last ten days, this was quite a blow to Father. First, he was forced to sell the farm, the house in Pr. Holland, and the business properties at far less than their value, eliminating the monthly income he was receiving from his leases. Now he was told that his remaining monthly income, the payments from Walter, would be discontinued as well.

This was a difficult moment for both Walter Falk and Father. They had been close for more than fifty years, as long as either could remember. They had grown up with each other. They had been raised as brothers. Walter Falk was part of our family. He was Uncle Walter to my sisters and me. When I was baptized, Uncle Walter became my godfather. Uncle Walter had stood by Father even after nearly all of our friends walked away from us because they did not want to associate with Jews. There was nothing more to be said. Their relationship was severed. There was no possible remedy. They would never speak to or see one another again.

Events flew by over the next three weeks as preparations were made for our move. Each day, it seemed that something more was lost, that some trust or old friendship was broken. Mother and Father had lived in Pr. Holland for close to forty years. My sisters and I had been raised there. Now, within a few short days, that life had been taken. There was little we could do. There was no recourse. These three weeks were difficult, compounded by the total lack of news. It was hard to separate rumor from fact. One day, we would hear one thing; the next day, we learned something else.

With the properties sold and most of our possessions destroyed, packing what remained was not all that difficult. We would take our clothes, jewelry, family albums, and family papers. No more. There was no time for emotion, for clinging to the past. We would take our memories, however melancholy they had become. Little else mattered.

A vital activity of those final days was to collect and organize our papers. We needed to have everything in order for the coming months: identification papers, my school records, birth certificates, licenses, health records, contracts and leases, deeds for the properties that had been taken. Father was particularly concerned about his military papers, those attesting to his good conduct in World War I. He still remained convinced that the regime in Germany would not last and that, at some point, we would return to our previous life. Mother was less sure, and I certainly did not have a clue. But, regardless of the outcome, we needed to be certain that we were prepared.

Father also had me apply for a passport. We received it only four days before we left East Prussia. I might have been unsure of my future, but it seemed clear that Mother and Father had already decided that I would leave Germany soon.

A significant problem was our deteriorating financial situation. The farm, the house, the properties, the automobiles, and the livestock had been sold for only a small percentage of their value. Still, when added together, there should have been a substantial amount of money available to us. Now, with the bank accounts frozen, we were denied access to these funds. We would be able to withdraw only a small monthly amount, enough to survive, but that was it. There was no way around this problem.

Mother's final act was to exchange rings with my sister Trude. Unsure of what the future would bring, Mother wanted to leave something of deep personal value to her daughter, Trude, to bind them together with one lasting memory. Mother gave Trude her three-diamond ring, her most precious family heirloom. And Trude gave Mother the single diamond ring she had received from Walter when Ruth was born. Their promise that day was that there would be a time when each would be returned to the other. But, until that time, they would never let the other's ring leave their fingers.

So, on the tenth of December, 1938, we said our goodbyes, I gave my old sled to Ruth, and we boarded the train to Berlin, never to return to East Prussia again. Life, as we knew it, would never be the same.

Day 9...

Joanie dropped me off at the Phoenix airport first thing in the morning. It gave us time to talk. We were both sad and helpless. Our conversation was mostly about Mom. What would she do? How would she cope? What would we do? There were no answers. Just questions. We would just wait and see. Others had dealt with this situation. We knew we could too.

We said our goodbyes, and I wiped my eyes. I hope I told Joanie how grateful I was. All my life, whenever I wanted to make my sister cry, I would wipe my eyes. It was almost like a secret code. And mostly I did this just to be a troublesome brother – not something I am particularly proud to admit. Today was different. Today, I wiped my eyes out of genuine love and caring. And, today, we both cried.

Chapter 48

Berlin, 1938

Since the 18th century, Berlin had been one of the centers of European power, politics, and culture. Berlin brought together nobility, the wealthy, politicians, industrialists, bankers, diplomats, scientists, scholars, world leaders, musicians, and artists. It was not only the capital of the Reich; Berlin was the center of Jewish life in Germany. More than one-third of Germany's Jews lived in Berlin.

Berlin has always been a busy, vibrant, cosmopolitan city. Only two years after the frenzy of activity in preparation for the 1936 Olympics, construction continued at a demanding pace. Hitler and his architect, Albert Speer, had plans to make Berlin a world-class city, with projects of gigantic size.

That was the Berlin that Father, Mother, and I entered when we moved there in December of 1938. Pulsating with big city life, building projects were underway everywhere. The streets were noisy. Cars honked. Streetcars overflowed. The sidewalks were filled with jostling crowds. Everything and every person seemed to be in a state of constant motion. I had visited Berlin three times before, so I was not overwhelmed or surprised by its bigness, but it was hard not to be caught up in the excitement and its hustle and bustle. I am sure my eyes were as big as saucers. We were small-town Germans who had arrived in the big city.

Father found Berlin confusing. Our situation was difficult, yet we found ourselves surrounded by Berlin's normal everyday life. Much appeared as if nothing had happened. Construction and commerce seemed to go on everywhere. Father must have admired the success that he saw. In a different time, he would have loved to be part of things, to be in the center of it all. All he could do now was stop, sit, and watch. It became a form of entertainment. Yes, he was angry and hurt by the way we had been forced from our home, yet he remained proud of the economic strength of his country. Despite what he and our family had already endured, Father always hoped these moments would pass and life would be restored to its former self. When he would sit and watch projects unfold, he watched like a child, with awe and intrigue. This was his Germany, his country, his home.

I do not think Father ever looked in the mirror and saw himself as Udo Wobser, the Jew. He always saw himself as Udo Wobser, the German. Even, here, in Berlin, there was little doubt. He would refer to Jews as "them" and seldom recognize that they were us. This has always remained an unspoken conversation, confused and conflicting. Having so many years to consider the question, I find myself still trying to figure out these issues, not so much about who I am, but rather, who Father thought he was. I know I repeat, but there were too many little signs, and very few denials. Despite his birth parents, Mother's family, the way we had been categorized by the Nazis, and the way we were now treated, he remained unconvinced. He was never raised as a Jew, and that made it hard for Father to accept his race. He was proud of who he was – and that was German.

In the real world, this confusion did not matter. Whether by choice or circumstance, we were thrown into our surroundings. We found ourselves tossed into the uncertain seas of the Jewish community in Berlin in 1938. We needed to find our way to survive and endure.

Berlin, then, was a city filled with contradictions. To visitors, little seemed out of sorts; there were few reminders of the horrible incidents that had occurred only six weeks earlier. At first glance, it seemed that the world had not stopped, not even blinked an eye. For most, the facts, the destruction of lives, real and true, had been rejected. What had happened was beyond rational belief. On the surface, little seemed amiss.

One needed to scratch deeply to find that there were complex layers to what initially appeared on the surface. There was the proud and vibrant city of Berlin, confident and strong. And there was Jewish Berlin, Germany's second-class citizens, who operated and struggled to survive in their own separate world. That was the world we found ourselves immersed in.

Ilse and Arthur, with their infant, Frank, met us at the train station, and we went directly to their apartment at 15 Steinmetzstrasse, which was to become our home for the weeks and months to follow. I remember how shocked we were to see Arthur so pale and gaunt. It had only been days since Ilse had arranged his release from Sachsenhausen.

Together, we would conserve our resources, gather our wits, and stay focused on what to do next. With our bank accounts frozen, our budgets were limited. We needed to save every penny. The inheritance that Arthur had received when his mother had died years earlier had all but disappeared, evaporating with Berlin's hyperinflation. The apartment was small and cramped, but we all made do. I know it may sound a little too simple, but being together gave us comfort and strength.

We had just arrived when Ilse was out the door and on her way to work. My sister worked incredibly long hours, as she always had and always would. I seldom remember Ilse ever stopping to rest and never remember her stopping to complain. Fortunately, Ilse was able to keep her job at the hospital. As a nurse, she could treat only Jewish patients. The pay was meager, but it was a job that paid, and with it, she managed to help keep our crowded household going.

Arthur supplemented as he could, but there was little work suited for his limited skills. We loved him dearly. But, throughout life, when it came to employment, Arthur was always miscast. On occasion, he would be asked to give a singing lesson to a promising Berlin student, but that was about it. In his own way, Arthur always contributed what he could. To Arthur's relief, for much of the time, Mother took over responsibility for tending to Frank. They seemed a very good match. Frank was only six months old and needed full-time attention. In doing this, Mother found a way to feel she was contributing too. Frank gave Mother so much happiness. Mother and little Frankie became inseparable.

With no work for a Jew of his age or trade, Father made it his full-time duty to take care of our affairs and to search for a way for me to leave Germany. Arthur became his assistant. Until we said our goodbyes at the train station a few months later, I don't think there was a single day when their determination wavered. The family had decided that sending me away from Germany was their first priority. Only after I had left would they concern themselves with their own survival.

Father seemed busy every waking hour of every day. In addition to worrying about what to do with me, he was struggling with the banks to get what money he could from the sale of his properties, and he had to deal with the Nazi rules and regulations that all Jewish families faced. I remember one time when Father said he felt like a dog on a leash. As still is true in many European countries, new arrivals in a city or town needed to register their presence with city officials within days. Father handled this chore, reporting to city hall with our identification documents. He also had to register with the Gestapo. And, now, follow up visits were required.

There was no wavering or avoiding these important rules. Failure to comply resulted in significant penalties. We were not in danger as long as we followed the regulations. But there could be no mistake. There was no margin for error. The penalty for a Jew with any infraction, even the most insignificant, might mean the difference between life or death, or transport to Sachsenhausen. Everything about us was known to the Gestapo – our origin, our address, our livelihood, our finances, our family tree. There were no secrets. There could be no secrets. It seemed that, at least weekly, Father had to spend his day at either the police station or the Gestapo headquarters reporting on the doings of the family. There was a tedious grind to this slow, demeaning, bureaucratic system. One could wait for hours and hours to accomplish an insignificant minute-long task. Too often, the wait would be useless when the result was an office door closed for the day.

Father struggled endlessly with his finances, trying to recover even a portion of his life's savings. He had spent years and worked hard to build his modest fortune. Under no circumstance would he leave Germany without making certain that there was a record of what had been taken by the Nazis. Fortunately, he found legal assistance to assemble these documents, something that would become important in future years. I'm not sure how he did this, as Jews were prohibited from hiring lawyers. For every rule, there was a way. Jews could not practice law, but they could help other Jews.

As for me, neither school nor a job was an available option, so instead, I was sent out each day to hone skills that would make me a better candidate for emigration. For many of those countries accepting refugees, odds could be improved by having specific technical and language skills. In many of the Berlin Jewish neighborhoods, there were intensive efforts to help young people meet these requirements. As soon as we arrived in Berlin, Mother enrolled me in an English class. I knew nothing of the language. And, three afternoons each week, my family paid an electrician to allow me to apprentice and to learn the rudiments of that trade. I have no idea where they found the money to pay for this opportunity.

So our time in Berlin was busy. It seemed that someone was coming or going every hour. We needed to be occupied. There was little else we could do but work to survive. We needed to find a way to put Germany in our past. By late 1938, Jews in Berlin were prohibited from strolling in public parks or going to the cinema, the theatre, exhibitions, or attending a sporting event. We were not welcome in restaurants. Certain areas of the city were deemed "Aryan zones" and off limits. We were banned from swimming pools. Police protection was non-existent. We were even prohibited from using bicycles. In February of 1939, Jews were required to turn over all gold, silver, diamonds, and other valuables without compensation. As to our good silverware, we were allowed to keep a bare minimum, enough for place settings for our family. Many broke the rules, but like I said, if you were caught, the penalties were severe.

I was barely sixteen. I felt much older than my years.

Chapter 49

Christmas 1938

hristmas was upon us only weeks after we arrived in Berlin. Celebrating Christmas was a longstanding family tradition. It had grown from when my three sisters were very young and continued as our cherished family gathering year after year. With rare exception, we were always all together: Mother, Father, the sisters, and me. The table would be set with our finest china, glassware, and linens, and the menu would be the product of several days' preparation. The carving of the Christmas goose was a much heralded ritual Father repeated each year. Christmas in the Wobser household was a time of abundance, a celebration of our family's good fortune. We told stories, we laughed, we relived our memories, we were thankful. Christmas was always a joyous occasion.

Mother and the girls would debate the selection of the tree, a careful choice by Father and me from the trees in the meadow. Was it better, wider, or taller than the previous tree? Trimming consumed hours of enjoyment. We took pride in repeating the customs of the past. The entirety of Christmas was a custom revered. The smells, the sights, the sounds, the tastes, the textures of Christmas would be shared by all.

This year, the contrast could not have been greater. The events of the past few months had made us lose our enthusiasm. Christmas of 1938 was cold and sterile, tiresome, and stale. I can think of so many words. It was survival, change, expectant, and unknown. It was forgettable, lacking, and barren. Our life in Berlin was unsettled and uncertain. We continued to struggle with disbelief. We all knew our circumstance and could do only what our circumstance permitted. We could not deny the reality: Christmases of the past would never return.

We dearly missed the rhythm of our Sunday afternoons in Crossen, our time spent with Trude, Walter, and five-year-old Ruth. These moments ended too abruptly, far sooner than we could ever imagine, leaving us left with only worry. Now not sharing Christmas together only heightened our awareness. It snowed that week in Berlin, a deep snow, the blizzard one remembers. I found myself thinking about my old sled. I wondered about Ruth.

Our mood was somber, and our moments poignant. Frank was still an infant, unlike Ruth, who, at five, was energy in motion, who loved to untie all the bows, and who made everyone laugh. Lotte, Trude, Walter, and Ruth were absent. Ilse had to leave early for her work at the hospital. We were weary and tired. Even our savings were better spent on the future rather than wasted on gifts destined to be left behind.

There are times when it is too sad to express certain emotions. I feel that way about that Christmas of 1938. I loved every person in the room. We were family and close. But that special feeling was gone. It did not matter how much we tried. Every aspect of our world was slowly being taken away.

Day 9, afternoon and evening...

Time zones made the return trip an all-day affair. The plane was delayed. By the time I drove from the Norfolk airport home to Corolla, it was well past midnight. It had been a long day.

Ginger greeted me at the door with exciting news. She had just gotten off the phone with Joanie and Mom. Everyone's prayers must have helped. Dad's status has improved. He is still heavily sedated, but he clearly heard them today. He answered their questions by wiggling his toes: one wiggle for Yes and two wiggles for No.

Joanie and Mom are thrilled and happy. He is still very sick. It will be a long recovery. But the doctor believes he should get better each day.

Ginger hugged me for a very long time. I was glad to be home. Maybe Joanie was right, and he heard my voice. It was a great report, but I am starting to feel like a yo-yo. We need to take this one day at a time.

Chapter 50

Where to Go?

We knew others in Berlin, friends of relatives, relatives of friends. The Jewish community in Berlin now numbered seventy-five thousand, a small fraction of the city's inhabitants and far fewer than the two hundred thousand who had lived there before. More than half the Jews in Berlin had left Germany, scattering as best they could. And most of the remaining were thrown into the same pot and stirred around in the same way. We all knew we were no longer welcome in Germany. The events of the past four years, particularly the past twelve months, the annexation of Austria, assaults on Jews, Kristallnacht, and property seizures, made it clear that Germany would no longer be our home.

Most recognized that they must leave. But saying and doing were vastly different things. It is difficult to leave a country that has been your home for generations. It is heart-wrenching to leave a country when family members are left behind. For those aged, frail, or weak, it is hard to find the strength and energy to leave. Most still believed this was their country, this was their home.

Many had trouble with the idea of going to a country that had a different way of life. We were Europeans, and European customs were familiar. Many of us spoke the languages of other European countries. Some of us settled in Germany from other European nations in the aftermath of World War I or previous conflicts. But, in 1939, a halo of uncertainty circled mainland Europe. Most agreed that leaving meant crossing the English Channel to Great Britain or an ocean to another continent. There were those that found this change in culture too hard to overcome.

Denial can be a terrible curse. We found ourselves in the midst of this confusion. Finding a way to leave might be difficult. But choosing not to leave was no longer a reasonable option.

We all faced the same problem, where to go? Many countries had quotas. Others required financial guarantees. Some denied the situation. Most countries had not yet recognized the scale and magnitude of the issue; that would take several more years. Countries were challenged by employment and economic difficulties of their own. Allowing large groups of refugees to enter might jeopardize job opportunities for their own populations. Almost without exception, nationalism and taking care of one's own had to come first. Only then would a country consider opening its doors.

While finding a place to go was the problem, the paradox, in early 1939, before World War II was to start, was that German policy officially encouraged emigration of German Jews. The German government wanted us to leave, to be rid of us. With one hand, they made our lives miserable and constrained. And the other hand helped, reducing bureaucratic hurdles so those who wanted to leave could leave more easily. Pack your bags, leave your valuables, give us your property and bank accounts, pay the necessary taxes, and we will wave goodbye and shout good riddance. We will be glad to see you go.

Sometimes, I think these times are misunderstood. In 1938 and 1939, it was not Nazi policy to deport German Jews to concentration camps for extermination. That would occur later. There were incidents. Even the most minor rule infraction was a serious issue, and punishment was severe and swift. Please don't allow me to understate the situation. It was cruel. It was demeaning. No one should ever be forgiven for treating people in the way that they did. Clearly, these were perilous times. But, at present, the situations in Austria and Poland, countries that Germany had invaded and controlled, were much worse than they were in Germany. Of course, everything would change dramatically in Germany and throughout Europe in 1941, when Germany invaded the Soviet Union. Then, the *Final Solution* became official government policy, and there was no way out. Millions would be murdered. The horrors and atrocities were unimaginable.

For now, we were outcasts. Our way of life had been severely curtailed and restricted. Yet, as long as we followed the rules imposed, we hoped to avoid further physical danger. We were all subjected to the taunts and harassment from bullies on the streets. We all saw the signs with their demeaning slogans. Mostly, we were despised and left alone. Apart from the thugs in neighborhoods we avoided, our immediate problem was not the German government. Our problem was where we might go. Would there be a country willing to take us?

For many, once the problem of where to go was solved, there remained much that was still confusing. So much was self-defeating. Problems ran in circles. The Nazis made it clear that they wanted us to leave. And, when we did, they reached deep into our pockets, taking money, property, restricting what could be transferred abroad from German banks, freezing bank accounts, and levying an increasingly heavy emigration tax. Everything we owned was viewed as German property. The German government had no intention of allowing us or other refugees to take anything of material value out of the country.

The result? Most were impoverished by the time we were able to leave. We were only permitted to take ten Reichsmarks (about $4) out of the country. We became destitute refugees, dependent upon a new country's generosity. Through no fault of our own, even the most self-reliant became paupers. Not every nation had the resources to share or the will to be welcoming.

The simple reality was that there were far more of us who wanted to leave than there were opportunities or places to go. Not everyone was lucky enough to have a relative in America with the resources to help or the willingness to guarantee their support. Most found themselves in an ocean without a ship.

Later, for Mother and Father, the decision would be even more difficult. They would not want to leave without knowing their three daughters and their families would be safe. Nothing was easy or simple. There were no guarantees. Failure could be final. When they finally left, I know that they were weary and hoping that they had done their best. I cannot imagine their agony and the tears that must have been shed.

For the moment, I was the problem and the priority. What they would and could do for themselves were issues and decisions for later months. Now their attention was totally focused on me. Where would I go? What was to be my future?

Chapter 51

Heinz Gets His Visa

It was during this time that we learned that the problem had been solved for my cousin Heinz. Mother's sister, Trude, wrote from Leiznig to tell us. Authorizations had been granted, and visas had been issued. Heinz would be leaving for Scotland on April 20. All the arrangements were set. A distant uncle on Heinz's father's side who lived in Scotland had given a financial guarantee. Heinz would have a job working in Edinburgh. He had a place to stay. His work would be menial and lowly paid, but that did not matter. He would get out of Germany.

We knew that Heinz was living in Berlin and staying with his father's brother, his Uncle Max. He had driven to Berlin shortly after Kristallnacht and had been here ever since searching for his way to leave Germany. Within moments of reading the letter, Mother was out the door to find Heinz. This was a cause for celebration, and a day or two later, we had a dinner party for Cousin Heinz to celebrate his good news.

Over dinner, Heinz told us his story. We knew that he had left the university in Cottbus on November 9, the day Aunt Trude called

Crossen to alert us to the fires and looting. When he tried to return to his classes, he learned that he and the four other Jewish students at the school had been expelled and would never be re-admitted. Concerned for his safety, mother's sister, Trude, had suggested that he drive to Berlin and stay with his Uncle Max until his future could be resolved.

He drove directly to Uncle Max's apartment, parking his automobile on the street. By sheer luck, there was nothing about his car to raise suspicions that it was owned or driven by a Jew. Unlike cars licensed in Berlin, where plates were numbered 350000 and higher to signify Jewish ownership, his car had been registered in Leiznig, where there were no such markings.

This had been important, as the Nazis had issued regulations in Berlin denying driver's licenses to Jews. Any Jew driving a vehicle would be subject to penalties, which Heinz had managed to skirt as he entered Berlin. Since arriving, he had kept the car parked, not wanting to take any risks. Within the last few days, he had found a buyer. He managed to sell the car on the street. While he did not get full value, he was able to sell the car for cash. And the Nazis did not know how much cash he had received.

Using some of the cash, he purchased an airline ticket to Scotland and even two bottles of wine for our dinner celebration. Talking to myself, I couldn't help but wonder how much he must have spent on that single ticket. There were so many who could barely afford transit on ships and trains. He planned to give his mother the remaining funds to help his sisters.

It was a good story, and we all rejoiced in Heinz's good fortune. I admit to becoming a bit depressed and jealous, perhaps because of the wine. I had a different problem. We knew no one outside of Germany. We had no guarantees. Our resources were limited. And I didn't own an automobile that I could sell. Still, I was happy for my cousin Heinz.

Chapter 52

Staying in Touch

elephones, a luxury of the past, were no longer as accessible and were far too costly to use. And the few times we had to use a telephone, we remained fearful about who might listen or how a misconstrued conversation could result in the Gestapo knocking at the door.

Earlier, in Crossen, and before that in Pr. Holland, we took the telephone for granted. It was the modern era. It was a modern convenience, although not as modern as today with much newer technology. Not everyone had telephones in the 1920s and 1930s, but we did. So did my sisters. So did my aunts and uncles. We didn't talk daily; no one did. We used the telephone when it was needed. It was part of our life.

In Berlin, letters became our preferred means of communication. Through letters, we kept up to date. We sent birthday greetings, learned family news, gave and received advice, celebrated and commiserated, planned arrivals, and planned departures. And, like with the telephone, we were concerned about privacy, about whether our letters would be opened and read. This became more of an issue later, once the war started, but even then, we remained concerned. The Nazis had issued a ban that even affected letters. Jews were not to own typewriters. This ban was seldom followed. Arthur owned one, and we kept it hidden from plain sight.

Mother often remarked that she enjoyed letters more than telephone calls. Weekly letters could be shared. They were read over and over, for clues, for details, for every bit of family news. Letters could be held in one's hands, and the words could not be forgotten. Letters could be saved.

Through letters, we learned that my cousin Inge, who was now twelve, was in Brussels. She was back in school and had made many new friends. It had been a very emotional and trying time for Aunt Hilda. Sending Inge away was a very difficult decision, but it was for the best. Aunt Hilda had wrapped up affairs in Wurzen and had been granted a work visa to immigrate to England. She had found work as a domestic and would leave soon to set up her new life. She would send for Inge as soon as she could make the necessary arrangements.

From Trude, we learned that Walter in Elbing was now in the German Army. He had already been away for three weeks. Trude still felt safe in East Prussia. She and Ruth would be alright. Their savings and Walter's military pay should carry them through. We were relieved to read that they had not been affected by recent Nazi decrees concerning mixed marriages. And we shared in the stories of Ruth's various adventures and her growing enthusiasm for entering the first grade later in the year.

Another letter told us that my sister Lotte planned to marry Ernst Jaruslawsky, the brother of Mother and Father's close friend Greta Lesser. This was very exciting news. We remembered that Lotte had first met Jarus at Trude's wedding years ago. They weren't yet sure when they would marry but hoped that it would be in Berlin within the year. They both needed to arrange time off from their work.

Mother's sister from Leiznig wrote that she was relieved to learn that Cousin Leni and her husband had made their way safely to Australia. They were living near Melbourne. Erna was still living in Belgium, where she was able to practice medicine. Aunt Trude told us she would remain in Leiznig. She did not want to leave. Her friends were there. Her children were now safe. That was most important. She felt that she could take care of herself in Leiznig.

Writing and receiving letters would continue to be our way to stay in touch with one another. Unfortunately, one day, the mail service between Germany and its enemies stopped. That would come later. Then, we were lost.

Days 10-12...

Real life is one thing, and fiction another. Over the next few days, Dad's improvement was not always certain. The damage from the stroke still could not be fully assessed. He had been put on dialysis to stem kidney failure from infections. One day was up, and the next day was down.

With mixed emotions, Joanie returned to her family and the frozen ice of Iowa. Mom continued her daily marathons to the hospital. She had vouchers to use the taxi, a workable but undependable convenience. For her, the drive was too long and difficult. I overcame my mixed feelings, and with blessings and encouragement, Ginger and I departed for our two-week trip.

Before leaving, Ginger asked me how I felt. Truth is, I felt like I ought to feel guilty, but really did not. Maybe I was pretending to feel guilty. I can't be sure. Sometimes, how I should feel and what I feel are not the same. What I did know, with absolute certainty, is what Dad and Mom would want us to do. And that is exactly what we did. Life ticked forward. Reality felt like fiction.

Chapter 53

My Way Out

As best we understood, I had three options available to leave Germany. The first was beyond our reach. Finding a relative to give a financial guarantee and vouch that I would be a self-supporting refugee was ruled out. Unlike Cousin Heinz, our family did not have relatives elsewhere, and we did not have the funds to pay for the guarantee. Ilse's husband, Arthur, had an uncle in America, but Father refused to consider that option. He wanted to pursue other alternatives first. Father thought Uncle Ludwig might be a lifeline for Ilse, Arthur, and Frank, and wanted to preserve that possibility.

The two remaining alternatives included finding a job and housing for me in Great Britain, or the Kindertransport program, which had been initiated just a few months earlier. British officials were amenable to granting visas to Germans if they had secured employment. And there were certain categories of employment where there were known shortages. Domestic help, laborers, and farm workers were a few. This was the option Aunt Hilda had successfully pursued. If someone was able and willing to perform this kind of work, and if a position could be prearranged, it might be possible to obtain a passport and a visa without posting a financial guarantee. Of course, the major problem with this approach was finding the connection with someone in Great Britain who could assist. Fortunately, by this time, through various churches and committees, there were a number of efforts underway.

The second option was the Kindertransport program. In November of 1938, the British Parliament gave permission for ten thousand children, mostly Jewish, aged six to seventeen years old, to enter the country. I was sixteen and therefore eligible, providing there was space. Kindertransport had some separate issues, however. One was the Nazi decree that Jews were not allowed to use trains or go into railway stations. While there were no barriers erected, this regulation created a problem for parents wanting to put their children onto the trains for this very emotional and lasting parting. The Quakers performed a major public service by standing outside train stations to receive children. They would accompany them to the port at Hoek van Holland to ensure their sailing connection to England. The Quakers also arranged to receive and provide care for the children when they arrived. Most were placed into Jewish foster homes, where efforts were made to keep siblings together.

Father chose not to use the Kindertransport program. I never learned why he made this decision, at least not with any certainty. I did not consider myself a child but did meet the age requirement for Kindertransport. We were in Berlin at the right time. I can only guess that Father wanted a different outcome for me. He gave me some hints, but never told me exactly.

My sense is that, unless he could not find another alternative, Father did not want me placed into a Jewish home or under the caring watch of a rabbi. That's the only conclusion I can draw. Nearly all the Kindertransport children were Jewish, and most were placed in homes that would preserve their Jewish faith and identify. Of course, now I can only speculate. I knew that Father wanted me to go forward in the Lutheran church. Perhaps because of the Jewish connection, the Kindertransport program was not his first choice for me. It may be that he thought this might be his last chance to influence my life and that his motivation was based upon our religious faith. That would be consistent with his beliefs.

How I was able to leave Germany seems such an old memory. At the time, there were no moments to ponder and speculate. Mother and Father were very practical people. Decisions were made given the choices available. We did not stop and debate what might have been. We didn't have the luxury, the patience, or, for that matter, the opportunity for that kind of thinking. That's not the way I am. That is not the way I was raised. It is something I resist. I was taught to look at a problem, consider the choices, make a decision, and then go forward. Don't look back. Deal with reality, not with foolish speculation.

That's why I have never been vocal on this issue. I don't want to speculate on what could or might have been. It makes me uncomfortable. A choice was made, and that's what we did. Would my life be different if I had left using the Kindertransport program? Probably. But what possible difference does that make now?

Uncomfortable or not, I suppose now is the time to say a few things about my beliefs. As an adult, matters of faith and church have meant little to me. The way I see it, religion has done our family more harm than good. For me, faith has never been a source of comfort. Mela and I don't always see eye to eye on these matters. When we married, I know she was hoping to go to the synagogue and to raise the children in the Jewish faith. For herself, Mela always missed having that sense of identity. She had a longing to belong. On that matter, I have always been respectful but unaccepting. Long ago, we found our compromise. Our children were not raised as Jews. We agreed to give them the knowledge to make their own decisions. I know this has made Ralph cynical about organized religion. I'm not sure what my daughter believes. I rarely spoke about my feelings. I never tried to impose my beliefs. But, now, if you were to ask me what I am, here is what I would say. In blood, I am a Jew. That is a fact I would never deny. In matters of faith and church, I am a Lutheran. That's how I believe. It has been that way since the day I was born. That has never changed. I am like my father.

We did receive help from the Quakers, but not with the Kindertransport program. Father worked with the Quaker office in Berlin. Through them, he made contact with a Scottish gentleman, Dr. G.C Cossar, who had an association with the London Refugee Committee and the Lad's Club in Glasgow. Born into a wealthy Glasgow family, Dr. Cossar, a philanthropist, had a long evangelical history of bringing displaced Scottish and Irish boys to New Brunswick, Canada, where they would work on farms. Dr. Cossar had retired from much of his earlier work but was willing to make the necessary financial guarantees in exchange for my commitment to work for one year in Scotland. Part of my wages would be withheld to repay Dr. Cossar for the guarantee. After that, the plan was to send me to Canada, where my farming skills could be put to good use.

With that settled, events unfolded quickly. The next issue was obtaining an entry visa. It helped that the first part of the problem had been solved. Now, with a prearranged job and housing in Scotland, a visa application could be pursued with the British consulate. Affidavits were required. Doctor's visits needed to be arranged. But those were minor hurdles. Most importantly, now an application could be completed and filed.

Even with the support from the British consulate, a day could be spent standing in line for a single piece of paper. The sheer volume of applications made long lines normal. Everyone was equally desperate. The simplest task could be difficult. Slow mail service complicated communication with officials in Scotland. Quickly meant more waiting.

The commitment from Scotland meant everything. Once we had it, Father devoted all his waking hours to the single task of securing a visa. With the Quaker's help, my visa was expedited. If it wasn't for Father, the Quakers, and Dr. Cossar, I doubt I would ever have been able to leave Germany.

During the third week of March, we received a letter posted on March 13, 1939. I have always believed that this was the most important letter of my life, the letter that saved my life. I was directed to go to the British Consul in Berlin, to the passport office. Only three months after we had arrived in Berlin, the German Emergency Committee in London authorized a visa to be issued to Gerhard Wobser. I had permission to leave Germany. I had permission to go to Scotland. My future was about to begin.

Chapter 54

My Celebration

For the second time in just a few short weeks, we opened a bottle, this time Champagne. I was barely sixteen. I was about to go forward with my life, on my own, in a place I hardly knew, and with a language almost completely foreign to my ears. All I remember from that evening was the excitement. I sipped my Champagne. This time, the room did not spin. My melancholy would set in a few days later, but not that evening. As I recall, Arthur bought the Champagne. He also found a bakery and bought a small torte. I'm sure he used his singing lesson money. It was exactly a kindness that Arthur would do.

To this day, I don't know who paid for what and where they found enough money. But, within days, I had been issued a passport stamped with a visa. Train and ship tickets had been purchased. I had been to a tailor, and measurements had been taken for two new suits. I received so many instructions, often conflicting, from both Mother and Ilse. I learned how to sew, how to do the wash, how to iron, how to replace a button. Ilse made it a point that I knew the facts of life. Later, these were carefully and graphically restated by Arthur.

I was tutored on how to write letters, how to mail letters, and how to buy stamps. I was drilled in table manners. While Mother supervised, Arthur tried to teach me to dance. Father came home one day with a new razor, a gift for me. That evening, for the first time, he taught me to shave. Nothing was left to chance.

So much had happened in the previous four years. It seemed like such a long time, but it went by so quickly. I know the two thoughts are contradictory, but the time was both long and quick. An eternity took an instant. And, now, so suddenly, I would leave.

Mela is right. Life is a balance. Smiles in one eye and tears in the other. There is no better phrase to describe how I felt.

Days 13-17...

Mom continued her daily reports by sending an email each evening making certain we all had the same story. Ginger and I arrived in Prague and spent a wonderful few days with my first cousin Manfred and his wife Marianne, who live in Germany. After Prague, Ginger and I ventured to Budapest, spent Christmas in Vienna, celebrated New Year's in Salzburg, and had a day or two in Copenhagen before returning home.

The reports on Dad showed slow but steady signs of improvement. And it became clear that Mom had found a manageable rhythm to her life. We called her every few days, but mostly left her alone.

We could tell that an important part of her felt independent and able as she managed her situation. She might have been tired, but she had a purpose. Her nightly emails stemmed the disruption of phone calls. She needed her space. She needed her privacy. She wanted her children to go on with their lives. Dad would have wanted that too.

Perhaps it was my way of rationalizing, but I believe she was proving something to herself. Because of her age, we should not treat her as old. Sometimes I wonder how old Ginger and I will be before Zak will ask whether we can take care of ourselves. How will we react? Is there a magical age when children become parents to their parents? Mom was great and needed to feel in charge of her life. There was a certain satisfaction to not needing our help. She would ask if she wanted help. We were all happy with that arrangement. But our antennas were also up to the stubborn issue. Mom has a way to be stubborn about these kinds of things. Joanie would know when to act.

As each day passed, I gained more hope. Mom's updates were encouraging, and every little success was a cause for celebration.

They were weaning Dad from dialysis and the ventilator, trying to let him breathe more and more on his own. She told us she talked to him for hours on end every day. Each day, she was more convinced that they were having a conversation. One day, she wrote that he knew she was there. He opened his eyes and nodded his head.

Another day, Mom reported that the tubes would be removed, that they would have him sit up, that he would be able to eat food. These were personal accomplishments that she and Dad shared. Most hours, he remained sedated and slept. She told us that Dad was not exactly the life of the party, but she was sure that within days, he would be able to talk. She could see it in his eyes and the way he moved his hands.

Chapter 55

Leaving Berlin

*S*unday, April 17, 1938, was the day I boarded a train and left Germany behind. I said goodbye to my family and the only life I had ever known. And, within a short time, all that was, was no longer.

The Berlin train station was crowded that day with people all harried and hurried. Some were crying and hugging and moaning and weeping. Others went about their business oblivious to the commotion of families torn apart. It seemed that there were two worlds and not much in between. By now, Jews were required to add Sarah or Israel to names on legal documents, including passports. My new name was Gerald Udo Israel Wobser. It was on all my papers.

I don't recall how we skirted the prohibition of Jews in the train station. It was probably just another meaningless regulation seldom enforced and indiscriminately used by the Nazis to harass the unsuspecting.

I do remember leaving Mother, Father, Ilse, Arthur, and Frank at street side. I recall hugging goodbye and picking up my suitcase. I was dressed in one of my newly tailored suits. Mother said I looked handsome. Father took his black onyx ring from his finger and pressed it to mine. He told me it was my turn and never to quit, to be proud, and always, to know who I am, to be true to myself. Both gave me handwritten letters, some advice to remind me of them. We all had tears in our eyes.

I remember walking through the station to board the train, how my footsteps felt hollow, how old I felt. And I remember looking at my reflection in the train window as the train began to move. I remember how my throat felt as it choked back the emotion. There was not a moment of that day that I don't recall.

The train was crowded. There were many leaving. It was easy to tell who the refugees were. There was something about us that all looked the same. Our destination was the seaport near Rotterdam in Holland. The train ride would take most of the day, but it seemed to go by in only minutes. By ship, we crossed the North Sea, and by morning, we docked at Harwich, England. I was in such a state of shock that seasickness never entered my mind. I will never forget that moment my feet touched land. I dropped to my knees and kissed the ground. We all did. We all cried. It was all that we could do. One life was over. A new life had begun.

Part Two
On My Own

Chapter 56

Scotland, April, 1938

*I*t hardly seemed possible. One moment, I was in Berlin with my sister's family and Mother and Father, and the next moment, I was in Uddingston, Scotland, living in the Clydeneuk House, a nineteenth century Scottish country estate under the care and guidance of Dr. G.C. Cossar. As well as I remember every moment of the trip to Harwich, I remember very little of the time after I first arrived. Papers were processed. Someone from the Lad's Club in Glasgow met me and fed me. Somehow, I was transferred from Harwich, England, to Scotland. Two nights were spent in a bed at a church. Another night was spent in a family's home. More papers were processed and health records checked. Uniformed policemen stamped my documents. Questions were asked. Answers were given. Some faces were friendly. Some faces frowned.

I was astonished, uncertain, and more than a bit scared. I knew what farm life would be like. But that would not happen at first. Everything else? As far as I could see, everything else was different, unfamiliar, and foreign, beyond my comprehension. I was overwhelmed by self-doubt.

My biggest problem was language. The little English I had learned in Berlin was nothing like what was spoken in Scotland. They spoke too fast. I had never heard words like these; the syllables were all strange. I could not process. For the first several months, anyone I met must have regarded me as mute. I did not speak. And, if I did, my vocabulary was limited to the shortest of utterances: please, thank you, hello, and goodbye. Mostly, I nodded. Mother would have approved; at least I was polite.

Before being placed on a farm, I worked in the gardens at Clydeneuk in Uddingston and helped care for the landscape by day. By night, I studied and practiced my English. My progress was slow and painstaking. I remained afraid to speak.

Some may find it odd, but I found a certain comfort in not speaking. I was reminded of childhood when my sisters filled all the space with their talking and I was left with little to do but listen. This trait would continue for much of my adult life. I did learn to converse. But it has only been in recent years that I have found a need to interrupt others, to share my thoughts and opinions. Now I imagine my family wishes I would keep my self-confident opinions to myself and would stop filling all the space with the sound of my voice.

When I was placed on a farm, it was in Balfron. I was sent to the Dalfoil Farm owned by the Christie family. The Christies were a hardworking lot, and the farm was demanding. Six days every week, we worked from sunrise to sunset. We worked side by side. They were a good family, kind and bighearted. They gave me a room and fed me. But they did not replace my family. I was the hired hand. They were someone else's family. I had no other expectations. I knew I was there to work.

Sunday mornings were for church, but the remainder of the day was mine. That was an unexpected luxury. I was never lonely. My years at the farm in Crossen had taught me how to overcome my loneliness. I was on my own. I had my own time. I only needed to answer to myself. The experience was new. Having always lived with Mother and Father, I was accustomed to giving answers to the questions they would ask. Now, for the first time in my life, there was no one asking questions.

I'm sure others might find my daily repetition less than appealing. I did not. For me, there was a simple steadiness to my new life, a steadiness that contrasted well with the uncertain months that preceded my arrival. The days went by in an ordered fashion. They were predictable. They were dependable. I worked. I slept. I ate. I dreamt. Then, I would awaken and do it all over again.

Chapter 57

Maud and Mrs. Mein

*A*t sixteen, life seemed to change with each heartbeat. I suppose that is true for most sixteen-year-olds regardless of time or circumstance. One moment this, and the next moment that. It was only weeks before my feeling of routine and steadiness was replaced by the feeling of monotony and standing still. I needed to do more, to be out, and to get on with it. And, most importantly, I knew I needed to learn my new language.

As fortune would have it, the Christies introduced me to a neighbor who lived just beyond the adjacent farm. She was originally from Switzerland, was fluent in both German and English, and, most importantly, the Scottish variety. Mrs. Marie Mein, the widowed wife of the retired local constable, and her fourteen-year-old daughter Maud became my angels. Mrs. Mein understood my plight. She was an immigrant. When she first came to Scotland, she worked as a domestic. She knew what it was like to have to adjust to entirely new surroundings, to find oneself far away from family, friends, and home.

For the remainder of my stay at the Christie farm, I spent nearly every Sunday afternoon and evening with the Meins at Edelweiss, the name for their home on Fintry Road in Balfron. They invited me to their church. They introduced me to their friends. With open arms, they made me part of their family.

The Mein home became my home away from home, and Mrs. Mein and Maud filled the void that I sorely missed without my family. Through them, I learned to understand and speak English. I was cautious and slow at first, but once I started, there was no turning back. Through them, I gained the self confidence I desperately needed to go forward with my life.

Mrs. Mein took it upon herself to correspond with Mother in Germany. She would always say that every mother needs another mother to give a report on her son. Mother and Mrs. Mein exchanged letters every week. It became a lifeline for me and, I am sure, the same for Mother and Father. It was an act of kindness I have never forgotten.

Maud was a quiet girl, almost too young for her age. She became a good friend. She helped me adjust to my surroundings. She had lost her brother, Thomas, years earlier. Perhaps I replaced him for her in some small way. I hope so.

Through Maud and Mrs. Mein, I was introduced to others. I was accepted and made to feel welcome. It was not long before I woke with a start one morning and realized that I had spent the night dreaming, no longer in German, but in my new language, English. That's when I knew I had finally arrived.

I will never forget the Meins and the people of Scotland. They didn't care if I was German, that my ancestry was Jewish, or that I was an alien in their land. They opened their homes. They opened their hearts. They asked for nothing in return. Few are as fortunate as I was during those days.

Sometimes luck simply strikes, and fate intercedes. Good people reach out and change a life. That's what happened to me. I will always be grateful.

Chapter 58

Dream or Memory?

So many memories are vague about the months I spent at the Dalfoil Farm, so vague that I wonder if I was living in a dream, whether I was really there. Even now, as I repeat the story, I cannot help but wonder if that time really occurred in my life. It seems so much more than a lifetime ago.

One moment, I was living with my family in Germany. All my surroundings were German, the signs, the sounds, the buildings, the automobiles, the clothing. The next moment, I was living in Scotland. Then, everything that I knew was in my past. It was much more than the difference between languages. It was visual. It was food. It was smell. It was color. It was the way laughter sounds. It was in the streets. It was springtime in Scotland and everything was green. The final days in Berlin, everything seemed cloudy and gray.

There is that feeling, that final, lingering moment before waking up when my dreams seem so real that I pause to consider whether they really happened, when I have the urge to reach out and grasp them with my fingers. There is that brief moment, when my eyes are still closed and my mind is not yet open, when I lay awake and do not think. That's what I sense when I think about those days in Scotland. It all seemed so real that it could have been a dream.

I should have been homesick at the beginning. Mother, Father, and I had shared so much during the preceding few years. I know I missed the comfort of familiar faces. But I wasn't. I never felt homesick. I never was sad at my circumstance. I never felt sorry for myself. My adventure was full of anticipation and expectation; it was uncharted and unknown. I felt the excitement of youth. I knew that I had a direction. I knew my life would go somewhere. I always had a compass, a lifelong gift instilled by my parents. What I did not know for certain was whether I was living in a dream or reality. That, I still needed to figure out.

Chapter 59

War

*A*s I settled in, my biggest worry was what would happen to my family who remained in Germany. I was able to leave, but they were all still there. The news reports on the radio were bad. The prospect of war loomed large for us all. We heard one thing one day, another the next. It was hard to separate rumor from fact. Nobody knew for certain, but the signals seemed clear. And, although my interest in world events had expanded and grown, my lack of education limited my knowledge of the world and its geography. Living as I did on the farm in Balfron, I had little access to the news. I also think the Christie family tried to shield me from the events that were unfolding. They knew the dangers for my family. They felt my worry and were concerned about me. I was no longer a child, but not quite an adult. I am sure they could feel my heartache.

On the evening of September 3, 1939, Prime Minister Chamberlain gave a nationwide radio address, and we were told that Great Britain and France had gone to war against Germany. That is when I first learned that Germany had attacked Poland only days earlier. Others can relate the details of these invasions and explain the prolonged negotiations between Great Britain and the Germans. My concern was what war would mean to my family. Would I ever see them again?

When war was declared, I had been in Scotland for only four months. The memory still overwhelms me. With my little English, was I able to fully understand the words that were being said? Here I was in Great Britain. They had just declared war against Germany. My parents, my sisters, and my family would all be caught in the crossfire. War meant destruction. War meant casualties. War meant the unimaginable. I remember my confusion. I was sorting through who the enemy was and who I wanted the enemy to be. I was helpless. There was nothing I could do. There was not a thing any of us could do.

Until that day when war was declared, Mother's letters arrived with great frequency – letters from my sisters too. I wrote from time to time. Their letters were usually lengthy. My letters were invariably short. Mrs. Mein and Mother were exchanging letters. Now all that suddenly stopped. We had no way to communicate, and I was left clueless.

Day 18, Christmas Eve....

This morning, there was an email from Mom. The news was better. They had taken the respiratory tube out. Dad had not tried to talk yet. His throat was still sore. It will be a slow recovery, but at least it is a beginning. She said that they kept the music going by playing his favorite tapes. It was their way to dance to the music.

Chapter 60

My Parents?

When war was declared, all German refugees over the age of sixteen who did not intend to leave Scotland immediately were required to report to the police. I had to bring my passport to the local constable and was subject to certain restrictions. For example, I needed to notify the authorities if I intended to travel more than five miles from where I lived. There were some curfew restrictions too, and I was classified as an "enemy alien." That classification might strike some as odd, but these were not ordinary times, and emotional labels and reactions were persistent. All refugees from Germany were classified that way regardless of the circumstance or the reasons we had left Germany. None of this made much difference to me. I had no place to go. I was staying put on the farm.

There was little I could do except work and spend my Sundays with Mrs. Mein and Maud that fall and winter of 1939. The war was escalating, and I had no idea how my family was faring. Before Mother's letters abruptly stopped, she had written that they had made their decision to leave Germany. I could only hope that was the path they were pursuing.

Rumors were circulating about the atrocities that were being committed by the Germans. Most seemed directed at the Austrian and Polish Jews. We could never be certain. Mrs. Mein said that she had no idea whether this was true or part of the propaganda to increase the war effort. While I worried, I remained convinced that my family would be safe. I knew that Father would approach their exit with the same focus and intensity as he had done for me. All I could do was continue my life, hope they were okay, and wait to hear something.

In her last letters, Mother had said that the decision to leave had been troubling and emotional. She was reluctant to leave until she was certain that her children would be safe. They had learned that my sister Lotte and her fiancé, Jarus, were making plans to leave for Palestine. As Lotte had told me, when we were together at Gut Winkel, preparing students for their departures had convinced her that this was what they should do. Palestine would be a good home for them. Jarus had been reluctant because his parents refused to leave Marienburg and there were other family members to consider as well. They would watch the situation and wait a little longer, but that was their plan. They would leave. It was only a matter of when.

Mother was concerned about Trude and Ruth. Trude had decided to remain in Elbing and to ride out the situation. She felt strongly about this. They needed to be there for Walter when he returned home from serving in the German Army. His service gave them some protection. Walter had stood by his family, refusing the pressures to divorce Trude and annul his mixed marriage. Ruth had started school. Elbing was far removed from what was happening in Berlin and elsewhere in Germany. Walter was certainly not in a position to leave. If Trude and Ruth were to leave now, they would have to abandon Walter, and that was not something they would do. Their situation deeply troubled Mother, but they had made their decision, and there was nothing she could do.

Father had heard from friends who were planning to go to Shanghai, China. Apparently, Shanghai's immigration requirements were seldom enforced or, at least, were changing. The key was purchasing passage to Shanghai. No one was being turned away. Unless one had connections and access to financial resources, Shanghai had become the most practical and viable option. Still, Mother mentioned there was considerable confusion and varying opinion about Shanghai. Some thought it a good alternative; others thought it to be a very desperate choice.

Her letters had said other choices were considered. South America and Australia were also on the list. America had been Mother and Father's first choice, but impossible. There were no visas available. The quota was filled. And even if that hurdle could be overcome by some miracle, they did not possess the resources to make America a reality. Perhaps Arthur, Ilse, and Frank would be able to make it there with Arthur's Uncle Ludwig's help, but even that seemed doubtful. His resources notwithstanding, the visa and quota problems were obstacles that could not be overcome.

The last I heard was that Shanghai was the choice. Together with Ilse, Arthur, and Frank, they would search for passage. As soon as they could, they would leave Germany in their past.

Obviously, agreeing to a plan and successfully implementing it were two decidedly different activities. Meanwhile, they needed to cope with daily life in Berlin. That was what Mother wrote in her last letter. Then, war broke out and all communications ceased. It would be months before I learned anything more.

Chapter 61

Waiting

All I could do was wait for my eighteenth birthday in October of 1940, still twelve months away. That was when my commitment to Dalfoil Farms and the Christie family would be fulfilled. Although it was stated on my visa, I wasn't really convinced that I wanted to move to Canada to become a farmer. But I really didn't have an alternative plan. My alien status and lack of education, skills, or, for that matter, resources, certainly limited the choices on my horizon.

It was clear that the war was escalating. And my days working on the farm in Scotland were soured by the lack of news about my family. I had no idea how they were faring.

Scotland had been good for me, a challenging time, a learning time. I had grown. More than anything, I had learned how to survive, how to take care of myself, and I had mastered the English language, something I was very proud of. Mastered might be an overstatement. I was able to speak the language, and I was able to understand what was said. Later, it would become a complete surprise to hear the English spoken elsewhere in Great Britain. I had no idea that it would sound so unlike the English I had learned in Scotland.

The countries of Great Britain had a long history of helping those in need of safe havens and political asylum. I will always believe that Great Britain and Scotland, in particular, saved my life. I certainly was not alone. Between 1933 and 1939, more than eighty thousand Jewish refugees had reached Britain and were fully supported by British Jewish and other church organizations. Whatever confusion I may have felt about my loyalties when I first arrived had long passed. For now, Great Britain had become my adopted home, and Germany was our enemy. Of course, the complication remained that I still had family living in Germany. It was difficult to imagine Trude's husband Walter, my brother-in-law, as my enemy.

I knew little of the war. Much was left to my imagination. Living in rural Scotland, I was largely protected. In many ways, if it were not for my family in Germany, I was unaffected. There was no denying, however, that war was all around me. We heard more news each day.

As I think back, I must have grown restless, and there is one incident that bears mentioning. There was another refugee my age staying with the Callenders, not far from the Christie farm. Through him, I learned that I could be paid more if I went to work at the Branshogal Mill in Balfron Station. They would also provide room and board, the same as the Christies. That didn't seem fair. I spoke up and told Mr. Christie at the farm I should be paid more. When he refused, I went to the Stirling Labor Exchange and asked to change my work arrangement. All of this caused quite a stir. Dr. Cossar became involved. The local constable was called in to investigate. The British Home Office was advised, and there was even some question as to my alien status. As a result, my relationship with the Christie Farm was ended abruptly, and I did move to the mill in Balfron Station, although not entirely by my own choosing. I learned my lesson. The authorities did pay close attention to aliens in their midst. Despite this unfortunate incident, I remained appreciative of the Christie family and the time I worked at their farm. The pay was paltry, but the food was hearty. I felt grateful from the day I arrived to the day that I left. I just didn't expect to leave four months early.

Winston Churchill became Great Britain's Prime Minister in May of 1940, and Great Britain was completely committed to defeating Germany. From the radio, we learned that Great Britain's new foreign policy would be no negotiations and unconditional surrender. Britain was facing Nazi Germany and its allies with little support. The Soviet Union and United States had not yet entered the war. By mid-1940, the Germans had invaded Denmark and Norway. Then, the Nazis invaded France, Belgium, Holland, and Luxembourg. In mid-June, 1940, Paris was occupied by the Nazis, and France signed an armistice with Hitler.

As I learned about the war, it became clear what I wanted to do next. It was an easy decision. I would not move to Canada. I would apply to extend my visa, and on my eighteenth birthday, I would enlist in the British Army and join the fight against Germany. There had been much debate about allowing German nationals into the British Army. New rules permitting this had just been adopted. I was grateful for how my new home had helped me. Now I wanted to serve. I felt my patriotic duty. Years earlier, I had felt patriotic about Germany. Now my patriotism was for Great Britain.

Chapter 62

They Are Going to Shanghai!

*I*t was about that time, mid-May of 1940, that I received the long awaited news that Mother and Father, along with Ilse, Arthur, and Frank, had safely departed Germany. Mrs. Mein received a letter from Mother, postmarked April 11, 1940, from Trieste, Italy. Passage had been secured on a ship to Shanghai, China. The trip would take several weeks. They would write more when they arrived.

I cannot come close to conveying my sense of relief knowing that they had left Germany. Nothing had been said about Trude and Ruth in Elbing, nor did I learn anything about Lotte and Jarus, or any other family members or friends, but this was a start. I knew that my parents and Ilse's family were safe.

It was years before I learned what my family went through that year in Berlin and how they made their way to Shanghai. As the war effort in Germany continued to build, the Nazi campaign to rid Germany of the remaining Jews increased. For our family, the same obstacles continued – where to go and how to get there. Now they had to accomplish this in a time of war when suspicions were rampant.

My parents didn't know it then, but the window of opportunity to flee Germany was rapidly closing. It would close within the year. For those who remained, the consequences would become fatal. Still, many German Jews refused to accept what was happening. They had been loyal citizens of their homeland. They, their parents, and their grandparents had served in the army. They had held government jobs. This was their culture. Their families had been Germans for centuries. This was where their friends were. This was where their parents lived. This is where their children lived. This is where their life was. Many shared the disbelief that the anti-Jewish laws were directed against them. Others were so assimilated that they thought the targets were the conspicuous orthodox Jews and certainly not themselves.

Mother and Father were able to overcome these emotions and denials. Father would have been disappointed, frustrated, and depressed. Mother might not have felt the same; in these matters, she was more practical and sensible. I am sure Mother must have felt betrayed. Mother must have been angry. One thing was certain. They were deeply worried about their children's futures.

Each day posed increasingly difficult challenges. The buildup and success of Germany's invasion of Poland and the declaration of war against Germany by Great Britain and France all served to bolster the confidence and arrogance of the Nazi regime. Father was removed from a streetcar one day because Jews had been banned from public transport. In the Tiergarten, Berlin's central park, only a handful of the hundreds of benches were painted yellow and designated for Jews. Laundries were banned from washing Jewish people's clothes. Jews were not allowed to go to non-Jewish barbers and hairdressers. When rationing began, food rations for Jews were constantly reduced with no regard for the sick. In certain sections of Berlin, coal deliveries were not made to Jewish families. During severe winter weather, thousands of Jews were enlisted for forced work shoveling the streets of snow and unloading coal trucks. Beginning September 1, 1939, Jews in Berlin were forbidden to be outdoors after eight pm in winter and nine pm in summer. Three weeks later, Jews were forbidden from owning radios. Each day, another regulation was posted. Each day, Jewish life was made more miserable.

Father continued his daily visits to every office that could help. And, each day, he was joined by thousands of others, standing in lines, sitting in waiting rooms for hours on end, all trying to find their way out. Many times, Ilse would join him, and Arthur too. Mother would tend to young Frank. Coping was the best they could do.

It was Arthur who delivered the answer. Arthur received a response from his Uncle Ludwig who lived in America. Tickets would be purchased for all five, Mother, Father, Ilse, Arthur, and Frank, to go to Shanghai. This was the news they needed. Uncle Ludwig had already helped Arthur's first cousins leave Naples. Now he would help Arthur's family, including his in-laws.

On March 12, 1940, they were all granted permission to leave Germany. On March 23, the passports were stamped by the necessary authorities, and all taxes and fees were paid. On March 28, train tickets to Italy were purchased. There they would board the ship to Shanghai. Finally, on April 2, 1940, their party of five left Germany.

Their lifetime in Germany ended with an empty departure. No one was there to say goodbye or see them off at the train station. Lotte and Jarus were now in Bielefeld. Trude was living in Elbing. I was in Scotland. Walter Stange, Father's son, born out of wedlock, was living in Berlin but chose to stay away. Guilt by association was a powerful weapon. He meant well, but he could not be seen in the company of Jews. Father would never see him again.

Day 19, Christmas Day...
Mom sent out this email on Christmas Day...

Dear Everyone,

Merry Christmas to all. Hope everyone got his or her wishes fulfilled. Jerry is improving, his kidneys are almost back to normal, and the dialysis machine has been moved out of his room. He has no pain and is off sedatives. I hope they will soon move him out of intensive care, and I will stop sending you these daily reports. I would like to thank each of you for not having called too much. I realize you care and are concerned, and I love you for it. My days have been rather strange.

Much love, Mela

We called Mom from Prague late that night. It had been a long day for her. Early Christmas morning, she waited for the taxi to take her to the hospital, but it failed to show up. It took several hours before she was able to see Dad. She cried as she told us that all she wanted for Christmas was to spend the day with her man.

It had all worked out. She was okay now. She said that sometimes she felt sorry for herself. She was grateful that she could cry on our shoulder for a few moments. We should not worry. She was happy we called. Dad keeps getting better. That's all that matters. Enjoy yourselves. I love you. This was an emotional call. We all shed more than a few tears.

Chapter 63

Trieste, April 1940

The train trip was lengthy, and the seats they could afford were stiff and wooden, not designed for comfort for this long trip. I imagine their excited conversation, punctured by awkward silent moments, as they made their way. From Berlin, the first destination was Munich, where they would change trains. That first eight-hour leg must have been colored with sadness for Mother as she passed by Leipzig and the places of her youth. She would pass not far from where her sister, Aunt Trude, lived, not far from where she attended boarding school, not far from many of her life's memories. Aunt Trude was one of the many convinced that these times would pass. Riding the train that day, Mother could not know the fate that awaited her sister. She would not survive. Two years later, Aunt Trude would be deported to a concentration camp in Poland where she would be murdered by the Nazis.

From Munich, the train continued south through the Brenner Pass into Austria. There, the border crossing would be easy. Austria was an early victim of Germany's dreams. After Austria came Italy. The trip through Austria was short, only an hour or two, but crossing the border into Italy was delayed. They were well into their third day by the time they reached Milan.

In Milan, Mother and Father left Ilse, Arthur, and Frank. They would meet them on the ship. Mother and Father would go to Trieste to start their voyage. Their next train would take them to Venice. A second would go to Trieste. A Lutheran organization in Berlin had arranged a room where they could stay until they were to board ship.

Ilse, Arthur, and Frank continued south by train. They traveled to Rome, through Florence and Bologna. In Rome, they switched trains, this time to Naples. There they would stay with Arthur's Uncle Paul and Aunt Elsa. Paul was Arthur's mother's brother and the brother of Uncle Ludwig from New York, who had paid for their trip.

The stop in Naples was important. In addition to the ship tickets that had been sent to them in Berlin, Uncle Ludwig had forwarded funds to help them in Shanghai. Arthur retrieved these funds in Naples from his Uncle Paul in order to avoid confiscation by the German authorities.

The Oulmans owned a small pensione overlooking the Mediterranean on the Bay of Naples. They, too, were hoping to leave soon and were waiting for visas. Their daughter, Emilia, and their three sons had already left and made their way to America with Uncle Ludwig's help. After a brief visit in Naples, Ilse, Arthur, and Frank journeyed to Brindisi to catch the ship carrying Mother and Father. Then, together, they would make their way to Shanghai.

For Mother and Father, Trieste must have felt like an oasis in the midst of all the madness. War would not come to Italy for another two months. They did not know that their crossing would be one of the last ones to Shanghai for their ship, the Conte Rosso. In early June, when Italy entered the war, this route to Shanghai would be closed.

April weather in Trieste, sunny and warm, with the Adriatic Sea as the backdrop, stood in sharp contrast to the cold winter they had just endured in Berlin. The little I know of their time in Trieste was from a letter Mother wrote to Trude and Lotte two days before their departure to Shanghai. I didn't see this letter until many years later.

Don't worry about us. With God's help, we will find a home in a foreign land. Everything is like a dream. Father and I are sitting by the sea. One cannot make demands, and we are very capable of adapting. The main thing is that we will live again as free people.

Their ship left the evening of April 11, 1940.

Chapter 64

Voyage to Shanghai

Shanghai was a long voyage from Trieste, 8,790 kilometers, and the trip would take nearly an entire month. They would travel in an easterly direction. After departing the Adriatic Sea, they would cross the Ionian, then the Mediterranean near Egypt before making their way through the Suez Canal. They would stop in Bombay, Colombo, Singapore, and Hong Kong before they would reach Shanghai. The Conte Rosso had traveled the route many times and was well equipped for the journey.

Their first stop would come quickly, the very next morning. They would stop in Brindisi to pick up additional passengers. There, they would be reunited with Ilse, Arthur, and Frank.

Their time on Conte Rosso would be rather uneventful. Her history would come a little more than a year later. Called into service when Italy joined Germany in the war, the Conte Rosso would be converted to an Italian troopship. She would be sunk by a British submarine off the coast of North Africa. More than twelve hundred lives would be lost.

The Lloyd Triestino line operated four ships used to transport Jewish refugees from Germany and Austria to Shanghai. The Conte Rosso was able to carry a little more than nineteen hundred passengers, two hundred in first class, two hundred and fifty in second class, and the remainder in steerage.

The little I know of their voyage is what Ilse told me years later. They were comfortable and well fed. They passed the time in quiet conversation with others literally in the same boat. They still felt numb and dazed. They were unsure what the future would bring. They worried about those who were left behind.

Chapter 65

Internment at the Isle of Man

My days in Scotland always remained troubled by the lack of news about my family. But, now, that issue had been overcome. Mother, Father, Ilse, Arthur, and Frank had made their way to Shanghai. Mail service was passable between Great Britain and Shanghai, and I was caught up on most news. And, since mail service was running between Shanghai and Germany, I now had a way to learn about the fate of my sisters and others, even if the information would be old and out of date.

War seldom stands still, and in September of 1939, when Great Britain declared war on Germany, Britain banned all further arrivals from Nazi-controlled territories. I was fortunate to have made it. That window was closed only months after I arrived. In fact, I learned much later that at this same time, Great Britain restricted Jewish immigration to Palestine, as it was under the control of British Mandate authorities. This closed the window for Lotte and Jarus and their desire to leave Germany for Palestine. We did not know it then, but their fate had been sealed. She and Jarus would never be able to leave Germany.

After Germany systematically invaded Denmark, Norway, Belgium, Luxembourg, Holland, and France during the spring of 1940, there was little surprise when the British public began to panic. There was an intense fear that there could be a German offensive directed at the British homeland. Fearing the possibility that anyone with a German accent might be a spy, the British government began screening and detaining Germans who had settled in Great Britain. Later, a similar activity would take place in America when the Japanese were detained at the start of the war in the Pacific. In Great Britain, some called it a Germanophobia. With a net that large, everyone finds themselves caught.

On June 21, 1940, at the summons of the British government, I reported to the Isle of Man detention processing center to be assessed to determine whether I posed a threat to national security. The Isle of Man is located in the Irish Sea between Scotland, England, Ireland, and Wales.

Internment camps had begun to appear all across Great Britain. They varied greatly in size and treatment of prisoners. The largest were on the Isle of Man. The camps located on the Isle of Man were universally considered the most comfortable and best maintained of all internment camps. I understand that 80% of the detainees at the Isle of Man were German refugees.

One of the ironies of my situation, and the situation of many others, was that we were hardly likely to be sympathetic to the Nazis, much less be spies. But, in these panicky times, those in charge needed to be certain, and this was a complication that no one bothered to try to unravel. My age was an advantage. I was still seventeen, a little underage by most standards, and a bit younger than most of the other internees. The manager of the Branshogal Mill in Balfron even tried to intercede by writing a letter on my behalf. He gave me good references and an assurance that I would have a job if they released me. But nothing worked. I was interned just like the others.

So the plan that I would move to Canada and become a farmer ended, a little more inconveniently than I had hoped. I was placed in the Isle of Man internment camp for several months while they figured out what to do with me. If I were to pick one word to describe my time as an illegal alien internee, it would be boredom, complete and utter boredom. After I got past my initial shock, I realized that there was little to do. We all felt useless. And we had little reliable news.

There is not much more that can be said. I was treated well. I shared my time with many others and even joined in on many of the English classes that were being held. My accommodations were fine. I ate well. Mail service, although closely guarded and censored, was good. I corresponded with Mrs. Mein, who corresponded with my family in Shanghai. I remember little of what we did to pass the time as we collectively were removed from the British population. I looked forward to my eighteenth birthday and the hope that I could join the British Army and get on with my life.

Day 21...

Today, Mom's email started, "Dear Everybody, I could make somersaults for joy. Jerry has started to talk, except, wearing hearing aids, I am not able to understand his mumbles." She also wrote that he was restless and irritable. Her assessment is that's a good sign. It means that he is improving.

She didn't mention yesterday's problem with the taxi, so we suppose that all of that is back to normal. We are still in Vienna and head to Salzburg in the morning. We will call her again in a few days.

Chapter 66

Lotte and Jarus

J was in the internment camp on the Isle of Man when I learned that my sister Lotte had married Ernst Jaruslawsky, or Jarus as we called him, in Berlin in August of 1940. I received the news nearly two months after the wedding. My sister Trude had sent a letter from Berlin to my parents in Shanghai. Mother, then, sent a letter from Shanghai to Mrs. Mein in Scotland. And, finally, Mrs. Mein wrote to me. This was my way of getting family news from Germany.

Trude and seven-year-old Ruth were able to travel from East Prussia to Berlin for the wedding. They were the only family members to witness the ceremony. It took them two days to get there by overnight train. I'm sure it was a complicated trip with the war underway.

Lotte had remained close to Jarus ever since they had first met and danced at Trude and Walter's wedding nearly ten years before. That seemed like an entirely different world now. Our family had known Jarus for years. Jarus, a druggist by profession, lived and worked in Bielefeld. The last I had heard, Lotte was teaching in Spreenhagen at the Gut Winkel camp, not far from Berlin and 400 kilometers east of Bielefeld.

This is where the story gets a bit sketchy. Here is the little I know. Lotte had moved to Bielefeld. I'm not sure what happened with Gut Winkel and what brought Lotte to Bielefeld. Lotte and Jarus never shared that story. In March 1940, a year after I left Germany and while I was still in Scotland, nearly all of the Jews in Bielefeld were rounded up by the Gestapo. They were forced to move into Jewish-only housing, where they were required to perform labor for the Nazis. Along with many others, Jarus and Lotte were caught in this process.

They were placed in the Schlosshoffstrasse 73, a re-education camp controlled by the Bielefeld Gestapo. From what I have been learned, about seventy-five persons lived in this camp, a converted restaurant and inn on the outskirts of Bielefeld. Some of the people there were from Bielefeld. Others were sent there by the Nazis from nearby areas.

The Gestapo selected Jarus to be the camp leader, with Lotte as his assistant. He reported to the Gestapo daily, followed their orders, and was responsible for seeing that the work assignments were fulfilled. Together, he and Lotte managed the camp. As best I can tell, they had no choice in this matter. It seems that the Gestapo left them alone as long as residents followed the rules. They were free to come and go, but were required to live there and do the work assigned. If they failed to comply, they would be sent elsewhere, to more severe surroundings. The work was very physical: building roads, clearing debris, and constructing bomb shelters. The Germans may have called it a re-education camp, but in reality, it was a forced labor camp. There was no escape. If they left and did not return, they were arrested. It was a prison for Jews, one without bars.

Lotte and Jarus were granted permission by the Gestapo to go to Berlin for three days for their wedding. It took place on August 27.

As I tell this, nothing makes any sense to me. How could Germany treat my sister Lotte like this? All she ever wanted to do was laugh and enjoy life. Our lives were untangled and untarnished. Then, everything changed. Mother and Father had literally fled to Shanghai with little more than the shirts on their backs. I was restricted in an internment camp on the Isle of Man. Lotte and Jarus were in a forced labor camp in Germany. Trude and Ruth were in East Prussia and certainly remained in harm's way. All that we had was lost. And, there was nothing we could do. We couldn't change anything. We were helpless. What did we do? What had we done?

I wondered how Mother and Father were coping. When they had left for Shanghai, they had left everything behind. Weddings were supposed to be joyous family events, but they'd had to leave Germany before they could attend. At least Trude and Ruth had been able to be there and witness the marriage. Given our situation, even that seems remarkable.

Everything sounded chaotic in Berlin. Trude wrote that the air raid sirens were going off constantly. Britain began its bombing campaign on Berlin the night of the wedding. They didn't hear the air raid siren the first night and slept right through. Fortunately, their hotel was not hit. The next night, they spent underground in a bomb shelter. They had no idea that there were separate bomb shelters for Jews. They went to the wrong one at first and were told to leave. What kind of people would refuse entry in a bomb shelter to a mother and her seven-year-old daughter in the middle of the night?

My news was two months late. I could only hope that everyone had survived and that Trude and Ruth had returned to Elbing unscathed. All we could do was go on with our lives. There was nothing else to do.

Chapter 67

Army Life

en days following my eighteenth birthday, only two weeks after I received word about Lotte and Jarus, I was called to the Camp Processing Office and given my release from the internment camp. I was given a category twelve release. That meant that it had one condition: I would be released provided I immediately enlisted in the British Army. I was thrilled. This was exactly what I wanted. This was my way out. And it meant that I had a job and a place to go. At eighteen, given my circumstance, I had no clue what the future might bring, but at least I was headed in a direction, and it wasn't back to working on the farm or the mill in Scotland.

On November 11, 1940, I joined the British Army, technically the Auxiliary Military Pioneer Corp (AMPC), which was the only British unit that enemy aliens were permitted to serve in. Only days after I enlisted, it was renamed the Pioneer Corp in an effort to bolster its image. Thousands of Germans joined the Pioneer Corp to assist the war effort, particularly Jews and political opponents of the Nazi regime who had fled to Great Britain.

My grandsons have asked me about my service in World War II. Military service carries a certain aura, mystery, and prestige. Young people are sometimes fascinated. At the time, I was certain they were really asking about what battles I fought, whether I killed any Nazis, seen bombs explode, what experiences I had when fighting the Germans, what medals I had won. For some, my reality might disappoint. Perhaps they expect a war hero. That is just fine. I am proud of the time I served in the British Army and am still alive to recount my experience. For me, that was a good result.

The Pioneer Corp was a non-combatant, light engineering unit. There was even controversy about whether we could be armed and carry rifles. And, when we did, most of us had little training. Our work during the war was basically constructing roads, camps, and huts. We mixed concrete, dug trenches, dug latrines, erected miles of wire defenses, and cleared bombing sites, all forms of manual labor. Our job was to support the fight, not to do the fighting.

Serving as a German national in the British forces did have its dangers. If captured, there was a high probability of being executed as a traitor by the Germans. Fortunately, the work I was assigned didn't really put me in a position to be captured. As the war progressed, some German nationals became special agents parachuting behind enemy lines. Their language skills and knowledge of German customs made them particularly suited to that role. My time in the British Army did not include that danger. My language skills, however, did prove useful. But that was much later, when I served as an interpreter assigned to the war crimes unit during the British occupation.

Today, I find it hard to remember what it was like to be eighteen years old and in the world where I found myself. Was I confident? What did I know? Did I have emotions? Was I afraid? I cannot recall. I suppose all that I could do was endure and survive. I don't remember laughing or having a great deal of fun, but I am sure that I must have. I don't remember falling in love, yet it remained a possibility. I don't remember falling down and crying, but I am sure that I did many times. What I do know for certain is that somehow I was taught to always get back up. I thank my family for that. Mela sometimes tells me that I must have been old for my age and that I missed much. That I don't know. Sometimes we are just simply what we have to be. I didn't miss what I didn't know.

When I watched my children turn eighteen, I thought they looked so grown and seemed so young. Was I any different? At least their lives were better. Or were they? They certainly had more opportunities. But were they any less confused than I was? They were so much smarter, better educated, and knew so much more of the world than I ever did. I have always been awed by my Joanie and Ralph. Now, sometimes, I wonder how my parents felt about me. Were they awed by me? I wish I could have known.

When I was eighteen, I really did not have any idea where my life was going and didn't have much of a choice. I still missed my family very much. I had no idea where I might live someday. I was sure that it would be near either my parents or my sisters, but who knew where that could be. I had once had plans for my future: first the university, then, perhaps, an engineering career. Now those plans were gone, and I could not see a way they would ever be achieved. While the future looked uncertain, I can't say I was depressed. I was alone, but at least now I was among others who found themselves in much the same situation. That helped. It's funny. When we are young, adults often ask what we want to be when we grow up. That hasn't changed. I ask my grandchildren the same question. Nobody dreams to be where I was now. No adult ever warns you that it might be a possibility. But here I am. I can just take one step at a time.

Army life was a good experience. I still was at an age where I needed to be told what to do. And that's what I did. I dressed the way I was told. Every day, I ate three meals the way I was told. I was told to work hard, and I did. I was told to sleep hard, and I did. And, the next day, I woke up and did it all over again, just as I was told. Army life gave me the strength, the discipline, and the order I still needed in my life. It challenged me. It set high expectations. It taught me about responsibility instead of excuses. I suppose what Army life did for me is what many hope it does for our children today. The Army sat me down and taught me what I had to do to become an adult. Life in Scotland did much of that too, but it was not the same. In the Army, I was around people whose job it was to lead me and help guide me. I had role models to teach me, and I began to recognize what made them each unique. In the Army, I made friends, the kinds of friendships I had missed so suddenly when events changed our lives in Germany. Already, that seemed a lifetime ago. How many lifetimes are we each entitled to have?

There remained a temptation to speak German. My English skills were much progressed, but many around me felt comfort speaking in their native tongue. I remember that feeling too. This was forbidden by the Army, but there were some who resisted. I developed resentment to those who continued to speak German, often in secret. I have felt that way from that time forward and find myself uncomfortable with those I meet who want to converse in German. Mela always thought it would be a good idea for the kids to learn German. She wanted to teach them. Mela was fluent in German. She learned it visiting her grandmother in Koenigsberg when she was a child. I disagreed, and that is why I refused to help when she taught them one summer.

The Army gave me a new name. They refused to call me Gerhard. Now they called me Jerry. At first, they referred to me as Jerry the

German. There was another Jerry in our unit. The called him Jerry the Scot. I was surrounded by others who had come from Germany. They didn't attach German to each of their names. Perhaps it was because it distinguished me from those who followed their Jewish traditions, something I chose not to do. It didn't matter. We were all friendly, so I knew it was a term of endearment. I was just happy. We all had nicknames. I remember silently wishing that my nickname was Udo. I missed my father very much.

Orders about our names came down later, in the summer of 1943. I would be given the chance to legally change my name. We all were. I had no hesitation. Some refused. Then, I was suddenly no longer Gerhard Wobser. I became Jerry Webster. I stepped away from my past. I still had an accent but was no longer a German. I began my new life. Initially, the new name was to protect any family still living in Germany in case of my capture. All records that I carried were rewritten, even my military pay book. Gerhard Wobser was erased. I was assigned a new military serial number; the old numbers were coded and our origins identified. The army had its reasons, but mine mattered more. The new name gave me a fresh start. It made me feel I belonged to a different world.

Armed with a new name, I began to discover my personality. I learned that, although I lacked education, I made up for it in smarts. I found out that my mind was quick, that I was able to analyze, that I was able to organize, that I had plenty of energy, that I was not afraid of hard work, and that I had an aptitude for getting things done. Others recognized it too, and that gave me confidence. I was practiced at listening, and it served me well. I still stayed quiet and kept my thoughts to myself. But, now, I was a sponge. I absorbed everything. I learned from everyone. I learned to be serious but not to take myself too seriously. And I learned that I had faults just like everyone else. I was quickly taught not to show anybody up and not to slow anybody down. I stayed in the middle and did my job.

I suppose there is a point in life when each of us finds our balance and what fuels us. We each do that in our own way. Some do it when they are young. For others, it takes more time. Sadly, some never find it. Army life did that for me, particularly during my first two or three years.

Many with whom I served were frustrated and disillusioned. They expected to be in combat. They wanted to be in the fight no matter what the risk. Serving in the Pioneer Corp, many others who were older and more skilled often found themselves unchallenged and their potential underutilized.

That was not the case for me. I discovered who I was, what made me excited, what made me sad. I learned to enjoy being me. I have always felt I was lucky to be taught these lessons at an early age. And I remain grateful. Regardless of how I got there, the British Army gave me a good start.

Day 24...

Mom wrote that things continue to improve and that she feels like she is in Vatican City passing out the Pope's health reports. Dad will sit up in a chair within a day or so, which should give him some new things to watch. He will be able to look out of the window, which will be much better than staring at the ceiling. He will also meet with the therapist. He was back on dialysis for a few hours, as his kidneys still need some improvement.

Chapter 68

The War Years

When my enlistment began, I was immediately sent to Training Centre No. 3 in Ilfracombe, England: a seaside resort about 220 miles east of London. Ilfracombe is located on the North Devon coast. Training Centre No. 3 was in operation from 1940 to 1942, and I was one of some three thousand refugees to go through there during that time. The centre requisitioned a number of tourist hotels to put us up, and my stay was quite comfortable compared to the months that I had spent in internment at the Isle of Man.

I found myself among men of all ages and occupations. What we shared in common was our past. We had all left somewhere. Most had left loved ones behind. Most had been in various internment camps for months and were happy to be out. Most were Jewish. I was among the youngest, but I was not alone. Others were well over fifty years of age. Most were originally from Germany, but there were also many Czechs, Austrians, Frenchmen, and even some Italians. I found myself among educated and accomplished people. There were lawyers, doctors, surgeons, bankers, artists, musicians, and scientists. This was quite an experience for me with my lack of formal education.

My time at the Training Centre was brief, hardly two months. Of course, there was training, and we spent our days engaged in various forms of practice and exercise, often repetitious. But there was also much to keep us busy and entertained in our spare time, a welcome relief from the boredom of the Isle of Man. There were many talented performers among us, and we were frequently treated to theater and musical performances. There were classes, lectures, readings, all forms of activity. Despite all that was going on in the world and all that I had been through, I thoroughly enjoyed my time in Ilfracombe. Some days, it was hard to believe that I was in the army.

Many of my fellow soldiers were disappointed to find themselves assigned to the Pioneer Corps, but there was little choice if one wanted to serve. They felt they had more to contribute to the war effort, whether in brains or in brawn. We all would have our chance. But that would be two years later when regulations were changed and those in the Pioneer Corps would have the opportunity to transfer to various combat regiments including the special services. I chose to remain in the Pioneer Corps at that time.

Our training was limited, not at all like the basic training provided in the regular army. Since we were to be assigned non-combat roles, we spent as much time on hygiene and marching as we did on learning how to use a rifle or a gun. Physical fitness was stressed, and training activities were set up a few miles from town, along the coast, at Morthoe and Woolacombe, where the long sandy beaches could be used for obstacle and assault courses.

Shortly after my arrival, I was assigned to 137 COY. Company 137 was one of eight alien Pioneer Corp companies raised at Training Centre No. 3. When I joined 137 COY in February of 1941, they had just finished clearing demolition debris in London in the bombed-out areas of Deptford and Bermondsey. There, one of the men had been killed by an enemy bomb while they worked. That had taken a big toll on the company. During the years that I served, there were a few similar events, but most of our time was spent well away from enemy confrontations and front lines. We were generally not directly in danger.

During 1941, we were based at a number of locations around the Somerset area, in the southwest of England. For a time, we worked on runway construction at the air base in Yeovilton for the Royal Navy Air Squadron. After that, we moved to Dunfries, Scotland, and helped construct the RAF camp there. This was backbreaking work, and much of our time was spent excavating rock from quarries. I can't help but laugh as I think about this. Unlike most of my fellow soldiers who were older and wiser, I knew that I still had much to learn. One might think that any fool can work with a pick and a shovel. But fools we were. There is much to be said for mastering technique. Otherwise, the fate was fatigue or blisters. We all learned our lessons.

For much of the next two years, we moved throughout Scotland building camps and assisting with an assortment of construction projects. It was during this time that my trade designation was changed. When I enlisted, I was designated a Farm and Forestry Worker. My new trade was Bricklayer. My military record will also show that I attended and passed a sanitation course. For this, I even received a commendation. I suppose that qualified me for managing the construction and daily care of latrines. All became important life lessons and added to my growing list of jobs I did not want to do when I grew up and left the army.

D-Day, the landing at Normandy on June 6, 1944, was the decisive battle that foreshadowed the end of Hitler's dream of Nazi domination. Seven weeks later, 137 COY moved south to Fareham at the tip of Portsmouth Harbor. We landed at Arromanches in Normandy on August 2, 1944, and proceeded to Caen to begin reconstruction of bomb-damaged roads. During the remainder of the year, we moved to various locations in Normandy, unloading supplies, constructing, and fulfilling a variety of manual labor requirements.

In late November, 1944, we left for Antwerp to continue our work. There was still bombing going on, and at times, we were told we were less than a mile from the German front lines, the closest I had been for the entire duration of the war. Within weeks, it became clear that much of the war there was over. In April, 1945, the mission for Company 137 began to wind down. That month, fifty-four of us were posted to the 21st Army Group Interpreter's pool in Hamburg. By June, the remaining members of our company were posted to similar duties.

For some, the war experience is action, glory, and guts. I was proud to serve my role. War is serious business, a dark and terrifying time. I learned that for each person engaged at the front, there is an entire army of people needed to bring up the rear. And that is what I did for most of my time during World War II. That is what many of us did. We were all part of the war effort. I was lucky. I made it through with my life. In October of 1945, I turned twenty-three years old. And, by then, the war was over.

Part Three
The War is Over

Chapter 69

Where Were They?

I can't begin to describe the wave of emotion I felt when I learned that I would be sent back into Germany. There had been no contact with Lotte or Trude through the course of the war. I had no idea as to their whereabouts or whether they had survived. What about my niece Ruth? She would be twelve years old. I had never met my nephew Manfred. I was surprised to learn that Trude had a second child. He was already four years old. And, my brother-in-law Walter? What had happened to him? We had all heard and learned about the atrocities committed by the Germans. The tragedies were enormous.

Worldwide, fifty to eighty million people, 3% of the world's population, were estimated to have lost their lives. More than two-thirds were civilians. Six million Jews, three million from Poland alone, were murdered by the Nazi regime. Russian casualties were estimated at twenty million, including fifteen million civilians.

Every day, new information was uncovered about the horrors of the concentration camps. I had seen some of these camps with my own eyes. I was unsure what news would await me. Who had survived? Had anyone survived? Would I be able to find anyone?

The war in Europe ended in April of 1945 when the Germans surrendered. Many fellows I served with were overjoyed with our transfer to Hamburg and the Interpreters Pool. They felt they would finally be able to put their mental talents to use, a big departure from the physical labor we had performed during the war.

I can't say I shared this joy. I had become accustomed to the tempo of military life. I actually enjoyed the physical work. Now I would have to overcome new challenges, and I was uncertain how well I would be able to perform. But I was pleased by the prospect of being posted in Hamburg. It was only four to five hours from Berlin, and I was hopeful that I would be able to learn more of my family.

I also knew nothing about the fate of my parents. It had been years since I heard anything from my sister Ilse or my parents in Shanghai. I presumed that they were alright but had no concrete knowledge. I had heard that there were some bombings in Shanghai. My understanding was that the attacks were very limited and the civilian population was unscathed. There was no way for me to get news about my family in Shanghai.

There were so many loose ends. It had been four years since I had seen Aunt Hilda in London, when I had asked her to keep my old suitcase with my belongings while I was off to war. Aunt Hilda had been able to leave Germany in August of 1939, only weeks before England refused any further immigration from Germany. When I went to see her in London, she was terribly upset. She had no information about the welfare of her daughter, my cousin Inge. Communication had stopped when Germany invaded Belgium in 1940. Inge would be seventeen years old and fully grown by now.

What about my cousin Heinz? What had happened to him? Our paths had crossed briefly at the internment camp on the Isle of Man.

It had not been as simple for him there. I was underage, but he was older. When I saw him, he was about to be sent to a prison camp in Canada, along with many others identified as dangerous to the British homeland.

What about the others we knew? I was not alone. We all felt the same. We all had family scattered everywhere. We all were hoping to be reconnected. We were all displaced. And, for those of us in the British Army, we all had responsibilities that needed to come first.

Day 25...

It's New Year's Eve, and in Mom's words, it is a "red letter day." They released Dad to an acute rehabilitation center and delivered him by ambulance to his new address. Mom reports he has a lovely bright room and, with proper sleep and exercise, he ought to improve quickly. While he tries to talk, he nods mostly and seems to understand what is going on. He will still have dialysis three times a week and a few other medications. His recovery will be slow, but he is a strong-willed person and will try hard. She says that she will stop the daily emails now. It is a good way to end the year.

For Ginger and me, this is a reason to celebrate. Of course, we were celebrating anyway. New Year's Eve in Salzburg will be a dress-up affair. We have been here before for New Year's. That's why we wanted to return. At midnight, they will pop the champagne, and everyone will go out on the veranda and watch the fireworks. It has been snowing all day. Salzburg looks like a fairytale.

We will call Mom in Arizona and Joanie in Iowa later this evening. The time zones help. We can all look forward to the New Year. It's time to put the old year behind us and get on with the new.

Chapter 70

The Interpreters Pool and War Crimes

Shortly after I was posted to the 21st Army Group, it was re-designated the British Army of the Rhine and became the headquarters for the British zone of occupation in Germany. At first, I was assigned to the Interpreters Pool. Later, I would be transferred to the War Crimes Trial Centre. All of this was based in Hamburg.

At the end of World War II, nearly twenty thousand alleged war criminals were in the custody of British authorities. War crimes tribunals were set up in the British zone of occupation to hear these cases. Some cases were highly publicized and well known, receiving much attention. Most were not. These cases had to do with crimes committed against British soldiers or against people liberated by British soldiers.

This posed a massive problem for British officials. Interpreting needs were significant. More than five hundred trials were scheduled to take place between 1945 and 1949. While many interpreters were needed for the actual conduct of the trials, a far greater number of interpreters were needed for the investigations that preceded these trials. The vast majority of defendants, witnesses, and even defending counsels spoke only German.

We were not investigators, and I never performed that role in any way. We were interpreters. We sat, listened, and translated. In British tribunals, the official language is English. It was our job to translate the proceedings into English. My work was never in the courtroom. I was not qualified for that level of work. I spent all of my time assisting the investigators who were interviewing witnesses and those accused with crimes. I never chased down or arrested war criminals. That was never my job.

When I was first assigned to the Interpreter's Pool, it was small; only several hundred people worked there. It grew rapidly, and there were close to two thousand within a few months. It was a big job, and there was much work. At the beginning, there was some controversy over whether German nationals in the British Army could be used for this work. Could we be reliable and objective in these positions? Some feared that we would have an axe to grind, that we would treat those Germans accused with crimes unfairly. That was part of the problem the British government had at first as they tried to find enough interpreters.

Few of us had any training. We learned by the seat of our pants, on the job. When I started, they sent me to Brussels for a week of training, but I can't say that I learned very much. In fact, one of my first assignments was to get a military driver's license so I could drive the investigators around. But I grew into my job and did lots more than just drive during my time.

The work was interesting, and I volunteered to stay on beyond my initial enlistment. Over time, I think I got pretty good at my work and was promoted to the ranks of corporal and then, sergeant. I stayed with the War Crimes Centre until I left the British Army in August of 1948. By the time I was discharged, I had served in the British Army for nearly eight years.

Chapter 71

Letters from Shanghai

*I*t took months for the mail situation to improve. I found trying to communicate with my parents in Shanghai nearly impossible. As I moved throughout England and Scotland in the early part of the war, and then through mainland Europe to Germany during the later war years, the little mail I did receive was months late, and none of it was from Shanghai. Mrs. Mein in Scotland was always my best mailing address. Early in the war, when I was given leave, I would return to Balfron to see her and Maud. But, as the war progressed, I found that more difficult to do. The result was that I had no news of my family in Shanghai, and they knew little of me.

My mail caught up to me shortly after I arrived in Hamburg. There were several letters from Shanghai. I remember reading them in the order they were mailed.

The first letter I opened was dated May of 1940. Much of this I had already been told by Mrs. Mein. Father wrote that they were all doing well. They had adjusted to their situation as best they could. They knew they had to adapt to their surroundings and start over again. They had no idea what the future would bring. Moving to China had not been their first choice. It had been their only choice.

When they arrived, their old friend from Pr. Holland, Mr. Aris, had met them at the ship and organized rickshaws to take them to the shelter where they spent their first several nights. Mother's description of their first day was that, one moment, they had been served breakfast on a European liner by uniformed stewards. The next moment, they found themselves lining up for lunch in a soup kitchen.

By the time their ship, the Monte Rosso, arrived in late April of 1940, an estimated seventeen thousand German and Austrian Jews had already fled to China. Nearly all were living in Shanghai, most in the Chinese areas of the city. These areas had been under the control of the Japanese since the 1937 Battle of Shanghai. Jewish refugees had been arriving since 1933 because of the situation in Germany. And, as Nazi pressure for Jews to leave increased, the numbers grew and became a flood. By the time my family arrived, it was the tail end of the flood, and life for refugees in Shanghai was already well established.

Their immediate priority was to find housing and a way to support themselves. They were not alone. Most of their fellow passengers were penniless families. Their resources had been taken by the Nazis before or as they departed. Most left all that they owned behind. The funds sent to Naples by Uncle Ludwig had helped, and fortunately, within a few days of their arrival, they were able to find one room in a building that housed seven other families in the Hongkew District. Thousands of refugees were living in Hongkew because they could not afford to live elsewhere. In their building, all seven families shared the one bathroom. After two months, Ilse, Arthur, and Frank were able to move to their own room three doors down.

Another letter advised that they had moved again. Father became the rental agent for the apartment house. For collecting the rents from the eighteen other families, he received a 10% share, enough to help with their living expenses. Ilse had found a nursing position at the refugee hospital in Hongkew. The hours were long, and Arthur, Mother, and Father were actively watching over my young nephew Frankie. Mother was even working at home and earning a little money. She was knitting cardigans to be sold in stores in Shanghai and was part of a collective with other women. Arthur had little success with his job search, but had given a few singing lessons and received language instruction in exchange. He was also an organist at an evangelical church.

In one letter, Mother wrote about a dinner party they held. Since no one had extra china, everyone brought their own plates. They used their old suitcase as a kitchen cabinet. I also learned that they had connected with Mother's first cousin who was also living in Shanghai with her family. They had taken the overland route via the trans-Siberian Railroad to get to Shanghai.

Ilse wrote that she took a temporary nursing assignment and spent several days in a beautiful villa owned by a German family. She was hired to care for their daughter's newborn infant. The family had servants, and she had been given a very nice room. They even sent their car and driver to pick her up. This had been the exception. Most of her work was not like this. Frank had grown considerably and knew all their neighbors. Soon, he would be old enough to attend school.

Mother shopped at the market each morning. All vegetables had to be cooked. They only drank boiled water. In the evenings, they sat outside. Their landlord had a radio. They would listen to concerts. They were all learning English. It was the language spoken on the streets. Mother wrote that she thought the Chinese were very clean and hard-working people.

In 1943, all refugees arriving after 1937 were directed by the Japanese rulers of Shanghai to move to the "Designated Area," a small zone located within Hongkew. This proclamation was an attempt by the Japanese to appease their German allies. The Nazi government in Germany wanted the Japanese to be more hostile to the Jewish refugees. Anyone who resisted would be prosecuted.

This one square mile area became known as the Shanghai Ghetto, and already, close to 40,000 people, many impoverished Chinese, lived there when my family made the transition. Conditions within the Shanghai Ghetto were deplorable. Housing was overcrowded, and most units were inadequate for the extreme winter and summer temperatures. There was not enough access to adequate health care. The water supply was contaminated, and the sewage system barely sufficient. No matter how hard everyone tried to keep the area clean, the streets were trash-lined. Disease was prevalent. Living in the Shanghai Ghetto, Frank was still able to attend school, and Ilse was able to secure passes out of the "Designated Area" to go to work.

While their living conditions were far less than desired, Ilse wrote that they didn't feel in danger from the Japanese. Although the Japanese were allies of the Germans, Japan had resisted many of Germany's demands.

It was the final letter I opened that stopped me. The letter started, "my dear boy now I have to tell you the worst news of your life." That's when I learned that Mother had passed away of dysentery the day after Christmas in 1944. Ilse had nursed her for seven weeks at the hospital.

Chapter 72

Mother

*H*onestly, I really don't remember what I felt when I learned that Mother had died. It had been six years since I had seen her. She was only fifty-seven years old. In many ways, the war and the events of the past years had hardened me. Like many others, I am sure that I had become immune to my emotions; news was received, and there was nothing one could do.

I can't say that I broke down and cried. I can't say that my eyes filled with tears. It just was that my heart was heavy and I ached. I had lost someone I loved dearly. I would miss her. Some things you just have to take in stride, and I suppose that was what I did. I wasn't the only one to receive this kind of news. Is it a surprise to lose a parent? I knew that generations pass. That is the order of life. But it still hurt.

What I did feel was longing. I longed to be with my family. I longed to be part of the family that I had grown up with in Pr. Holland and Crossen. I longed to have their arms around me the way they used to, like the way Father did when we rode the sled when I was five. I longed for a better future and for brighter days. I always knew that my mother was proud of me. I just wished I could hear her say those words one more time. I felt bad for Father and Ilse. I hoped she had not suffered.

I smiled when I thought about the time Father told me he hoped I would care for him when he became old, and how odd it was that he hadn't said anything about Mother. I remembered the times when she and I would sit together and visit while I ate my dinner. I remembered the look on her face when we learned about the teenage clerk being murdered in Pr. Holland. I thought about what she told me of the way she had grown up and how she lost her mother when she was young. I have wonderful memories of how she and Aunt Trude laughed together those summers at Kahlberg.

I will always remember Mother. I always expected to see her again. I think she would be disappointed about not seeing me and how she would miss seeing Trude, Lotte, and her grandchildren. I wish she had known we would survive these terrible times and had seen how my life turned out. She would have loved Mela. She would have loved our children and their families. My world was not the same. I was lonelier today than I had been yesterday. That's how I felt.

Days 30-39...

We returned from our trip shortly after the first of the year. Things seem to have settled down in Arizona. Joanie, Mom, and I talk frequently. Mom assures us that all is well. Dad continues to improve. He still is not able to speak very well, but they are working on it.

Dad is even able to walk a bit. She laughed as she told us that they are a fine old pair. When they walk, he shuffles, and she weaves. When they try to have a conversation, he can't talk, and she can't hear. This has been a tough road. It is good to see that she has kept her sense of humor. She did tell us that she bought a small chalkboard. Sometimes, when they visit, Dad uses it to answer rather than trying to talk. Sometimes they play tick tack toe or hangman. I don't really know what the issue is with his ability to speak, but they seem to have it under control.

Mom has managed to take a few days off. A friend has sat with Dad. Mom says they both were in need of new company, so she has played bridge with her friends a few afternoons.

Joanie and I have had our own conversations. Neither of us have a clue where this is all heading. We agreed that Ginger and I will go out to Arizona for a few days this month. She and Marv will try to do the same next month. We can't be there all the time. This is their life. We know that they want us to live our lives. Mom has been very clear about that.

Chapter 73

Finding Trude

*I*t was September of 1945 before I was granted enough leave to begin my search for Trude and Lotte. In the aftermath of the war, life was anything but normal. Searching for someone was complicated. Many were missing. Train tracks had been bombed, making getting anywhere difficult. The occupation was still being organized. Passes were needed to enter most areas. Communication lines were being repaired. Utilities were being rebuilt. Nothing was simple. The Red Cross was organizing much of the effort to locate people. They were maintaining registries where one could search or be listed. If everything was working, Berlin was at least a four-hour train ride from Hamburg. Since my half-brother Walter Stange might have survived the war in Berlin, I wanted to start my search there. Walter might have some news.

The destruction was unbelievable. When I left Berlin for Scotland only six years earlier, Berlin had been a beautiful city filled with wide, tree-lined streets and boulevards, pleasing buildings, and carefully cared-for public areas. Now, the city I returned to was just a shell of itself, burned out, bombed, and destroyed. Only months earlier, in April, the Russians had unleashed their brutal power of armies, tanks, and aircraft, crushing German resistance and capturing Berlin. Then, they had proceeded to fight street to street and house to house, destroying much in their sights as they blasted their way towards Hitler's underground bunker in the city's center.

Even before the Russian invasion, Berlin had been bombed very heavily, pounded continuously since the first air raid in August of 1940. The city was almost completely destroyed; palaces, museums, churches, and monuments were all leveled. I was told that Berlin was bombed nearly four hundred times by British, American, and Russian aircraft. More than fifty thousand civilians had been killed. They were burned, suffocated, and buried under the ruins of the bombs. Apparently, six hundred thousand apartments were destroyed. The population of four and one-half million had been cut to almost half as much as the population fled.

The Red Cross office was functioning but had no record of either Lotte or Trude. I was able to locate Walter Stange. He had survived but had heard nothing from either of my sisters. Ours was a strange reunion. We had never been close before. He had only known me when I was a child. Now he seemed uninterested. He had been through a lot. Having seen the destruction, I can't imagine what it would have been like to survive the war in Berlin.

I took my chances. With several more days leave, I tried to get to Elbing, where my sister and her family had lived. The reports from Elbing were terrible. It had been spared for much of the war. But, in late December of 1944, as the Russian Army moved to the west, advancing on Germany, Elbing was right in its path. All I knew was that in January of this year, much of the city had been destroyed. Most of the population had fled. Many lost their lives. The Russian troops had been on a rampage. They had retaliated for their losses. Death and destruction were everywhere.

Poland was now administering the entire area of East Prussia. The remaining Germans were being forced to leave. The area was still in chaos. To get there was impossible. I was denied entry, and there was nothing I could do.

It would be several months, actually May of 1946, a year after the war had ended, before I was able to try my search again. There were many investigations and trials underway, and the Interpreters Pool was overwhelmed. We worked seven days a week. I needed to wait my turn to be given enough leave to return to the Red Cross office in Berlin. Travel remained complicated.

This next time, in May of 1946, I met with success. There was no record for Lotte. But I learned that a Trude Wobser Sprung had passed through their offices just a few days earlier. She had been searching for Lotte Wobser Jaruslawsky too. Trude had registered her address. She was living in a small town near Bremen, less than two hours from my base outside of Hamburg.

It took me a full day to get there. The trains would not go fast enough. I found the address that had been listed, a war-torn, three-story apartment building on a small side street in Delmenhorst. I'm sure I ran there from the train station.

As I entered the hallway, an older man passed by and doffed his hat. I blinked and looked at him a few times and said in German, "Walter, kennst Du mich nicht mehr. Ich bin dein Schwager, Gerhard." It was my brother-in-law, Trude's husband, Walter. He turned around and looked at me confused. He hadn't recognized me in my British Army uniform. It had been eight years since we had seen one another. The last time was at the train station in Pr. Holland when we said our goodbyes, when Mother, Father, and I left for Berlin, the day I gave Ruth my old sled. I was sixteen then. I couldn't believe my eyes. We had served on opposite sides in the war. I don't remember who spoke louder or who spoke more.

What a day. I learned that Trude was at the hospital with Ruth. The night before, Ruth had suffered severe stomach pains, and Walter had used the pay phone on the street to call an ambulance. Walter had stayed with Manfred while Trude went with Ruth. When I arrived, Walter had been on the phone again and had just learned that Ruth had undergone an emergency appendectomy. Everything had gone as expected. She was out of surgery. Manfred was being watched by a neighbor. We should hurry and go directly to the hospital.

And that's where I saw my oldest sister, Trude. She was sitting by the bed, silently watching Ruth, and holding her hand. She looked tired and worn. Her night had been long. She seemed older and thinner than I remembered. When Trude first spotted me, she looked at me confused, that brief moment when nothing made sense. Then, she suddenly jumped to her feet, ran to me, and hugged me, just like the way she hugged me when I was a child. We held each other as if we would never let go. Neither of us could say a word, our emotions were that drained.

I understood that Trude's first concern was Ruth. I was concerned too. So we sat shoulder to shoulder at the bedside, quietly enjoying our closeness, and waited for Ruth to wake up. There would be plenty of time to talk later.

When Ruth opened her eyes, I was there looking at her, the first face she could see. She shared the same momentary confusion as her mother. Then, her face erupted in a smile. She was my young niece, whom I had taught to sled and who flew my kites. She was still the little sister that I never had. All the heartache that I had felt the last eight years disappeared in that single moment, replaced by long-forgotten memories that reappeared just as instantly. I had found my family. We all had survived. This time, I cried. We cried together. This time, the tears in our eyes were tears of happiness.

It would be several days before Ruth recovered enough to be sent home. For most of the time, Trude and I stayed huddled in deep conversation by Ruth's bedside. There was so much to say, but only so much that could be said in front of Ruth. We could hardly find a place to start. And, when we took breaks, I would meet and get to know my nephew Manfred. Now, at age five, he was a delight. Just like his mother, he talked all the time. He seemed impressed with my uniform and having a British soldier by his side. We paraded up and down hallways as he introduced me to everyone in his sight.

Our stories were difficult and took time to explain. Often, it took days for details to emerge. Many were deeply buried and not easy to share. Many memories were awkward and not deserving of light. I quickly learned that Trude knew nothing of Shanghai and the last eighteen months. It came as a complete shock when I told her about the death of our Mother. I reacted similarly when Trude told me that Lotte's husband, Jarus, had died suddenly of a heart attack not long after they had been married. And as for Lotte? Neither of us had any news about her whereabouts. There had been no contact for close to four years.

For so many years, I had been Trude's young brother, and she my oldest sister. Now there were times when our roles became reversed. They would reverse again when we thought of each other as we had once been. At times, that became difficult because we both had changed. It was clear that the war had extracted its toll. Now we would need time to recover.

My leave ended quickly, and I returned to my base. There were so many questions that still needed answers. Slowly and painfully, we would learn more.

Chapter 74

Organization Tod

One of the first stories I was told was about my brother-in-law Walter. I knew that in Germany's build up to the war in 1939, he had been drafted. Actually, he had been recalled since he had already served in the German Army during World War I.

Walter and Trude had married before the Nuremburg laws were passed in 1935 and mixed marriages banned. When Walter joined the German Army, marriages between Aryans and non-Aryans that had taken place before 1935 were still allowed to continue. And, by then, there were fewer than twenty thousand mixed marriages in all of Germany. Shortly after he joined the army, Nazi authorities eased the conditions for divorce in mixed marriages and openly encouraged the Aryan spouse to divorce. Their objective was to be rid of all mixed marriages. At first, they hoped to encourage the Aryan partner to get a divorce by granting easy legal divorce procedures, even granting common property to the Aryan spouse. Then, the Nazis stepped up the pressure. Those who stuck to their spouse suffered various discriminations such as dismissal from public employment, exclusion from various civic organizations, and the like, many of the same discriminations that had been brought against the German Jews.

Walter resisted and stayed with his marriage just as he had told Father and me he would. Because of this, he was immediately dismissed from the German Army and, as a penalty, reassigned to the Organisation Tod, or OT as it was commonly referred to. As he told me the story, Walter said that he now knew that, had he filed for divorce, Trude, Ruth, and Manfred would have been sent to a concentration camp and murdered. He had no doubt in his mind.

The OT was a huge labor force, over one and one-half million strong, used to perform major manual labor projects. In the 1930s, it had been used to construct much of Germany's Autobahn. During the war, it was used to build miles of defensive walls throughout Germany, to clear bomb debris, and to perform a variety of dangerous tasks.

Listening to Walter's description of the Organisation Tod, I thought it sounded similar to the work we had performed as part of the Pioneer Corp. But he strongly disagreed. The Nazis had gone further. They used the OT as punishment, not for all units, but for a number of special units. Many of these units were filled with criminals released from jails. Some were filled with Jews taken from concentration camps. Others were filled with persons deemed undesirable by Nazi standards. These units were assigned the most hazardous duties, the duties where human life was expendable, activities like clearing land mines, various forms of backbreaking labor, activities where it did not matter if laborers were killed. Walter had been assigned to one of these units as punishment for not divorcing Trude.

Fortunately, his camp commander quickly realized that Walter was older and less physically able than many in his unit, and that he really was not a criminal or an undesirable. Once Walter explained why he had been assigned there, the commander protected Walter by making him his driver. He also reached out and tried to help make sure that Trude, Ruth, and Manfred were not mistreated.

During the later stages of the war, shortly before the Red Army invaded Elbing, Walter lost all communication with Trude. For a time, he was convinced that Trude, Ruth, and Manfred had lost their lives and that they were among the thousands of Germans who perished in East Prussia. He had no way to find them. The same was true for Trude. She had no idea whether Walter had survived the war, whether he was alive or dead. They found each other only months before I arrived, in late 1945, when Trude and the children fled East Prussia and made their way to Berlin. Even then, they were reunited only by accident.

Day 40...

I suppose when things happen, they mostly happen suddenly. We have reservations to fly to Arizona tomorrow and will stay with Mom for three days. Today, she called. They rushed Dad back to the hospital late last evening. We are not really sure what occurred, something to do with internal bleeding. Mom is pretty shaken up. They called her a bit after midnight. She couldn't understand everything said. Her hearing aids have been acting up. She hasn't been to the hospital yet.

If we can change our reservations to get there sooner, we will. Otherwise, we will stick to the original plan and fly out tomorrow. There is really nothing we can do. I talked to Joanie. She can go to Arizona after we leave, if needed. We will just play this by ear. It may be nothing. I can also stay longer.

Dad had been doing really well. Ginger and I were hoping to take Mom to look at some rehabilitation facilities. They thought they could move Dad to one next week while we were there.

Chapter 75

Trude – Surviving in Elbing

What my sister Trude and her children, Ruth and Manfred, experienced in Elbing was a horror that will never be forgotten. Manfred was much too young to have memories. He was born in 1941, after the war had started, and Trude did all that she could to give him a normal childhood. She has always been very protective of Manfred. For my niece Ruth, it is the opposite. She remembers everything, every last horrible detail. She was six when the war started. She was twelve when Trude and the children fled from Elbing. Her memories are vivid and will be etched in her mind as long as she lives.

I will tell you their story, but I have to do it in parts because there really are three distinctly different episodes – the war years, the Russian invasion of Elbing, and when the Poles took control. That was when Trude, Ruth, and Manfred found their way to Berlin.

To understand what happened in Elbing, one needs to recall the broader framework of World War II and to know some of the history of East Prussia. I'm no historian. I just need to outline their situation.

When World War I ended, Germany was stripped of its territories in West Prussia, East Upper Silesia, and Danzig. These lands were handed over to Poland. Elbing and the rest of East Prussia remained in German hands. Elbing, with a population of one hundred thousand, was the second largest city in East Prussia. Koenigsberg, further to the east along the Baltic, was the largest.

Germany viewed the loss of their lands as a great injustice. Regaining these territories became one of the reasons leading to the Nazi takeover of power in 1933. In 1939, the Nazi government in Germany struck back and invaded Poland to reclaim what they had lost. Poland suffered terribly at the hands of Germany. There were massive casualties. There was mass destruction. And, later, when World War II was over, Poland would extract its revenge. Poland would push most of the remaining German population from Elbing and the rest of East Prussia, resettling these lands with Polish citizens. Many left with little more than the clothes on their backs.

But that is not all there is to the story. The Russian invasion of East Prussia occurred shortly before World War II ended and greatly contributed to Germany's defeat and surrender. For most of the war, Elbing and the northern part of East Prussia along the Baltic Sea had been spared from attack. Germany had advanced to the west, invading Denmark, Norway, France, the Low Countries, and the Balkans, and attacking England. In the east, Germany amassed its troops on the border of Poland and proceeded to invade the Soviet Union, killing millions in their way as they marched to Stalingrad. The Battle of Stalingrad is considered one of the greatest battles of World War II. The Russians stopped the German advance, a tremendous humiliation for Hitler, and helped turn the tide of war in favor of the Allies. And that is when the Russian armies began their merciless march through Germany

Elbing and Koenigsberg were in the crosshairs. From mid-January until late April, 1945, the Russian armies rampaged and pillaged, destroying everything in their sights. They severed all road and railway routes, cutting East Prussia off from the rest of Germany. It was an endless nightmare for those who remained. The Russian troops took their revenge and retaliated. Thousands upon thousands of civilians in East Prussia lost their lives.

We all know that there was much more to the horror of World War II. As Germany waged its external war, internally it was building the Aryan nation, eliminating all populations deemed undesirable, and, in particular, the Jews. At first, German Jews had been pushed out of Germany. After the June, 1941, German invasion of the Soviet Union, the Nazi government authorized the complete extermination of the Jews in Germany and the countries that Germany had invaded. By 1942, millions of Jews would be murdered and systematically eliminated throughout Europe. By the end of the war, the number would grow to six million.

Elbing and the northern part of East Prussia lived these horrors. While most of the Jewish population had already left their homes and moved elsewhere, it would be a far more chilling story for the Jews who remained. They, like the Jewish populations in the countries Germany invaded during the war, would be sent to gas chambers.

When the Nazis came to power, there were about five hundred Jews living in Elbing, a fraction of the one hundred thousand residents. By 1939, the number had decreased to fifty Jews. The Nazi policies had worked. The Jews had fled Elbing. They had moved to Berlin. Many had left Germany. By 1942, only seven Jews remained in Elbing. All were protected by marriages to a non-Jewish partner. And the others? It is fair to assume that the rest had been sent to concentration camps and murdered.

Trude and her children, Ruth and Manfred, found themselves part of this tiny world of seven Jews, identified and known to the Nazis, and left to survive the war in Germany. Having been told this, it came as a surprise when Trude told me that, for the first four years of the war, life for most residents of Elbing had remained much unchanged. The war was being fought elsewhere. News reports each day proclaimed German victories. The biggest change was that Walter was away. She had missed him terribly. Nearly all of her friends and neighbors were in the same situation, and that had helped. They had all missed their husbands.

At first, she feared reprisals because the local Gestapo knew she was Jewish. Her identification papers made that very clear. The Jews in Elbing had been treated shamefully and tragically, but she had been shielded by her marriage to Walter. The Gestapo had left her alone as long as she went about her business and caused no disruption. Her fear remained throughout the war, but it had quieted after the other Jews were removed and she was allowed to stay. It had happened suddenly. One day, there were Jews in Elbing. The next day, they were gone. She really did not know any other Jews. There had been no reason to. Why would she? She had never been to a synagogue. She had no idea of their fate. No one was told. She had only heard rumors. Her fear? She always knew that she and the children could be next.

It had been very difficult for Ruth. At the beginning, she had been too young to understand. She had missed her father terribly. She had worried. Other children had treated her cruelly. There was a horrible boy in their neighborhood. He lived diagonally from their apartment, near where the streets crossed. Every day, he would dress in his Nazi uniform and sit on his window ledge. Whenever Ruth left the apartment, he would shout nasty things as she walked by, terrible things. He would tell her she should be gassed like the other Jews, and that she should be exterminated. How could a child begin to understand? Ruth would get very upset. There was nothing Trude could do to make the boy stop. His father was an important Nazi official. His parents laughed when they watched him taunt Ruth.

They encouraged him to continue, and he did, day after day. The smallest complaint, and Trude and the children would certainly be shipped off to a concentration camp.

For many months, Ruth had nightmares. She would wake up screaming. Her screams would wake Manfred. Trude worried that the neighbors would hear the disturbances and report them to the Gestapo. It had taken time for Ruth to outgrow her frights. As she got older, she was able to cope, to keep things inside. But what had that done to her? Trude told me she worried about Ruth. Now they hardly talked to one another. She had been much too young to see the things she had seen. Some things could never be discussed. Trude was afraid that Ruth would be haunted by these memories for the rest of her life.

Trude rarely shared much with me. Even though we were sister and brother, our age difference had kept us far apart. I was closer in age to Ruth than I was to my sister. I had always felt more emotion with my other sisters than I ever had with Trude.

As we talked, Trude said something I had not heard before, something Mother had told her shortly after I was born. They had talked about my baptism. Mother told Trude that my baptism meant that I had joined the non-Jewish world. Even though Mother had been raised Jewish, I would not be Jewish. My baptism had ended that. The Wobsers were not Jews. We had been baptized, so we would no longer be Jews. The same had happened to Father when he was adopted. His adoptive-parents, Albert and Marie Wobser, had him baptized so he would no longer be a Jew. Trude told me that is why she never thought of herself as Jewish. She actually denied being Jewish. Lotte and Ilse didn't feel quite the same way. They were more accepting. Lotte had married Jarus, who was Jewish. Trude believed that one of the reasons she, Ruth, and Manfred had survived in Elbing during the war was that they were not Jewish.

It hadn't mattered what Trude thought. She could not protest. The Nazis said she was Jewish, and that was the way she had to live. The rules were clear. There were no outings to movies or theatre. Household help? Not allowed. Disagree? They will send you away. The big J on her identification papers made everything perfectly clear.

Despite their situation, Ruth had been able to attend public school. Ruth had proven to be a marvelous student. She was bright, attentive, and serious. She earned the praise of her teachers. On the first day of school, Trude made sure Ruth knew to say, "Ich bin 50% Arier und 50% Jude," if asked. Ruth was taught that there were serious penalties for misstating your race.

By the fourth year, Ruth had excelled in her placement exams, top in her class. It had been a great disappointment when she was told that, no matter her grades, because she was mixed race, a *Mischling*, she would have to attend the lesser school, the one for the inferior, the ones destined to work with their hands instead of their minds. Ruth had been humiliated. She had cried for days. Fortunately, there was a teacher who took a special interest and tutored her privately, making sure that she continued her studies. But the tutoring, as well as her accordion lessons, had to be held after dark so no one would know. Imagine a young child having to walk the streets in the dark just to be able to get to her lessons.

Manfred was born in 1941, after the war had started. Trude hoped that he wouldn't remember what they had been through. She would not let him be scarred with these memories. Walter had missed the birth. He had been away with the army. From the moment he was born, Trude became almost overly protective. Even Ruth was not allowed to hold him. Care for him? No way. Ruth should go out and do something. When she was nine, Trude told her she could catch the boat to the beach at Kahlberg. She could go on her own as long as she didn't drown and was home before dark. She could play with friends there. Ruth grew up to be independent. She learned to take care of herself. Trude would take care of Manfred. He would know little of war.

The buildup to the war had improved the German economy. The depression was over, and business had rebounded. Walter had been paid well at the store. They had saved their money. They were fortunate. When the war came, they had the resources to take care of themselves. With Walter's government pay and their savings, there was enough to support the family. Later, when things turned bad, money meant little, particularly when there was not enough food or fuel. Then, they would scavenge the streets for whatever they could find.

It was 1943 when things started to change. That was when Germany started to suffer defeats. The Russians had beaten back the Germans in Stalingrad. The Allied bombings had taken their toll all over Germany. Berlin and the cities were bombed day after day. German industries were finding it harder to meet the army's demands. Manufacturing was under pressure. Transportation routes were disrupted. Food was in shorter supply. Although the news continued to report that Germany was winning, they all knew that something was different. They had lived with rationing since the war began. Rationing was patriotic and part of the war effort. Everyone needed to make some sacrifices. Now there was less, and the army needed more. Each day, it seemed that there were more and more shortages. Each day, they had to sacrifice more.

These conversations with Trude were difficult. While the Nazis had mistreated her terribly, Germany was still her home. It was hard for her to open up, hard to accept defeats, hard to talk about mistakes. She was unwilling to admit her uncertainty. She would never show her emotions. She refused to discuss her fears. Clearly, she was anti-Nazi. There was no question about that. But the war had not made her less German. In many respects, the war had made her more German. The war had not made her more Jewish. In some ways, it had made her more certain that she was not. It had been a terrible time for herself and her family. Yet I was still her little brother. It would take years for her to tell me her story and how much she had been hurt. I would never learn all the details. They were too deeply buried. They would never be revealed. They would follow Trude to her grave.

Days 41-44...

We had a good visit with Mom. It was the right time to visit. Unfortunately, Dad is not doing well. He was in intensive care the entire time and totally uncommunicative. It is pretty clear that he is not going to get better. We took Mom to see a few rehab centers just so we know what the choices are, but none of us are optimistic. Ginger and I are more concerned about Mom right now than Dad. He has people to watch out for him. Mom is alone and is tired. We don't want her to fail.

She realizes now that, whatever the outcome, she needs to be prepared to live alone. Even if he comes through this, chances are he will never be the same. She said that she and Dad always knew this would happen to one of them someday. They both knew that they were getting older. It just doesn't make it any easier. She wasn't prepared for someday to be now.

She wonders if Dad would have made the choice to have the surgery if they knew then what they know now. He knew it was a risk. She isn't sure that he considered the consequences. She just wants what is best for him now.

Before we left, she asked me to do two things. First, she wanted me to teach her how to use the "damn" remote. She had not been able to watch TV since this all started. Second, she needed to fill up the car with gas. She had no idea how self-service gas stations work. All we could do was laugh.

Chapter 76

The Russian Invasion

There had never been a winter in East Prussia that was as cold as that winter of 1944-45. There was no way to stay warm. Coal was nowhere to be found. Firewood was scarce. Food was whatever could be found.

By early December, 1944, it was clear that the Russian Army would invade and destroy everything in their way. Koenigsberg had been almost completely demolished by Allied air attacks only months earlier. The Red Army had initiated its offensive into East Prussia as early as October, 1944, but was driven back by the Germans. Now planes could be seen flying overhead. The tanks would be next, and the Russian troops of the Red Army, on horseback and foot, were right behind.

Day after day, horse-drawn wagons passed through the streets in a continuous line. People were fleeing with whatever they could take. Freezing and bundled, they were running from the Russians, running for their lives. It was not only civilians that were on the move. The German Army had decided to withdraw the POWs from their camps, and they joined the hundreds of thousands of people on the move. The procession was endless. People were coming from the east and moving to the west, one after the other, again and again.

Automobiles had been confiscated. They were needed for the war. It didn't matter since there was no fuel. A few trains still ran, but that would stop in days. Cars were overflowing, and men clung to their sides. If the horses refused, there was no choice but to walk. It was a mass of humanity, day after day.

Some chose to cross the Vistula River, which was frozen with ice. Even though a pathway had been outlined and marked, it must have been terrifying, in the pitch black of night, not knowing if the ice would hold. Those who were lucky would make it; many would not. It didn't matter what route they took; they needed to head to the west, to get away from the fighting. If the cold didn't get them, the starvation would, and if the starvation didn't get them, the Russians would.

It was after dark on Trude's birthday, January 20, 1945, when they took my old sled and pulled it down the street. They were looking to see who had left and who had remained. Ruth watched the sky light up in orange from the firing of the tanks. They knew they would hear the rumbling of the tanks on the street within the day. Trude asked eleven-year-old Ruth whether she thought they should leave. Close to ninety thousand had already left Elbing, and fewer than ten thousand remained. Ruth told Trude she thought they should stay. Manfred rode as they pulled my sled back home.

Later that night, they put the sled away, packed a few belongings, and joined the others in the cellar. It would be their bomb shelter while they waited for the war to be fought above their heads.

The fighting in Elbing would go on for several weeks. Elbing was a pivotal, strategic location. The Germans were determined to make a stand. The battle was intense. By the time it ended, bombs and shells destroyed 65% of the city. On the ground, the fight was fierce, street to street and building by building.

It was February 9 when the cellar was opened and they, along with fifty others, emerged from their shelter. The Russians had been victorious. The German Army was destroyed. It would still be two more months before Berlin would fall and the Germans would surrender. The nightmare was far from over. The invading Russian troops would rape and pillage what was left of Elbing. Close to twenty million Russians had been killed in the war. It would be difficult for their soldiers to not take revenge.

It would be August before the Red Army would hand over the region's territory to Poland and the Polish government would take over administration. Meanwhile, those who remained would have to fend for themselves.

Winter would not be over for many more weeks. Icy temperatures would continue. Food would remain scarce. There would be no place to purchase any kind of food for six months, not until the Polish population started to settle in Elbing. There was no running water, no electricity, no sanitation, and no medical facilities. While it was still cold, snow was melted for water. When it became warmer, buckets of water were drawn from old factory wells. Nobody knew if the wells were contaminated. Disease and illness were rampant. Those left became scavengers simply trying to survive. While Trude watched Manfred, Ruth would join others combing the destruction for whatever they could find. They ransacked vacant buildings and stores, looking for anything that had been left behind. At night, horses would be stolen and butchered for meat. They had little choice. The punishment for stealing from the Russians would mean death. Not having food would lead to the same.

These were terrible, horrible days. There was no escaping that reality for Trude and Ruth. It would get better, but it would take time, too much time for far too many. On the streets, women and young girls would find themselves defenseless. Rape was prevalent.

Some would be rounded up and taken away for days. The troops had not seen women for months. It was not uncommon in the evening for groups of soldiers to go door to door. With no husbands to stop them, they would satisfy themselves. The women complied. There was little they could do to send the soldiers away. Ruth spoke of her fright of the bare-chested Russian Cossacks riding horseback through the streets. It would take many weeks before the Russian command center could take control and offer any protection. They would try to bring order to the chaos. Soldiers with Red armbands marked with a "K" would help when called. But there were far too few, and the horror would continue.

When I heard these stories from Trude and, later, from Ruth, I never knew what words to say. Trude was reluctant to speak of these times. These are stories nobody should tell. These are secrets no one should ever have to share. These are horrors that will remain untold.

Chapter 77

Finding Walter

One evening, Trude told me the story of how she found Walter. After the war, she had resigned herself to a life in Poland. She really had no choice. By the summer of 1945, there was nowhere to go. Although most of Elbing was in rubble, their apartment building was still partially standing, and by some miracle, their unit was still inhabitable. They had nothing else.

Many of the Germans who had survived the war had left. They had relatives elsewhere. They had been found, or they had found their families. The Polish government had issued them exit papers so they could leave. A few months later, they would require most of the other Germans to leave. They wanted to repopulate the region with Polish citizens.

For Trude, there was nothing. There was no mail service. She had no money, at least any that could be used. She had heard nothing from Walter. She knew nothing of Lotte, or Ilse, or the parents in Shanghai. She knew nothing of me. Again, she, Ruth, and Manfred were left to fend for themselves.

The Polish administration had assisted. They had given her a job in one of their offices. Others had helped too. A young Polish officer, a courier for the Russians, had taken an interest in them. He was Jewish and had lost his wife in the war. He enjoyed their company. Sometimes he brought special foods from the commissary and treats for Ruth and Manfred. He brought them new identity papers, in both Russian and Polish, so they would not be mistaken for German Nazis. They would be allowed to stay. Poland would become their home.

There had been a few issues. One warm, sunny day in early May, Trude had been playing the piano and opened a window to let the fresh spring air in. A redheaded Russian officer listened from the street and appeared at the door, encouraging her to continue to play. A few days later, he returned with some bread and asked her to play some more. On his next visit, he offered to take eleven-year-old Ruth to his quarters where he could feed her a warm meal. Having gained her trust, Trude sent Ruth off with him on his motorcycle. There had been an unfortunate incident. All Ruth told her mother when she returned was that she didn't like the food.

Another day, the police came to the door and accused Trude of stealing. She was taken to the jail for interrogation. That day, Ruth took charge and found their friendly Polish officer. He and Ruth ran to the station. He demanded that Trude be released. That had been a close call. What would have happened to Manfred and Ruth if she had been kept in jail?

It seemed that, every day, there was a new problem. As the weeks went by, she found herself thinking of Walter as in the past, convinced that he had been killed in the war. If he had survived, he would have found them by now. There had been no word from Walter for more than a year. That November of 1945, a postcard arrived. It was delivered by the train conductor. All it said was, "Come to Berlin. I have seen your husband."

Frau Kirsch, the mother of Ruth's friend Lieselotte had left Elbing months earlier, after the Russian invasion. She was a widow.

During the war, when her husband, a chimney sweep, died, she was left to care for her three children. To make ends meet, she operated a vegetable stand in front of her house, just down the street from Trude's apartment. Trude bought vegetables from Frau Kirsch, and they had become friendly. Now Frau Kirsch and her children lived in Berlin.

It was Frau Kirsch who sent the postcard. With no mail service, she sent her son to the train station to find the next train to Elbing. The train conductor was paid to deliver the note to Trude. All Trude knew was that Walter was alive.

It took them several days to arrange their departure. Getting the exit papers was complicated. Finding seats on the train to take them to Berlin was even more difficult. Finally, word was sent to Berlin that they were on their way. The train trip took several days more.

They could only take what they could carry. Everything else they owned was left behind. Their apartment would be given to new Polish owners. Trude knew they would never return to Elbing. With Walter, they would begin a new life.

They were careful to hide anything that might be confiscated at the German border. Polish officials would not let them take any valuables to Germany. Their belongings would be carefully searched.

Trude was concerned about the necklace that belonged to Lotte. After Lotte's wedding in Berlin in 1940, Lotte had given it to Trude for safekeeping. There was also the diamond ring that Mother had traded with Trude years earlier, when Mother and Father had left Pr. Holland. During the Russian invasion, they had woven the ring into Trude's hair to conceal it from the soldiers. These heirlooms were stored with other jewelry hidden in the hollowed wooden heels of Trude's and Ruth's walking shoes.

In Berlin, they made their way to Frau Kirsch's apartment. There, they sent word to Walter. It would be several days before he would arrive. Trains did not run on a regular schedule. Then, they located Walter Stange, Trude's half-brother. Trude and the children could stay with him while they waited.

Later, they would learn the story. After the war, Walter had no way to return to Elbing. Germans were not allowed to go east. He was stranded and had no place to go. His only means of transportation was an old bicycle. He had no money. There were no jobs. All he could find was work as a day laborer on a farm near Stendal. Finally, he was able to take a train to Berlin. He, too, would find Walter Stange. Maybe Walter knew something about Trude and the children. He had become convinced that they had not survived in Elbing. He had heard terrible things about the Russian invasion. Only by sheer accident, at the train station in Berlin, did he encounter an old customer from Elbing. They hardly recognized one another. This friend asked about Trude. He had seen her in Elbing after the war and knew she survived. He took Walter to see Frau Kirsch, Trude's old friend from Elbing. She had written the postcard and sent her son to the train station to bribe the conductor to take the postcard to Trude in Elbing.

Trude rarely displays her emotions. Now she cried. It was early December, 1945, when Trude, Walter, and the children were reunited. It was the happiest day of her life. They had survived the war.

Chapter 78

Two More Years

When I found Trude and her family in Delmenhorst, they had only been there for a short time. Walter had not wanted to live in Berlin. He was concerned that eastern Germany would come under the control of the Soviets. With time, he was right. His predictions would come true. Delmenhorst, near Bremen, was a city of close to fifty thousand where they could begin a new life.

It had been less than six months since Trude and Walter had reunited. We were all adjusting to the traumatic times we had been through. Today, there are counselors who can assist through difficult times. After World War II, there could never have been enough counselors to meet the needs of the survivors. Not just in Europe, but throughout the world, people learned to cope as best they could. That is what we all had to do.

At about this same time, I had a choice to make. My enlistment with the British Army was over. I had to decide whether to end my military service or volunteer for another two years. By now, I had already served for nearly six years.

When I gave it some honest thought, I realized that the British Army had become my home. I knew I wanted to be near family, and Trude was here. As for Ilse and Father, they remained in Shanghai. They were struggling to sort things out for themselves. They were still adjusting to the loss of Mother. Father had suffered badly. And, by now, we all sadly realized that, no matter the story, we would never see Lotte again.

I chose to sign up for two more years. The army allowed me to transfer to the BAOR base in Delmenhorst where there was a small war crimes unit. I could spend more time with Trude, Walter, and the children. There, I could lead a more normal life. In two years, I could make another decision. I was sure the others would leave Shanghai by then. I imagined their choices would be to return to Germany or move elsewhere in the world, possibly America if they could get visas. As for me? Either I could choose to make the British Army my career or I would follow them and see where that took me.

Day 46...

The news from Arizona has not changed much. Dad continues to live, and they are doing nothing extraordinary to keep him alive. He continues with dialysis and remains sedated all of the time. There are indications that he suffered another stroke. Mom goes to the hospital each day. No more emails are being sent to family and close friends. Everyone knows that there is nothing to report.

Joanie did send out one quick note. Today is their fifty-fifth anniversary. I'm glad she did. I had forgotten. I remember, when they had their fiftieth, Dad told me he had once heard that even the richest man in the world can't buy a fifty-year marriage. He said that made him feel pretty good that day. We had a nice time on their fiftieth. We all got together for a weekend in New Orleans, our families, the grandkids. I bet Dad would feel pretty good about fifty-five years too. I am sure that he never imagined this would be how his life would turn out.

I know nobody remembers the song, but his favorite was "I'm Sitting on Top of the World." And, that's exactly the way I think of Dad. That's a pretty good way to live. Most of us would like to feel that way.

Chapter 79

Cigarettes for Umbrellas

When I was transferred to the BAOR in May 1945, Europe was celebrating Germany's surrender. It took place on May 8, only days before I arrived in Hamburg. The Battle of Hamburg had been one of the final battles of World War II, and British troops had only been in control of the city since the third of May.

In 1945, when the British occupying forces arrived, Hamburg was in shambles. Most of it had been destroyed. Hundreds of thousands remained homeless, thousands were living in cellars and shelters, food was scarce, and all utilities were in ruin.

Even now, a year later, when I moved 140 kilometers southwest to Delmenhorst, much was still at a standstill. Economic activity was still beginning. Thousands remained homeless. Many attempted to return to homes that no longer existed. Utilities, communication, and transportation would continue to be in a state of repair. Everywhere throughout Germany, people were trying to rebuild their lives, and infrastructure was being restored.

Delmenhorst had been relatively undamaged by airstrikes during the war. The damage in nearby Bremen, only 10 kilometers away and in the American Zone, was much more severe. Nearly 60% of Bremen had been destroyed. It had been pounded by air attacks. Eighty percent of the port city of Bremerhaven was destroyed.

Within the British zone of occupation, Delmenhorst became home to thousands of refugees. Between 1945 and 1946, Delmenhorst's population grew by nearly 20%, from 40,000 to 48,000 persons. New arrivals included German civilians evacuated from cities, those who had escaped from fighting on both Eastern and Western fronts, former forced laborers from across Europe, and ethnic Germans expelled from Czechoslovakia or from former German eastern territories, like East Prussia, that had been ceded to Poland.

Food supply was a constant problem, particularly in the British zone. Rations were reduced to near starvation levels, 1,000 calories a day, in March 1946. It would be more than two years before these would substantially increase. The supply of housing was equally stressed. The demand for housing far exceeded what was available, and more people were still arriving daily.

As a British soldier in the occupied zone, I was spared much of this discomfort. Living on the army base, I was well fed. My quarters were luxurious by my standards, better than any since I had been in Crossen, which seemed a lifetime ago. And, personally, the year and one-half I was to spend in Delmenhorst marked a big change for me. With the war over, I felt the air of possibility. The army became my day job. My military pay went far in post-war Germany. And, now, for the first time as an adult, I had the freedom and resources to take charge of much of my life.

I know that many members of the British occupying forces felt as if they were strangers in a strange land. My feelings were more mixed. I knew that I would never become a German citizen again, but even after having been away for many years, I felt familiar in Germany. I had family here.

Trude, Walter, and their children became my first priority. My brother-in-law, Walter, had lost everything. He was starting over at middle age. Trude and her family needed to regain their life. Ruth and Manfred needed opportunity. I wanted to do as much as possible to help them get back on their feet. Having family nearby meant a great deal to me, and I spent as much time as I could with them. I wanted to get to know my nephew Manfred, and I wanted to renew my friendship with my niece, Ruth, who had blossomed into a teenager during the war.

As a member of the occupying forces, I was very conscious of the rules and regulations concerning relationships with the local population. We were warned daily. Immediately after the war, the rules were very strict. No fraternizing with the local citizenry. But, within the first two years after the war, instructions issued to British soldiers changed completely. At first, we were banned from all contacts with German civilians other than those necessary for work. Later, all forms of activity that promoted mutual understanding and personal reconciliation were supported.

Stereotypes promoted in wartime had portrayed all Germans as aggressive, militaristic, and not to be trusted. After the war, the number of young women in Germany far exceeded the number of men. I would be the first to admit, it was a curious time to wear a British uniform.

For me, at first, I found my situation awkward. The rules were not entirely clear as to how they applied to German nationals who served in the British Army and now were back in Germany. I was one of a very small number now living in the same area as their German family. The army's concerns were very real, but I wanted to spend time with my sister and her family.

I had only been in Delmenhorst for a few months when I was called to appear before my commanding officer. There had been a report that I had been seen in the company of an attractive young German girl. The penalties for this infraction could be significant. The matter was under review. My future could be in question. Obviously, this was quickly resolved once it became understood that this was my niece Ruth. But, given the serious nature of the inquiry, I'm not sure what they thought when it was first reported.

For Trude and Walter, there was much to figure out and do. They were in need of a decent apartment for the family. The temporary housing they were in was inadequate, too small, and too cramped. Manfred would be beginning school, and Ruth was resuming her education, this time at the school for students with potential. It was important that their family get their home life settled. They needed to get adjusted to their new lives. Fortunately, we spotted a vacant unit in a building controlled by the British Army, and I was able to help them secure their apartment.

Since I had arrived in Scotland, and throughout the war, I had saved my money. There had been little opportunity to spend it. Now I spent some. My transportation problems were solved when I was able to purchase a used motorcycle. By some odd circumstance, I also found an old bicycle I was able to repair. And, since the commissary on the base was well stocked, I was also able to supply Manfred and Ruth with treats and supplement Trude's meals occasionally.

For a time, the black markets flourished. For many, it was the only way to get needed supplies. Ironically, after the war ended, many German citizens still had money. The bigger problem was the shortages. Basic items were often not available. Walter and Trude had neither money nor adequate supplies.

I can't remember exactly how we did it, but one day, Walter asked me to help him trade cigarettes for umbrellas. I would get cigarettes at the commissary. He would take the train to the Knirp umbrella factory, where he would exchange the cigarettes for umbrellas. Then,

I would take the umbrellas back to the barracks, where they could be sold or exchanged for more cigarettes. Somehow, Walter profited with each transaction. That was how many things worked at first. People survived. Ingenuity helped.

Chapter 80

Gisela

My day job was mostly spent interviewing witnesses. Actually, I did not do the interviewing. I was simply the interpreter. Nobody should be confused on this issue. Others were asking the questions. My job was only to make sure that the British Army investigators could communicate with the witnesses. Mostly, I sat quietly in a corner, since many of the investigators had become fluent in German.

Many of the interviewees were young German women who had witnessed various alleged war crimes. Some were impressed with British Army officers. As an officer whose native language was German, I caught the eye of one, and that's how I met Gisela. She was a close friend of a woman we interviewed.

Gisela became my first girlfriend. I know that for some, that must sound strange. I was twenty-four years old and had never had anything beyond a casual encounter with a girl, let alone a woman. And, by casual, I mean very casual. To answer the question, yes, I was still a virgin. I was not proud of that fact, nor was I interested in maintaining my virginity. It was only due to circumstances beyond my control. Keep in mind that I was twelve when we moved to the farm in Crossen. Then, even in school, I did not participate in any social activities. After that came Berlin, then Scotland. In Scotland, Mrs. Mein encouraged me to attend a few of the dances at her church with Maud and her friends. I had no luck there. From Scotland, I went to the army. When I took leave from the army, I usually went to stay with Mrs. Mein and Maude or went to London to see Aunt Hilda. My encounters with the opposite sex had been very limited. Most of what I knew I had learned from the well-used, dog-eared magazines passed around the army barracks at night. I had a sense of the thrill, and the up and down motion, but in a singular, one-handed way. As you might imagine, I had some pretty strange notions of what a relationship should be like. And, without prolonging this discussion, I should add that Father had never been a particularly good role model when it came to interactions with women. I had no idea how to behave. I suspect Mela might offer that this remains true.

My limited experience didn't stop me. I was twenty-four and had survived the war. I had plenty of self-confidence. What stopped me, at first, were the army regulations. I had some flirtatious encounters with women but none that I pursued until the regulations eased. That's when I met Gisela.

Given the circumstances, I suppose that it is not surprising that I fell pretty hard. This was my first crush. Gisela was one year older and more experienced in the world. But her experiences had been limited too. Most boys and men had been sent off to war by the time she was old enough to begin dating. Also, her father, a Lutheran minister, held much influence. She and her brothers and sisters had grown up with a strict moral code. They were a large, close-knit family. When she had left her family home in Oldenburg, she had gone to Bremen and studied art. Her dream was to have her own ceramic studio.

During my stay in Delmenhorst, we spent most of our free time together. I became very close to her family. She became close to mine. I suppose some might say we were inseparable. Ruth liked her very much. I know that Trude and Walter pictured us marrying and living our lives in Delmenhorst, where we would be nearby. I still remember the time we rode our bicycles to the park and swam in the lake. Walter followed us and stole our clothes. Ruth and Manfred loved that story. I'm sure they imagined much more.

Chapter 81

Letter from Heinz

One day, I received a letter postmarked London. It had been sent to Mrs. Mein in Balfron and forwarded to me. It was from my first cousin Heinz, whom I had not heard from for more than six years. The last time I had seen him had been our brief encounter at the internment camp on the Isle of Man, right before he was to be sent to Canada. Now, the first thoughts that crossed my mind were of the days we had spent together when we were kids at the beach in Kahlberg.

His letter was long. I will just summarize it. There was much to report. First, he was healthy. He had survived the war. After I had seen him, he had been shipped to Canada, where he had spent several months in a large prison camp. He had been together with many German nationals, illegal aliens as they were called. Many of his fellow prisoners were famous and well known, names I would recognize. Heinz had been given an important job. They had made him assistant camp postmaster. Helping deliver the mail, he had met everyone. He had even received a commendation and certificate for his service. I laughed at that last part. It reminded me of the way Heinz sometimes talked when we were children. Same old Heinz.

Heinz went on to say that, after six months, a determination had been made and that his group had been reclassified. They had been deemed reliable to serve in the British Army and had been shipped back to England. There, he had been recruited for special services because of his aptitude and language skills. Since he knew the German culture, he could blend into the population. In 1943, after training, he had been sent behind enemy lines to spy on the Germans. He had spent time first in Germany and then in Sicily. It had been quite an assignment. There had been a lot of technical training. Now he was done with the army.

His girlfriend from Cottbus, where he was at the university, had been able to flee Germany right before the war too. She had been sent out through the Kindertransport program and had lived with a British family. Somehow they had reunited. In 1943, the week before the army sent him behind enemy lines, they were married. They were very happy together. She was the love of his life. Within the year, they would move to America. An uncle there had invited them.

The war years had been tough. He asked about my family. He had heard little news. He wanted me to know that his mother, my Aunt Trude, had perished. She had not survived the war. The Nazis picked her up in Leisnig and deported her to a concentration camp in Poland, where she was murdered. His sister, Erna, had been murdered too. She had been rounded up by the Nazis in Belgium and deported to a camp. He had very few details. He knew that Leni had survived. Thank God she had made it to Australia. His writing was emotional; my summary is too brief.

He finished by asking about Opa Helft's gold chain. Was I able to get the chain out of Germany? Did I still have it? He wanted me to know that he still had the watch. He had always kept it close. It was a memory that only he and I shared. Perhaps, someday, when we meet again, we can put the two together. That would be special. He signed the letter, "Henry." He was no longer Heinz. Like me, he had changed his name. Like me, he had begun a new life.

It was a wonderful letter. I wish I still had it now. Over the years, somehow, I lost it. All of our children would have loved to read it. The war had taken its toll. First, Mother, now my cousin Erna and Aunt Trude. How many others? In our hearts, we knew that my sister Lotte was gone. What about my cousin Inge? What had happened to her?

Day 49 ...

I suppose in some ways it's easy to be logical about these matters. We all know that our parents will die. I am resigned to that. Dad will not last long. As parents, we pray that it will happen to us first. Nobody wants to outlive their children. As husband and wife, Ginger and I consciously know that it will happen to us. More than likely, it will be one before the other. We don't know the script. We just know the ending.

But here is the thing. I count myself as one of the lucky ones. Few can be as fortunate as me. My parents have lived longer than most and have expected very little. We have been blessed in too many ways to count. I will miss my Dad. I wish everyone could miss their Dads as much as I will. But I know that's not always true.

Today, I know that he is still dreaming. And I believe his dreams will never stop. He has always lived his dreams. I know that will continue forever.

Chapter 82

Becoming a Naturalized British Citizen

$\mathcal{E}$nlisting in the British Army did not make one a British citizen automatically. While I had no idea whether Great Britain would become my permanent home, it was the country I had served, and I thought becoming a British citizen would be a good idea. Applying for citizenship was complicated and controversial. It would be 1948 before Great Britain revised its naturalization laws. My application was subject to the British Nationality and Status of Alien Act of 1914. Becoming a British citizen had a different set of rules and required a case-by-case review and an approval by the British Home Secretary.

Virtually no citizenships were granted to German nationals during the war. There were many arguments surrounding this issue. There were those who argued that anti-Semitism would increase if more German Jews were allowed to become British citizens. Others argued that this continued to be an employment issue and that there were not enough jobs. Some felt that citizenship was not necessary, that most German nationals would leave and return to their homeland after the war. And others questioned whether German nationals would conform to the British way of life.

Of course, these arguments had little to do with me. I felt that Britain was my home and I had served her well. Whether I spent my career in the British Army or not, there was a reasonable possibility that I would live the remainder of my life in Great Britain. In May of 1946, the British government issued a new application form that gave priority for aliens who had served in the British armed services. My base commander encouraged me to apply and offered his complete recommendation. In addition to time in the armed services, the rules required British residency before the war and five years in the UK, counting time overseas in the British Army. I met the qualifications and applied.

For all its complications, my application was received with speedy approval. Six months later, I received notice that I would be approved after submitting a statement that I would not retain my German citizenship and including ten British pounds sterling. In February of 1947, I officially became a citizen of Great Britain. I was no longer Jerry the German or Gerhard Udo Albert Wobser. Now I was Gerald Webster, the Brit. You can still call me Jerry.

Chapter 83

They Are Moving to America

It was February 1947, the same month I became a British citizen, that Trude received the letter from Ilse in Shanghai with the exciting news. Ilse, Arthur, Frank, and Father had been granted visas to immigrate to the United States. They would depart in early March on the General W.H. Gordon, a converted navy troop transport ship. Their journey to San Francisco would take two weeks. Ilse wrote her letter the day they heard the news. It was postmarked Christmas Eve, 1946; mail from Shanghai was still taking nearly six weeks.

Memories are curious. When Trude read me the letter, I immediately remembered listening to the radio years earlier with Father, when we imagined the construction of the Golden Gate Bridge and how I tried to build a bridge for my toy train. I wonder if Father thought of this too when he learned they would be going to San Francisco. I am sure that when we were listening to the radio that day, he would never have imagined that he would move to San Francisco someday.

There were two letters in the envelope. The first was dated months ago, in August. Trude read that one first. Ilse's letter was lengthy. Ever since the war had ended, everyone they knew in Shanghai was anxious to leave and find a permanent home. Shanghai had always been temporary, a safe refuge, away from Germany and the war. They had fled to Shanghai because there was nowhere else to go. Now they had been faced with the same decision that they had confronted years earlier, where could they go? Which country would take them?

As a temporary home, Shanghai had been good. Ilse had been able to work. Frank had done well in school. When they had first arrived, the transition had been difficult, particularly for Mother and Father, who were of an older generation and more set in their ways. For Frank, it had been easy. He was an outstanding student. They were always amazed at his ability. He had known no other life and had adjusted well. Mother's death had been very painful. Father's health was not so good. They had adapted. It had not always been easy, but that was life. Arthur was always supportive. Now they knew it was time to move on.

The political climate in China was rapidly changing. Chiang Kai-shek and the Nationalists had expressed various disturbing views concerning the European refugees. Arthur was unsure about Mao's Communist party. What role would it play in the coming years? Staying in Shanghai was no longer a good option. With the war over, they would face an uncertain future should they try to remain.

America had been their first choice. Arthur's relatives were few, but the ones he did have all lived in America, and they would help. Uncle Paul and Aunt Elsa, whom Ilse had met when they had stayed in Naples, had moved to America. They had not been able to leave Naples until 1941, almost a year after Italy had joined the war. Then, they had gone to Cuba and lived there for most of the war. Now they were living near Chicago with Aunt Elsa's sisters. Their grown children, Arthur's first cousins, had settled in America and were raising their own families. Only their daughter, Mela, was unmarried, and she was in Chicago too.

Arthur was not quite as certain as Ilse. He didn't know much about America. And he did not know his cousins too well. He had only met them once, and that had been nearly thirty years before, around the time his mother had died. He had been raised in Germany. They had grown up in Italy. Arthur was comfortable with the German way of life but knew that there was little for him in Germany, no profession to return to, no remaining family. Arthur would do whatever Ilse wanted, whatever would be best for the family. He would follow her wherever she wanted to go.

One alternative was Palestine. Several people they knew in Shanghai were attracted to the possibility of a Jewish state. But they had rejected the notion of going to Palestine. Neither Ilse nor Arthur was interested. Neither felt Jewish. Father would not like it. In Palestine, they would be outsiders. It was not the place for them.

Their other choice might be to return to Germany. Ilse was torn over this decision. Trude was there. I was there too, but they had no idea what I would do, except for the notion that maybe I would end up in England or Scotland. Ilse wrote that she knew Trude was hoping I would marry Gisela and settle in Germany. Ilse was convinced that Frank would do well in America. He had learned English at the school in Shanghai. Frank could speak English better than he could speak German. In America, they would be able to make a new life, to have a fresh start, and to be able to leave the past behind. They would never be able to live the life they'd once had in Germany. It would be painful. Father had grown older and his health was not as good. They were concerned that he might have had a small stroke in the past year. He didn't believe his life would be long. He would go wherever they wanted.

Ilse's first letter ended by saying that she had made their decision. She knew what was best for the family. There were too many bad memories in Germany. America would be best for Frank. She could use her nursing skills anywhere. Arthur would adjust. First, they would see if they could go to America. If that option was not possible, then they would consider returning to Germany.

The second letter was dated Christmas Eve, the day Ilse had written it. This one contained the good news. Nothing had happened quickly. Much of the world was hesitant and reluctant when it came to the issue of refugees. Many countries continued to have the same restrictive immigration policies that they had had before the war. Refugees in Shanghai worried that they had been forgotten. It seemed that the world had failed to notice that they were still there. International attention had been entirely focused on what to do with displaced persons in Europe. Only recently had it become realistic to leave Shanghai. Within the last several months, refugees had started to leave. Now, nearly one thousand refugees were going to America each month. Even more were returning to Europe.

They had struggled to get visas, find financial support, and to book transport. Finally, everything had been arranged. Packing would be easy. They had little to take, even less than they had brought. A refugee placement service in San Francisco would assist them in finding work and getting settled. America was a big country, and they had no idea where they would live. The little money they had was probably worthless. When they arrived in San Francisco, they would find out what was next.

I was thrilled when I learned this news. It helped me make my decision. I knew that when my enlistment ended, I would also try to go to America. I wanted to see Father again. I missed Ilse. I wanted a chance to get to know my nephew Frank. I knew that Germany was not the place for me. It was the past.

And, if that didn't work, I now had my British citizenship. For the first time in my life, I had a choice for my future.

Chapter 84

Lotte

We were all haunted by our questions about Lotte. Even today, I know Joanie still wonders. For Joanie, her Aunt Lotte will always remain a mystery, a life that is forever unknown. Every few years, someone in the family has tried to learn more, but the answer has always stayed the same. Trude, Ilse, and I came to know it shortly after the war. I am not certain Father ever did. Even later, when he once saw Ruth, he called her Lotte, thinking his daughter was still alive.

It wasn't that it was something we refused to acknowledge or discuss. We simply did not want to think about it. It was too painful. Of all people, Lotte was the one who could always make everyone laugh and everyone smile. We not only loved her, we adored her. I will forever believe that lasting memories should be the best memories. It's too difficult to dwell on the dark ones. That's not the way I want to remember Lotte. I only want to remember her life.

After Jarus died early in 1942, Lotte remained in Bielefeld. She was given no choice. The Gestapo made her the camp's leader, the same position Jarus had held at Schlosshoffstrasse 73a. And, just as

Jarus had been directed to do, Lotte managed the work assignments. She met with the Gestapo commandant each morning and arranged the day's schedule.

Schlosshoffstrasse 73a was a forced labor camp. Of that, there is no question. While it was able to accommodate seventy-five persons, often there were more, as there were also facilities for those older and infirm. They were all prisoners. Each day, they would be told what to do. Each night, they would return to the camp. If they failed, they would be sent to another camp, to another destination. Whenever someone left, a new person would arrive to take their place. The work varied at times. Some days, they cleared debris. Other days, they were sent to work in factories.

At first, Trude had managed to stay in contact with Lotte. They were able to communicate by mail. On rare occasions, they spoke by telephone. Sometime in 1942, Lotte had told Trude that frequently trains would pass through Bielefeld. In broad daylight, people would be loaded into railroad freight cars in large groups. They were herded like animals. They were told to leave most of their belongings behind and could only take one small bag. Some said they were being sent to Poland or to Austria. More workers were needed there. There were other rumors. They couldn't be sure. Nobody wanted to speak about it. Nothing seemed real. So much seemed inhumane.

It was March of 1943 that Lotte moved into the house of the manager of a small factory, a bicycle factory, Trude thought. They had a brief phone call. Lotte had told her she thought that everyone else at the camp had been sent away by train. Lotte had told her nothing of her relationship with the factory manager. All she knew was that Lotte was caring for his house. Lotte hoped to stay there, that this person might be in a position to prevent her from being sent away like the others. That was the last Trude heard.

After the war, in 1946, and after I had moved to Delmenhorst, Trude went to Bielefeld to look for the factory manager, to see what she could learn. She was desperate to find out more. Here is all we know.

A deportation took place in Bielefeld on June 28, 1943. Lotte was in the group that was taken that day. The factory manager was powerless to prevent this. There was nothing he could do. The train went to Theresienstadt, arriving June 29, 1943. From there, Lotte was transported to Auschwitz. She may have broken her arm. For work, she was useless. Lotte was murdered in Auschwitz. The exact date is not known. Officially, her fictitious date of death is December 31, 1945, a date for those whose dates of murder will never be determined.

In 1943, Lotte Wobser Jaruslawsky, wife of Ernst Jaruslawsky, daughter of Ludwig and Alice Wobser, sister of Ilse Behrend, Trude Sprung, and Jerry Webster, was 32 years old. She would be forever missed.

Day 51...

Joanie just called. She is on her way to Arizona. Mom called her to say that if she wanted to see Dad while he is still alive, she ought to come now. Mom said she was shaky and hadn't felt well. She needed Joanie by her side. She needed Joanie's support. Joanie said that Mom didn't call me because she knows how I feel. Ginger and I had been there within the week. Mom didn't think it was necessary that we return now.

We have all been prepared for this to happen. This has been going on for more than seven weeks. There are few surprises. When I am honest with myself, I admit that I gave up weeks ago. I wish his life had ended more quickly. If assisted suicides were legal, I might have considered it. Knowing Dad, I am sure he would have felt the same way. Mom has carried the brunt of the pain and suffering. He would never have wanted that.

I've made my peace. He will always be part of me. I don't need to watch him die. I am just glad I was able to watch him live.

Chapter 85

Preparing for America

*D*eciding to go to America was one thing. Informing others was another. The earliest I could leave would be August of 1948. That was when my enlistment with the British Army would end. Telling my commanding officer that I would be leaving posed no problem. He was always supportive. I knew that he would write me a good recommendation.

There were also a few details that needed to be arranged. Most were minor. I would have to apply for a British passport. My old German passport was of no use. I also needed a visa for the United States. With my new British credentials, that would not be an issue. As for money, with what I had and what I would save, I knew that I would have enough. It was still 1947. I would not leave for more than a year, plenty of time to save for my airline ticket. Having my British citizenship helped not only with the visa. I knew that if America turned out not to be the place for me, I could always return to Great Britain. I was certain I could make a life there, but it wouldn't be in the British Army.

I had no regrets about the time spent in the British Army. It had taught me much. After nearly eight years, I was sure that I did not want to make the army a career. Even as a British citizen, there would be little opportunity for me. There would always be work, but the prospect for advancement would be limited. I didn't have the qualifications, background, or education. In the army, I would always have a sign on my back that said I was a foreigner.

The most difficult conversations would be with Trude, her family, and Gisela. I chose to wait for these conversations until the weeks preceding my departure.

Gisela was a wonderful companion. I had become close to her family. She had become close to Trude, Walter, and the children. We were viewed as a couple. I knew that they were all expecting us to marry someday. Perhaps she would join me. Although I had made my decision to leave for America, we had become very close to one another, and I was torn. It was my brother-in-law Walter who helped. He told me that someone had once given him a quote from the German poet Goethe and that it had served him well, particularly when he was being encouraged to divorce Trude. *"As soon as you trust yourself, you will know how to live."* This was good advice. It convinced me to trust my decision.

From the start, Gisela and I had always been honest with one another. Our relationship had grown. Perhaps, in certain ways, it had not grown quite as far as I had hoped, but my hopes had not been entirely thwarted, and the future still held promise. Gisela had her family in Germany. She had many friends. She was not prepared to leave, and I was not prepared to stay. Others may have expected something different, but that was not to be.

Trude respected my decision. She understood. My relationship with my sister was sometimes complicated. Our difference in age was a gulf we could not bridge. She would always treat me like her young brother or even her son. At times, she failed to recognize that I was now a grown man. We would always feel love for one another, but we both knew that I did not have to live near her to be happy.

One afternoon, I took Ruth for a long walk. She understood that Ilse had always been the sister that I loved the most. I told her that my father had grown older and I still wanted to feel his arms around me again. She supported my decision. She told me that at her first opportunity, she would come to America too. That is where she would live.

Then, it all happened quickly. On August 9, 1948, I received my discharge from the British Army and began my journey to America. My first stop would be London. I would collect my belongings that I had left with Aunt Hilda. I returned to Scotland for one last farewell. And, when I stepped on the plane, I knew I would never return to Germany again.

Chapter 86

The Last Time I Saw Aunt Hilda

y visit with Aunt Hilda was bittersweet. She had learned the basic facts from the Swiss Red Cross. She knew that her daughter, my cousin Inge, had gone missing. But that was all she had ever been told. Only a few months earlier, someone had written from America, a girl who wanted to tell her the story of Inge. She had been a classmate in Brussels. She had wanted to visit. Aunt Hilda had resisted. But the girl had insisted. The story was too complicated to write in a letter. She needed to tell Aunt Hilda in person.

Aunt Hilda told me that the girl did come to visit. She came from America just to see Aunt Hilda. She was close in age to Inge, in her early twenties by now. Only two months earlier, the girl had finished her college education. Now she was engaged to be married. She had her whole future to look forward to. They spent several hours together. It took that long to hear the whole story. When the girl finished, Aunt Hilda told her to leave. She never wanted to see her again. She would never understand why so many of the others had survived, but not Inge. Inge was all the hope she had ever had in the world. Why hadn't Inge survived? Why hadn't Inge been saved? Aunt

Hilda would never understand. She would live with this question for the rest of her life.

Within days following Kristallnacht, in November of 1938, Inge had been sent away to Brussels, Belgium. She was only twelve, too young to be on her own, but Aunt Hilda had insisted. She had wanted her to be away from Germany. She had wanted her only child to be safe.

The destruction in Wurzen on the night of November 9 had been terrible. The department store that had been owned and operated by the family for over forty years had been totally burned and destroyed. There was nothing they could do to save it. The inventory was gone. It would have taken everything they had to rebuild. The Nazis would have taken it from them anyway. Ever since Uncle Alfred had died, it had been difficult for Aunt Hilda. The store had been losing customers since the boycott in 1933. It was too much to operate the store and to raise Inge.

With the store gone, there was no other reason for Aunt Hilda and Inge to stay in Wurzen. The Nazis had made it clear that they had no future anywhere in Germany. The best thing would be to try to immigrate to Palestine or England and create a new life. In the meantime, sending Inge away made the most sense. She would be safe and continue her education. Once Aunt Hilda was settled, she would send for Inge.

After Kristallnacht, nearly one thousand Jewish children from Germany and Austria, including Inge, were sent to Belgium. The rescue effort was closely connected to the Belgian Red Cross. Most of the children were sheltered in private homes, and about eighty in two large children's homes, one for girls, the other for boys.

On the outskirts of Brussels, the Home General Bernheim housed about thirty girls ranging in age from seven to fifteen. The home was run by a highly respected Belgian couple, the Franks. All the girls attended a nearby school, where they received a good education. At first, Inge had been placed in a private home, but it seemed that she had done better living in the dorm room at the Home General, where she had made many new friends. Aunt Hilda had seen pictures of the home. It was an imposing three-story house surrounded by a six-foot-high brown brick wall. The home looked quite new. It was built like a large villa with Mediterranean styled shutters and windows.

Inge had written every few days. She had overcome her homesickness and adjusted to her new surroundings. She always had interesting stories to tell. Inge had sounded excited and happy. Perhaps there were times when it was not the best situation, but it was the best they could manage until Aunt Hilda was settled and could send for Inge.

Aunt Hilda explained to me that moving to Palestine had not worked out but that, in early 1939, her application to move to England had been accepted. She had applied to become a domestic worker. It was the only skill that she had, and in early 1939, England was approving applications by German Jews agreeing to this kind of work. Things had happened quickly. She had moved to England at about the same time that I had gone to Scotland. But Inge could not join her then. She needed a separate visa.

Her correspondence continued with Inge, and Aunt Hilda applied for a visa to bring Inge to England. As it was being considered, Germany invaded Poland, and Great Britain declared war on Germany. That's when everything stopped. No more visas were being approved. Mail service was disrupted, and nearly all communication was lost. Aunt Hilda had become desperate, but she was helpless. In England, she had neither connections nor resources. There was nothing she could do. Great Britain would accept no more German nationals as long as they were at war with Germany. Inge was stranded in Belgium. Aunt Hilda told me that the girl who had come to visit had told her the rest of the story.

When Poland was invaded in September 1939, panic erupted in Brussels. Everything closed. People were convinced that Belgium would be next. And, just like in England, there were debates about putting German nationals into detention camps. At the Home General, the German girls were even cautioned about speaking German in public. With time, the panic subsided, and the girls were able to continue with their studies. But everyone had become worried. They knew the world was different.

By May, 1940, Inge had turned fourteen years old. She had been in Brussels for nearly one and one-half years. On the tenth of May, the girls were awakened by loud explosions and bright flashes of light. When they looked out the windows, they could see parachutes falling from planes. The Germans were invading Belgium. The girls had practiced for this moment and knew to gather in the basement. It was their shelter. The basement was large, and there was room for all. As the day wore on, the sounds became more distant, and their tensions relaxed. Cautiously, they resumed many of their normal activities. But they always listened. They knew for certain that the Germans would be coming. They would arrive before long. It was only a matter of time. Some of the girls were able to reach relatives, but most were not. Those who remained recognized that they were vulnerable and that there was little they could do.

For the following four days, the girls spent nearly all of their time huddled in the basement. It was the safest place in the house. One by one, they would go upstairs to eat. They would take turns using the bathroom. At the first sound of bombs, they would hastily retreat back to their shelter. At night, they would create makeshift beds. In the dark, they would whisper to one another. They would tell the younger ones stories.

It was on the fourth day after the invasion began that they were told to prepare to leave. They should wear as many layers of clothes as possible. Extra clothing, shoes, and food should be put into their rucksacks. Take only what you can carry. They would leave Brussels by train and would not return, at least not until the Germans were out of Belgium. A bus would take them to the train station. No one told the girls where they were going.

So it was on May 14 that the twenty-five remaining girls from the Home General Bernheim made their way to the old Brussels train station. The bus ride took them through the downtown area of Brussels, and they saw the damage and destruction, the bombed out streets, the shattered windows, and the broken walls.

When they arrived at the train station, they were joined by others. They would now be under the care of the Salvation Army. That's when they learned that they, along with a group of other Jewish children, were being sent to France, where they would have a better chance of being out of harm's way.

They waited several hours at the train station, not knowing whether more bombs might fall. Finally, the train arrived. They were told they would be riding in a large freight car, the kind normally used to transport livestock and horses. Trains were at a premium; this was all that could be found.

The freight car would be their home for the next seven days as the train made its way to France and beyond the border. The trip was frightening and uncomfortable, but there was little choice. They were without windows to the outside, and as they rode, they could only hear the explosions of the bombs as they fell. At times, the train would stop, and the girls knew nothing. All they could do was curl up together using their extra clothes as mattresses. There was nowhere to sit.

As they slowly made their way, the train would stop at small villages. There, they could use the facilities. They would be greeted by local villagers who would provide them with sandwiches for the next leg of the journey. Word had been passed along the route that their train was coming. The French people were encouraging and helped as they could.

On the seventh day, they reached their destination, a small village some forty kilometers southeast of Toulouse, France. As they departed the train, they found that there were others, and that their group had grown. Now they numbered one hundred, half boys and half girls. Together, they walked a narrow lane, the final six kilometers, to Seyre, a small village of less than one hundred with only a few small buildings. They were directed to a long, gray, two-story building, a large barn belonging to the farm of the Chateau de Seyre. This would become their home for much of the next year.

Their new home was nothing like the Home General Bernheim in Brussels. There was no furniture or beds and little to eat. The winter of 1940 was very harsh, and there was much illness and suffering. Now they needed to survive in isolation, and the group was much larger and required more organization. They would conduct classes. Education would continue for the younger children. The older children helped care for the younger ones and worked on nearby farms. Food and clothing were in short supply. Fortunately, a group affiliated with the Swiss Red Cross agreed to provision the young refugees' camp and began to supply clothing and basic needs. There was little contact with family or friends. Mail service hardly existed. And, if they were to receive mail, it would be slow and censored.

Eight months after they arrived in Seyre, they were told that the Swiss Red Cross would make available an old castle in a more secluded site closer to the Spanish border, 80 kilometers away, not too far from the Pyrenees. It was vacant and deteriorated. At first, the older children were moved there so they could help with its renovation. Wells and latrines were dug to make the old chateau habitable.

By late spring, May of 1941, a full year after they had left Brussels, the Chateau la Hille was ready to accommodate everyone.

During the summer of 1941, seventeen of the younger La Hille children were able to leave for the United States through the efforts of U.S. organizations. But, by this time, France was occupied by the Germans, and the French police were well aware that more than eighty Jewish children were still being housed at the Chateau la Hille. French law gave them some protection, at least until their 18th birthdays.

By the following year, a number of the older children were nearing or had reached the age when they would no longer be protected. Inge was now sixteen years old. Every few weeks, French police officials would check. Already, some of the older children had slipped away during the night. In late summer, they learned that entire families in Paris were being taken away by the French gendarmerie. Age no longer mattered. All the Jews were being deported. They knew that they would be next.

On the morning of August 25, 1942, the police appeared and announced that they had orders to make arrests. Everyone was instructed to assemble in the courtyard. By order of the Nazis, all boys and girls over the age of fifteen were told to pack one small suitcase or rucksack. Thirty-seven children were arrested by the gendarmerie. All valuables were to be left behind. They were put in an old police van and deported to Camp le Vernet, a concentration camp near Pamiers. Inge was one of those arrested that day.

Frantically, the Swiss Red Cross interceded, and on the fifth day of detention, as they watched other internees from the camp being loaded into freight cars for deportation to Auschwitz, the thirty-seven children from the Chateau la Hille were released and sent back to the Chateau. As soon as the children were returned to La Hille, they began organizing illegal escapes of the older girls and boys over the

Pyrenees to Spain and the Alps to Switzerland to save them. Other older children found work and shelter with farmers in the region. Twelve of the teens joined the Resistance.

It was during the week of December 24, 1942, that they were told that the Swiss Red Cross was no longer able to protect them. It was a certainty that all would be arrested within days, and this time, they would not be released. The remaining children were divided into groups of five and instructed on their routes. They would need to walk to Foix, where they would catch the train to Toulouse. There, they would catch a train to Annemasse and walk to a Swiss Red Cross home. At the home, they would be given a small map and final instructions on how to cross the border. Dividing the children into small groups and sending them out at separate times gave them the best chance to ride the trains to Annemasse undetected. Each was given a Swiss sounding name and an explanation should they be detained by the police. No one was to speak German. They were all to hide their German accents.

Inge's group of five left on January 8, 1943. They successfully made their way to Annemasse and the Swiss Red Cross home. Even the German soldiers riding their train did not detect them. At the home, they received their final instructions on how to cross the border. They walked for about thirty minutes, crossing three barbed wire fences. As they walked for ten minutes along the third fence, they saw a light in the distance. One of the five went ahead. It was the light from several German soldiers. The five, two boys and three girls, were arrested.

The following day, they were interrogated one by one. Their identities could no longer be concealed. One in their group managed to escape through a bathroom window. The others did not. That winter, nearly ninety of the one hundred children from the Chateau le Hille escaped and found their way to safety and survived. Inge was one of those who did not. She was deported to Auschwitz and murdered by the Nazis. My dear, sweet, cousin Inge was sixteen years old when her life was cruelly taken.

I can't imagine Aunt Hilda's heartbreak when she first learned this story. Listening to her recount these details reconfirmed my decision to start a new life in America. I had to leave Germany and these horrible nightmares behind. Too many lives had been destroyed. To this day, I can't imagine the terror and horror the Germans imposed on millions of innocent people like Inge. That day, I told myself that I would have nothing to do with Germany for as long as I would live. Now, nearly sixty years later, I feel exactly the same.

Before leaving Aunt Hilda, I asked for my old suitcase, the one containing my old clothes and the few possessions I had taken when I left my parents in Berlin and went to Scotland. Aunt Hilda shook her head and told me she no longer had the suitcase. She told me she had never expected me to survive the war and had given it away. What would she do with my old things?

Much in the suitcase held no meaning. The suits made for me in Berlin might still fit, but could be easily replaced. But my treasures could not be replaced: family pictures taken at the farm in Crossen, the letters of advice Mother and Father had written and given to me on the day that I left Berlin, the family tree that Lotte had created and given to me for my children, papers from my childhood, the few Reichsmarks I had taken from Germany, an address book Mother had made listing all the people in the world that we knew, even papers from Father's childhood. These were my worldly possessions. Now, even these were gone.

Though Aunt Hilda managed to live for nearly fifty more years, sadly, I decided to leave her behind too. I would have nothing more to do with her. I still felt kindly towards her; it is just that I could not bear these memories. I never saw her again.

It was many years later that Ralph and Ginger found Aunt Hilda in London, a few years before she died. I never told them about her, but others did. She still lived in that small flat near the Golders Green underground station, where she had told me the story of Inge. One day, when we were visiting the Outer Banks, Ralph phoned her in London. Aunt Hilda was ninety-five years old by then. My disappointment had subsided with time. She had continued to live alone, never remarried, and had spent her life working as a maid in London. Forty-five years after I had last seen her in London, we spoke for the first time. I didn't mention the suitcase. All Aunt Hilda remembered was Inge. Why hadn't her Inge survived?

Day 52...

Joanie called first thing Arizona time. It was too late to call last evening when she'd gotten in from Iowa. Dad was in pretty bad shape, worse than she had expected, no recognition, nothing. Mom was holding up, but she was very tired. Joanie thought she was on the verge of collapse. It has been nearly two months since he had his surgery, and she has been by his bedside every day. There has been little change since Ginger and I left ten days ago. He is a fighter. But, now, there is no fight left. Mom is ready to let him go.

They met with the doctor this morning. There is no hope. Mom and she wanted to check with me before they arranged for hospice. Mom knew it was the right thing to do. She wanted Dad to rest comfortably. That was all she could do for him. She knew he could not hear her anymore. She had said everything she needed to say. Mom told Joanie this is the way of life. It happens to everyone. Cherish your time together. Life will not last forever.

Chapter 87

America

I left London on September 15, 1948. It was a Wednesday. It had been nine and one-half years since I had left my parents and my old life in Germany. I was sixteen then. Now I am twenty-five years old. I feel much older, like I have lived an entire lifetime since we said goodbye to one another at the train station in Berlin.

My flight takes me first to Montreal. There I catch another, this time to Chicago. In Chicago, I take a two-hour bus ride to Rockford. I know nothing of these places. They are only dots on a map. Rockford is where Ilse, Arthur, Frank, and Father now live. That is where I will live. I should be there by Saturday morning.

When Ilse and her family arrived in San Francisco in March of 1947, the refugee placement organization searched for work and housing for the family. The church in Rockford was in need of an organist. That's why they moved there. Ilse wrote that the community is very nice. People have helped them get settled. Father has aged considerably and doesn't remember things so well but he is content and has his own room in the house. He enjoys sitting on the front porch. Arthur has a second job as an elevator operator. Ilse is able to work as a private nurse. Frank, nine years old by now, is in school. Their house has room for me.

As we taxi the runway at London's Heathrow Airport, I see my reflection in the plane window. It reminds me of the day I saw my reflection in the train window when I left Berlin. I wasn't old enough to shave then. Each day has seemed long but when I think about all the time that has passed it seems to have gone by in an instant. I know I should sleep, but I am too excited.

We were landing in Montreal when I woke up. I had no idea we were there. Excited or not I slept the entire way. My plan was to send a telegram to Rockford, to tell them when to expect me at the bus station. But, I will wait. I will send them the telegram from Chicago. We should arrive there in another few hours. Then, I will know for certain when my bus will arrive.

I wonder how they will look, how much they have changed. I am sure that they wonder the same about me. Now my thoughts are all tangled. I stare into nowhere and see nothing. I don't think. I just wonder. It was so simple when Father and I rode the sled down the hill at the old Jewish cemetery in Pr. Holland.

Epilogue

I know that some will ask whether this story is true. It is. The people are real, the places are real, and so are the events. I admit to connecting the dots at certain points, but the fiction was kept to an absolute minimum. Dad, his sisters, and other family members were described exactly as they were. Dad really was a quiet man who kept his thoughts and opinions to himself. He was always reluctant to talk about his life. He enjoyed his privacy, but I don't think he would mind that I shared his story. I like to think he would be amazed.

Joanie and Mom were there to watch Dad take his last breath, and his death was peaceful. Since Ginger and I had been in Arizona with Mom the week before, I chose not to return for this final moment. It was not something I was wont to do. For me, I could not bear that being the last memory of my father. There were other memories of Dad that I wanted to remember.

Mom and Joanie shared that final moment, and I know it was special. We had all shared the past two months together, and we knew that we cared for one another. Those last few days were emotional, but after eight weeks, even emotional tends to become relief. On that we all agreed.

It had been Mom's journey. The rest of us, Joanie and Marv, Ginger and me, friends and family, were pretty much bystanders. This was their life together. We were ready to help when she needed us. We stayed away when she needed her privacy. That was the way she wanted it to be. Like Mom always said, this was her man, and it was her job to take care of him. He would have done the same for her. It is all part of life. We will all have our turn. Every life ends with death. On balance, I think Dad was a pretty lucky guy.

No funeral, no memorial service, just a quick goodbye and cremation. That is our family's tradition. Each has their own. We all mourn in our own private way. We knew Dad would rather we spend the time with our own children. He always said the past was the past. He always thought that the present was more interesting.

Joanie stayed for a few days to help Mom take care of things before returning to Iowa. She and Marv would be back in a few weeks. Ginger and I waited a few days. Mom needed time and space to recover before we returned for a visit. She was exhausted. We could see that she had used up her tears of a lifetime. The last two months had drained her, physically and emotionally. She would be okay, but it would take time.

Mom had already cleaned out most of Dad's things by the time we got there. I suppose we all grieve differently; she did it her way. In Arizona, we took care of some details, took Mom to see friends, visited the casino, and went out for a few meals. Mostly, we talked. That's what she wanted to do. As I said at the beginning, Mom likes conversation.

Each evening, I mixed the martinis. Then, the three of us would sit down to visit. The first evening, after a few minutes, Mom said she wanted to talk about how she and Dad met.

We both knew much of the story. She had been living in Chicago. Her parents were there too. With Uncle Ludwig's help, she and her three brothers had come to America from Naples before the war. Her parents wanted to come too, but it had been difficult because of quotas. Instead, they stayed in Naples and continued to operate the pension until they could find a place to go. In 1941, when they did finally leave, they spent a few years in Cuba before arriving in the United States. Her father's brother, Uncle Ludwig, had helped Mom's parents as well.

Mom had a remaining first cousin in Berlin who had married a girl from East Prussia. Uncle Ludwig had helped this cousin, too. The cousin left Germany to survive the war in Shanghai. It was the only place he and his family could go. Uncle Ludwig helped pay the transportation to China for Arthur, his wife, Ilse, their son, Frank, and Ilse's parents, Udo and Alice Wobser. Arthur, Ilse, and their baby even stayed with their Uncle Paul and Aunt Elsa, Mom's parents, in Naples before they caught the ship to China. Uncle Ludwig had wired funds for them there.

Two years after the war, Mom's first cousin Arthur emigrated from Shanghai to America. With his family, he settled in Rockford, only eighty miles from Chicago. When Mom went to visit her first cousin, she had no idea that his wife, Ilse, had a younger brother who had recently left the British Army and was living with them in Rockford. Their romance was brief. Dad had seemed very inexperienced in affairs of the heart, Mom claimed to have taught him much, and after two weekends, they decided to marry.

Then, Mom smiled and said she had never told us what Dad said when he proposed. Dad, the guy who rarely asked a question or ventured an opinion, the guy who listened more than he spoke, the guy who didn't like to debate the unsolvable matters, got down on one knee and solemnly asked if she believed in fate.

Dad told Mom that there were many things in his life he could explain, but didn't understand. And that there were many other things in his life that he understood but could not explain. He was convinced that fate was the only answer. His entire life, he had thought about fate.

Fate had drawn them together. An invisible hand had been leading him to her. There was no denying it. Despite all the choices he had made in his life, some things just happened for the strangest of reasons. There was no explanation. His choices were not random. He could not change this. They were meant to be. Since the day he was born, it was certain that he would fall in love with her. They were destined to marry. They would raise a family together. That's why she must agree to marry him. He knew it was her destiny too.

What were the odds that a boy growing up in Preussisch Holland, East Prussia, Germany, and a girl who grew up in Naples, Italy, would meet in Rockford and fall in love? Dad claimed that the only possible answer was fate. How else could you explain it?

I refilled our martinis. Ginger, Mom, and I sat quietly reflecting on Dad's beautiful proposal. That's when Mom's eyes twinkled, and she grinned with that grin that she could only make and asked, "Did you ever wonder if Uncle Ludwig had arranged it?"

Acknowledgements

I have the good fortune to be surrounded by an incredible family who has made this book writing adventure an absolute joy. None of this would be possible if it were not for my lifelong partner and love of my life, my wife Ginger. During the eight months that it took to compose these pages, there was not a day that I was able to talk about much of anything else. Ginger knew what I was going to talk about it before I even opened my mouth, and she was always there for me. Every time she listened thoughtfully and was patient with her critique. When it became time to read what was written, Ginger approached the process with unwavering attention and advice. Some journeys need to be shared, and many days I needed a cheerleader. On other days, Ginger was my coach. I will be forever grateful. I know that I am the luckiest man alive. Like Dad said, some things are meant to be, and yes, I'm sitting on top of the world!

My adventure was not simply one of research and writing. I also spent time getting to better know and enjoy my first cousins, more than I can ever recall. Writing a book about family is a perfect excuse to make up for all those years where there were never enough moments. My father and his sisters have left a wonderful legacy. Our generation has not only all survived. We have prospered. America has been good to us.

My cousin Ruth who grew up in Elbing, East Prussia, now lives in Florida. She has an encyclopedic memory. I have come to learn that she is one of the smartest people I know. I have had the pleasure of her support and assistance on an almost daily basis and am sure she has read each page at least five or six times. It made me cry when she admitted her tears. And, each time I have asked for her help, she has given it with total enthusiasm and complete dedication. Through this process, Ruth has become so much more than a cousin and a collaborator. She has become one of my closest friends. It is a friendship we both know will last a lifetime.

My cousin Frank, who was born in Berlin and spent many of his early years in Shanghai, now is a retired gynecologist living in Indiana. Frank has undoubtedly scratched his head and wondered what I could possibly have been doing these many months. I have interrupted too many of his days with obscure questions. He has always been a source of information and always provided it with wit and conversation. Frank's daughter, Nicole, is working on a family history for her own children and has been an enthusiastic contact for needed details.

I also want to give a shout out to my nephew Abram. Years ago, when Abe was in high school, he wrote a report about his grandfather, my dad, Jerry. Abram interviewed dad on several occasions. The report was a document that I relied upon throughout and is a wonderful testament to the idea of grandchildren interviewing their grandparents. Abe was a big reason why Dad told his story. Well done, Abe.

There were many others, too, people who I corresponded with for background information: my cousin Manfred, who lives in Germany, any number of people at the British Archives, local historians in

Europe. I know I should, but I can't begin to list the number of books that I have consulted in my search for descriptions of various events. Any story like this requires lots of help.

Most of all, I want to thank my sister, Joanie. Words cannot convey the depth of my gratitude. I hope one day she will assemble her own version. I can't wait to see it, and I know it will be special because we do see things in our own individual way. Having a brother like me is definitely not easy, particularly when undertaking a project like this one. I can't think of a time when I needed her help that she didn't drop whatever she was doing and come to my rescue. And, no matter what, she did it with grace and kindness. Joan is the unsung hero. Writing a book like this is a process replete with emotion, and Dad and Mom had only two children, Joanie and me. Everything in this book, we share in common. I couldn't ask for better. And a special thanks to Joan's husband, Marv. I'm sure this process disrupted his life too.

Even with all this wonderful support and help, I imagine this book is flawed with errors and omissions. And I'm sure there will be some who take issue with faulty opinions; some may even spark a bit of controversy. I hope whatever judgments I have offered have always been respectful. Whether fact or conclusion or any part in-between, please know that these are my words and my interpretation of events. For the mistakes, I take credit. Whatever the fault, the responsibility is mine.

Finally, every journey should be enjoyed and savored. Mine has been the journey of a lifetime. I hope this adventure will prompt others to take the same trip. It is a labor of love. I recommend it with my head and all of my heart.

Ralph Webster,
June, 2016